# 4000
# QUESTIONS
*and*
# ANSWERS
*on the*

# BIBLE

# 4000
# QUESTIONS
## *and*
# ANSWERS
## *on the*

# BIBLE

### A. DANA ADAMS

Testament Books
New York

This 2001 edition is published by Testament Books™,
an imprint of Random House Value Publishing, Inc.,
280 Park Avenue, New York, NY 10017,
by arrangement with Broadman and Holman Publishers.

Testament Books™ and design are trademarks of
Random House Value Publishing, Inc.

Random House
New York • Toronto • London • Sydney • Auckland
http://www.randomhouse.com/

Printed and bound in the United States of America

**Library of Congress Cataloging-in-Publication Data**

Adams, A. D. (Alice Dana), 1864-1934.
4000 questions and answers on the Bible / A. Dana Adams.
p. cm.
Originally published: Nashville, TN : Broadman and Holman, 1996.
ISBN 0-517-21923-9 (alk. Paper)
1. Bible—Miscellanea. I. Title: Four thousand questions
and answers on the Bible. II. Title

BS612 .A29 2002
220—dc21
2001044275

10 9 8 7 6 5 4 3 2 1

# CONTENTS

## 1. THE BEGINNING (Gen. 1:1–2:7)

**1. What is the name of the first book of the Bible?** Genesis, which means "Beginnings."

**2. What do we know of the beginning of the world?** "In the beginning God created the heaven and the earth." Gen. 1:1.

**3. What is the difference between "created" and "made"?** "Created" means made out of nothing; "made" means formed or developed out of something already existing. In the account of the beginning of this world the word "created" is used three times.

**4. By what power did God create the world?** By his word. Heb. 1:3; 2 Pet. 3:5.

**5. Who is called the Word of God?** Jesus Christ. John 1:14.

**6. How do we know that Jesus Christ was with God in the creation?** *"In the beginning was the Word, and the Word was with God. . . . All things were made by him; and without him was not anything made that was made." John 1:1, 3.*

*"Who is the image of the invisible God . . . for by him were all things created . . . Col. 1:15, 16.*

**7. What was the last thing created?** Man, who was made in the image of God.

## 2. THE FALL (Gen. 2:8–3:24)

**1. Where did God place man when he had created him?** In the Garden of Eden. Gen. 2:8–17.

**2. Where was this garden?** Probably near the present river Euphrates, in Asia.

**3. What description have we given to us of this garden?** That God made to grow in it the tree of life, the tree of knowledge of good and evil, and every tree that is pleasant to the sight and good for food.

**4. How was it watered?** By a river that flowed to the sea in four branches, one of which was called the Euphrates, and may very likely be the river now known by that name.

**5. Was man idle in the Garden of Eden?** He was put into the garden to dress it and keep it.

**6. Were there any restrictions in the use of the garden?** Man could eat of every tree or plant of the garden save of the tree of the knowledge of good and evil.

**7. Did man obey God's command?** He did not; he ate of the forbidden fruit. Gen. 3:1–24.

**8. Who was the first transgressor?** Eve.

**9. How came it about?** The devil, in the form of a serpent, deceived her by a lie, saying that they would not surely die, as God had said, but be as gods, knowing good and evil.

**10. What foolish plan did they adopt to hide their shame?** They hid themselves amongst the trees of the garden.

**11. Can any place conceal us from God?** None.
*"Whither shall I go from thy spirit? or whither shall I flee from thy presence? . . . Yea, the darkness hideth not from thee; but the night shineth as the day: the darkness and the light are both alike to thee." Ps. 139:7, 12.*

**12. What is it that makes us fear to meet God?** The consciousness that we have sinned and that he knows it.

**13. What ought we to do when we know that we have sinned?** To confess and be truly sorry for our sin; to come to God, through Christ, for pardon; and to forsake it.

**14. How did God clothe the bodies of Adam and Eve?** In coats of skin.

**15. What punishment came because of this sin?** Satan and the serpent in whose form he appeared were to be finally conquered; Man was to be driven from Eden, and forced to work for his support, and finally to die; and Woman was to endure suffering, and be ruled by man.

**16. How was man to know that the ground also was cursed?** By the weeds it brought forth, and the labor required to till it.

**17. Was there not a special mercy granted to the woman?** Yes, that she should be the ancestress of Christ. Gen. 3:15.

**18. Why could man live no longer in the Garden of Eden?** Lest they should eat of the tree of life, and live forever upon earth in their fallen condition.

**19. Is the tree of life ever mentioned again in Scripture?** In Revelation, as standing by the river of the water of life, in the midst of the paradise of God. Rev. 2:7; 22:1, 2.

**20. How did God guard the gate of Eden?** By cherubim and a flaming sword.

**21. Why did Adam name his wife Eve?** Because she was the mother of all living; and the word means "living" or "life."

## 3. CAIN AND ABEL (Gen. 4)

**1. What are the names of the first two sons of Adam and Eve?** Cain, meaning "possession," and Abel, meaning "vanity."

**2. What were their special occupations?** Cain was "a tiller of the ground"; and Abel "a keeper of sheep."

**3. What difference was there in the offerings of the two brothers?** Cain offered of the fruit of the ground, and Abel the firstlings of his flock.

**4. Were both equally acceptable to God?** No.

**5. Was this because of the different kind of offerings?** Probably not; at least we have no hint of any previous command regarding sacrifices. Offerings of the first fruits of the harvest were commanded later; and each would naturally offer the fruits of his own labor.

*"By faith Abel offered unto God a more excellent sacrifice than Cain, by which he obtained witness that he was righteous, God testifying of his gifts; and by it he being dead yet speaketh." Heb. 11:4.*

**6. Do we know what proof God gave that the sacrifice was accepted?** No, it is impossible; but it was something of which the offerer could be sure, for Cain was very angry.

**7. How did God reprove him?** He told him it was sin which prevented the acceptance of his offering.

**8. To what awful act did Cain's anger lead?** To the murder of his brother Abel.

**9. What fearful lie did he tell?** He told the all-seeing God that he knew not where his brother was.

**10. What words did he use that we should say?** "Am I my brother's keeper?"

**11. How should we answer this question?** That we are so far our brother's keeper that we must be careful to do nothing which will hurt him bodily, mentally or spiritually; but on the contrary to do all possible to help him.

**12. What was Cain's punishment?** To be a fugitive and a vagabond in the earth.

**13. How did Cain feel when he heard God's curse?** That his punishment was greater than he could bear.

**14. What did God do to mitigate his punishment?** He set a mark upon him to prevent his being killed.

**15. What do we read of Cain's descendants?** They were men of strength and skill, showing great inventive genius in making tents, weapons, tools, and musical instruments. And they were the first who kept herds of cattle as private property.

## 4. THE WORLD BEFORE THE FLOOD (Gen. 5)

**1. What son did God give Adam and Eve after they had lost both Cain and Abel?** Seth first; and after that others whose number or names are not given.

**2. How long was the life of a man as here indicated?** Nine hundred years or more.

**3. What three names in this chapter are specially to be remembered?** Methusaleh, the oldest man; Enoch who "walked with God"; and Noah in whose days the flood came. Vs. 24, 27, 28, 29.

**4. Who had the shortest life and why?** Enoch only lived three hundred and sixty-five years; "and he was not, for God took him."

**5. What remarkable prophecy of Enoch does the apostle Jude repeat?** "Behold, the Lord cometh with ten thousands of his saints." Jude 14.

**6. To what does this refer?** To our Lord's second coming.

## 5. THE FLOOD (Gen. 6–9)

**1. What two races of men seem now to be living in the world?** A godly race, worshiping the true God, and called "sons [and daughters] of God"; and a worldly and perhaps idolatrous race, called [sons and] "daughters of men." Gen. 6:1–6.

**2. Did these continue to exist separately?** No.

*"The sons of God saw the daughters of men that they were fair; and they took them wives of all which they chose."*

**3. What was the character of their descendants?** They were "mighty men"; "men of renown"; and very wicked.

**4. What did God resolve to do?** To destroy both man and beast. Gen. 6:7.

**5. Did he find one faithful family?** Yes, Noah's. Gen. 6:8–22.

**6. What command did God give Noah?** He commanded him to build an ark in which he and others with him might be saved from the "flood of waters" which God was to bring upon the earth.

**7. What is Noah said in 2 Pet. 2:5 to have been?** A preacher of righteousness.

**8. To whom did he preach?** To all he met, telling them of the flood which was coming to destroy them. But they would not believe.

**9. What was the consequence?** "The flood came and took them all away." Matt. 24:39; Gen. 7:21–23.

**10. How were Noah and his family preserved?** In the ark which Noah built at God's command.

**11. Of whom was the ark a type?** Of Christ, as the appointed means of saving men from destruction.

**12. Of what was the flood a type?** Of the future destruction of the world.

*"The world that then was, being overflowed with water, perished; but the heavens and the earth, which are now, by the same word are kept in store, reserved unto fire against the day of judgment and perdition of ungodly men." 2 Pet. 3:6, 7.*

**13. What living beings were saved in the ark?** Noah; his three sons; the wives of all four; seven pairs of every clean beast and bird (such as could be used for food or for sacrifice); and one pair of every other sort. Gen. 6:18–20; 7:2, 3, 13–16.

**14. Could other men and women have been saved?** If they had believed Noah and been willing to take refuge in the ark they would have been saved.

**15. How long did it continue raining?** Forty days and nights. Gen. 7:12–24.

**16. How long did the waters prevail upon the earth?** One hundred and fifty days.

**17. How did Noah know when the waters had abated?** He sent out a dove. Gen. 8:8–12.

**18. What was Noah's first act when he came forth from the ark?** He built an altar and offered a sacrifice. Gen. 8:20–9:17.

**19. What promise did God give Noah at this time?** That he would not again curse the ground for man's sake, etc.

**20. What did God give him as a token?** The rainbow.

**21. Did God make any change in man's food at that time?** He gave him animal food in addition to his former vegetable food.

**22. Under what restriction?** That "the life thereof, which is the blood" should not be eaten.

## 6. THE TOWER OF BABEL (Gen. 11:1–9)

**1. As the population grew what did they plan to do?** To build a city and a tower "whose top may reach unto heaven," for their own praise and glory.

**2. Where was it to be?** On "a plain in the land of Shinar," which most probably is what later became Babylon.

**3. Of what did they build it?** Of mud dried bricks, joined together with mortar made of bituminous slime.

**4. What did God do about it?** He "confounded their language" so that they could not understand each other, which, of course, put a stop to the work; and he "scattered them abroad . . . upon the face of all the earth."

**5. Why was God so unwilling it should be built?** It was to be a monument to the power of man as distinct from the power of God.

**6. What name was given to it?** Babel, which means "confounded."

## 7. ABRAHAM (Gen. 11:27–23; 25)

**1. Which line of descent from Noah is most fully described, and why?** The line from Shem, because in that line were the Jewish people who wrote the books of the Bible; and from whom, after the flesh, Christ came. Gen. 11:10–26.

**2. From what sons are the Gentiles descended?** The other white races are supposed to have descended from Japhet, and the black race from Ham.

**3. What was Abraham's name in his early life?** Abram.

**4. Where was Abram born?** In Ur of the Chaldees, S. E. of Babylon. Gen. 11:28.

**5. To what land did his father remove, and why?** To Haran, still on the river Euphrates, but in the northern part of Mesopotamia; perhaps because of God's call to Abram while in Ur.

**6. Which of Abram's brothers died before they left their native land?** Haran, the father of Lot.

**7. After his father's death did Abram stay in Haran?** No. God told him to leave his home and go to a land he would afterward show him. This was Canaan, or Palestine. Gen. 12:1–9.

**8. Who went with him?** Sarai his wife, Lot his nephew, and their servants.

**9. What promise did God make to Abram?** That he should have many descendants who should form a great nation owning the land of Palestine, and that "in him should all the families of the earth be blessed." See Gen. 12:2, 3, 7; 13:14–17; 15:5; 17:5–8; 22:17, 18.

**10. To what finally did the promise refer?** To the coming of Jesus Christ.

**11. Where did Abram first settle, and what was his first act in the land of Canaan?** At Sichem, or Shechem, where he built an altar to God.

**12. Where do we again hear of Shechem?** See Josh. 24:1, 25, 26; John 4:5–42.

**13. Where did Abram then make his home?** Between Bethel and Hai, about twelve miles north of Jerusalem.

**14. Was Abram a rich man or a poor man?** He later became very rich; and was certainly not poor at this time. Gen. 13:2.

**15. How had Lot prospered?** Very much.

**16. What was the result?** A quarrel between the herdsmen of the two.

**17. How did Abram behave on this occasion?** He proposed that they should part, and gave Lot the choice of the land.

**18. Do you think that Lot behaved as well as Abram in this affair?** He made no liberal offer in return, and thought more of the goodness of the pasture than of the character of the people with whom he was to live.

**19. Had Lot cause to repent his choice?** He suffered constant distress of mind, and at length narrowly escaped with his life, with the loss of his wife, many of his family, and of most or all of his property. Gen. 19:15–29.

*"Delivered just Lot, vexed with the filthy conversation of the wicked: (for that righteous man dwelling among them, in seeing and hearing, vexed his righteous soul from day to day with their unlawful deeds)." 2 Pet. 2:7, 8.*

**20. What doleful news did Abram soon hear of Lot?** That Lot and his goods had been carried away with other captives from Sodom, by the kings of Elam, Babylonia, etc. Gen. 14:11, 12.

**21. What did Abram do?** He armed his own trained servants and went in pursuit. He divided his men, attacked the enemy by night on several sides at once, routing them and recovering the prisoners and booty.

**22. Who met Abram on his return?** Melchizedek, king of Salem, which probably was Jerusalem.

**23. Is this mysterious person ever alluded to again in the Bible?** Yes, in Heb. 6:20; 7.

**24. Of whom was he a type?** Of Christ in being both king and priest.

**25. Did Abram take of the spoil of the battle?** No, he refused to take anything but food for his men, and the share of his allies among the Canaanites.

**26. Who was Hagar?** One of Sarai's waiting maids, whom Abram took to wife, thinking thus to bring the fulfillment of God's promise of descendants. Gen. 16.

**27. Who was her son?** Ishmael, the ancestor of the modern Arabs.

**28. What especial covenant did God make with Abram soon after this?** The "covenant of circumcision," where God renewed his promise of many descendants, and promised to be their God; and enjoined upon him the rite of circumcision as a sign of the covenant. Gen. 17.

**29. How did God change the names of Abram and Sarai?** From Abram, or "high father," to Abraham, or "father of a multitude"; and from Sarai, "my princess," to Sarah, "princess" (for all the race).

**30. Where was Mamre?** Near Hebron, in Judah. Gen. 13:18.

**31. What remarkable event happened to Abraham there?** The Lord with two angels, or heavenly visitors, appeared to him in the form of men. Gen. 18.

**32. How did Abraham receive them?** With true Oriental hospitality, asking them to rest while he prepared food for them.

**33. What did they promise to Abraham?** That he and Sarah should have a son.

**34. How did Sarah receive the news?** She laughed, for it seemed to her impossible.

**35. When the three visitors had** eaten for what place did they start? For Sodom, to destroy it and rescue Lot.

**36. Why were they to destroy Sodom?** *"Because the cry of Sodom and Gomorrah is great and because their sin is very grievous." Gen. 18:20.*

**37. How did Abraham plead for the city?** By six times asking the Lord to spare it if there were fifty, forty-five, forty, thirty, twenty, and even ten, righteous persons in it.

**38. How did the Lord answer him?** He put no check on his prayer, and consented to do all that he asked.

**39. Would the Lord have saved the city if Abraham had asked for it for the sake of Lot alone?** He might have; but its destruction would only have been postponed, for Lot alone could never have reformed the city.

**40. What warning did the heavenly visitors give to Lot?** *"Whatsoever thou hast in the city, bring them out of this place: for we will destroy this place, because the cry of them is waxen great before the face of the Lord." Gen. 19:12, 13.*

**41. How many of Lot's family believed the warning and fled with him?** His wife and two daughters. But his wife looked back, and became a pillar of salt. Gen. 19:16–26.

**42. Does there remain any relic of this event?** The Dead Sea probably covers the place where they were.

**43. When did God perform his promise to Sarah?** At the end of a year, the time fixed. Gen. 21.

**44. By what name was the child of promise called?** Isaac, which means "laughter."

**45. What occurred on the day Isaac was weaned?** Abraham made a great feast; and Ishmael mocked at the young Isaac.

**46. What did Sarah wish Abraham to do?** To send away Hagar and Ishmael.

**47. Was this in accordance with the wishes of God?** Yes, he so told Abraham.

**48. What became of Hagar and Ishmael?** After some hardships they lived in the wilderness of Paran, in Arabia, and Ishmael grew large and strong, and became the ancestor of a race whose present representatives are the Arabs.

**49. What was the greatest trial of Abraham's faith?** The command of God to offer as a burnt offering his only son, Isaac, whom he loved. Gen. 22.

**50 Where was this sacrifice to take place?** "In the land of Moriah," usually supposed to be the mountain of that name in Jerusalem.

**51. Did he tell his son what he was about to do?** No. When Isaac inquired for the lamb he replied that God would provide one.

**52. When Isaac knew of his father's intention did he resist it?** No.

**53. Was he able to have done so?** Yes, as he was probably twenty-five years old, and his father was old.

**54. Did God allow the sacrifice?** No, the angel of the Lord spoke from heaven and said:

*"Lay not thine hand upon the lad, neither do thou anything to him: for now I know that thou fearest God, seeing thou hast not withheld thy son, thine only son, from me." Gen. 22:12.*

**55. How did God provide the burnt offering?** Abraham found a "ram caught in a thicket by his horns," and offered him as a burnt offering.

**56. By what name did Abraham call the place where this occurred?** Jehovah-jireh, meaning "the Lord will see, or provide."

**57. What is said in the New Testament of this act?**

*"By faith Abraham, when he was tried, offered up Isaac: and he that had received the promises offered up his only begotten son, of whom it was said, That in Isaac shall thy seed be called: accounting that God was able to raise him up, even from the dead; from whence also he received him in a figure." Heb. 11:17–19.*

**58. How old was Sarah when she died?** One hundred and twenty-seven years. Gen. 23:1.

**59. Where did Abraham bury her?** In the cave of Machpelah, near Mamre, or Hebron, which he bought for the purpose from Ephron the Hittite.

**60. What more do we know about Abraham?** He married a wife named Keturah, and had six sons. Gen. 25:1–6.

**61. Did these sons share the inheritance with Isaac?** No, Abraham gave them gifts and sent them away.

**62. How old was Abraham when he died?** One hundred and seventy-five years. Gen. 25:7.

## 8. ISAAC AND REBEKAH (Gen. 24)

**1. How did Abraham obtain a wife for Isaac?** He sent his steward to his own kindred in Mesopotamia for the purpose, after pledging him not to seek for one among the heathen around him.

**2. Did the steward succeed in his mission?** He was led by God's providence to the house of Abraham's nephew

Bethuel, and obtained his daughter, Rebekah.

**3. What did he give to her?** Golden earrings, bracelets, jewels of silver and gold, and raiment, according to the custom of those lands and times.

**4. How did he describe his master's possessions?** That the Lord had greatly blessed him, and given him flocks and herds, silver and gold, etc.

**5. Who came to meet Rebekah as she neared Isaac's home?** Isaac himself.

**6. Where did he take her and how did he feel toward her?** To his mother's tent, "and she became his wife, and he loved her; and Isaac was comforted."

**7. How old was Isaac at this time?** Forty years. Gen. 25:20.

**8. What was Isaac's occupation?** That of a herdsman and shepherd, as a great part of his wealth consisted of sheep and cattle.

## 9. JACOB AND ESAU (Gen. 25–27)

**1. How many sons had Isaac?** Twin sons, Esau and Jacob. Gen. 25:26.

**2. What was the difference personally between these two boys?** Esau was red and hairy; and Jacob smooth skinned.

**3. Did they grow up alike? Describe them.** Esau was a skillful hunter, but passionate, careless, attracted to the wild life of the people among whom he dwelt. Jacob was a quiet man, fond of his home, a shrewd business man, but with great capability for good when once enlisted on God's side. Gen. 25:27–34.

**4. Which was the firstborn?** Esau.

**5. What was the "birthright"?** The right of the eldest born to the possession of the larger proportion of the family property. Here, besides, the heritage of the promises made by God to Abraham and his seed: the blessing of the world through the Messiah.

**6. Did Esau value his birthright? The proof?** He sold it, when hungry and faint, to Jacob for a dish of stewed lentils—"red pottage." So many sell their birthright for a mess of pottage, imperiling their souls for present pleasure.

**7. Did Isaac know of the selling of the birthright?** Manifestly not, as he later planned for a feast at which the birthright blessing was to be given to Esau. Gen. 27:1–4.

**8. Whom did Esau choose as his wives?** Judith and Bashemath, of the idolatrous tribe of the Hittites. Gen. 26:34.

**9. Did his parents approve his choice?** No, they were grieved by it.

**10. Did Jacob allow Esau to obtain the blessing of the birthright?** No, at the instigation and by the planning of his mother he pretended to be Esau in order to obtain the blessing himself. Gen. 27:6–29.

**11. Did he go the right way to work to obtain the blessing?** No, he should have left it to God to secure him the blessing in his own time and way. It was right that he should have the birthright; but it was neither right nor necessary to obtain it by deception.

**12. How did Esau feel when he found he had lost his blessing?** He was in great distress of mind. Gen. 27:36–38.

**13. Whom had he to blame for it?** Chiefly himself, for he had voluntarily sold it to Jacob about forty years before.

**14. Whom shall we have to blame if we, like Esau, despise God's blessing now?** Ourselves alone.

## 10. JACOB (Gen. 28–35)

**1. How did Esau treat Jacob after Jacob had obtained the blessing?** He hated him and determined to kill him. Gen. 27:41.

**2. What did Jacob's parents resolve to do?** To send him to Padanaram, his mother's home, to keep him out of Esau's way, and also to get a wife among the daughters of Laban. Gen. 27:42–28:5.

**3. Did Jacob ever see his mother again?** Probably not, as there is no later mention of her, although Isaac is mentioned in Gen. 35:27–29.

**4. What remarkable thing occurred to Jacob at Bethel on his way to Syria?** He had a vision by night, and a renewal of God's promise and blessing. Gen. 28:10–22.

**5. What was the vision?** A ladder reaching from earth to heaven, and angels ascending and descending on it.

**6. Of what was the ladder a type?** Of Christ as the ladder of communication between heaven and earth.
*"Hereafter ye shall see heaven open, and the angels of God ascending and descending upon the Son of man." John 1:51.*

**7. What covenant did Jacob make at this place?** That since the Lord had promised him his blessing, he should be his God, and that he would devote to him a tenth of all he should give him.

**8. How did his uncle Laban receive him?** With kindness and affection. Gen. 29:13–28.

**9. What did he promise him?** That he should have Rachel for his wife, in return for seven years' service.

**10. Did Laban fulfill his promise?**
No, he gave him Leah instead.

**11. Did he later marry Rachel?** Yes, he served seven more years for her.

**12. How many wives had Jacob?** Both Rachel and Leah; and afterwards their handmaids Bilhah and Zilpah by their mistresses' desire, and according to the custom of the time. See 7, 26; Gen. 16:2.

**13. How long did Jacob remain with Laban?** Twenty years, serving fourteen years for his wives, and six years for his cattle. Gen. 31:41.

**14. Did Jacob obtain large possessions of flocks and herds?** Yes. Gen. 30:43.

**15. How did the sons of Laban feel when they observed this?** They were displeased at his success. Gen. 31:1.

**16. Were they justly displeased?** No, their own flocks had increased much more than if Jacob had not cared for them. Gen. 31:36–41.

**17. What did Jacob and his wives resolve to do?** At the command of God they resolved to return to Canaan. Gen. 31:3–55.

**18. Of what wicked act was Rachel guilty?** Of stealing her father's images.

**19. What did this prove?** That she and her father still worshiped heathen gods.
*"Joshua said unto all the people, Thus saith the Lord God of Israel, Your fathers dwelt on the other side of the flood [the Euphrates] in old time; even Terah the father of Abraham, and the father of Nachor: and they served other gods." Josh. 24:2.*

**20. What did Laban do when he found that Jacob had left him?** He pursued him.

**21. How did God protect Jacob from**

**Laban's anger?** By warning Laban in a dream.

**22. How did the interview between Laban and Jacob end?** It ended peacefully and in a covenant.

**23. What is the meaning of the word Mahanaim?** Two hosts or camps. Gen. 32:1, 2.

**24. Why was the place so called?** Because a company of angels met Jacob there.

**25. How ought Jacob to have felt when he saw this angelic guard?** That he was secure against all harm.

*"The angel of the Lord encampeth round about them that fear him, and delivereth them." Ps. 34:7.*

**26. How did he feel when he heard that his brother Esau was coming to meet him?** He was greatly afraid and distressed. Gen. 32:6–23.

**27. How did Jacob act?** He divided his people and flocks into two bands, so that if one were destroyed the other could escape.

**28. What happened to Jacob before he went over the brook?** A heavenly Being wrestled with him during the night, until the break of day. Gen. 32:24–32.

**29. What name did Jacob give to the place where this occurred?** Peniel, or "the face of God."

**30. What change was made in Jacob's name here?** It was changed from Jacob, "supplanter," to Israel, "a prince of God."

**31. What is pictured by this wrestling with Jacob?** Perhaps God's efforts to bring souls to a full and complete surrender to him. Others regard it as typifying prayer.

**32. How did Jacob and Esau meet?** In brotherly affection and peace, in answer to Jacob's prayer. Gen. 33:1–16.

**33. Where did Jacob live when he returned to Canaan?** At Shalem, a city of Shechem, where he bought the first land owned by the family in Canaan, except the burying place in Machpelah. Gen. 33:17–20.

**34. What did God desire Jacob to do?** To go and live at Bethel.

**35. How did Jacob prepare for this journey?** By calling upon his people to put away their idols, and be clean, and change their garments. Gen. 35:1–7.

**36. What great loss came to Jacob when near Bethlehem?** The death of Rachel. Gen. 35:19.

**37. How many sons had Jacob at this time?** Twelve. Gen. 35:22–26.

**38. How far south did Jacob travel?** To Mamre, near Hebron. Gen. 35:27.

**39. Who resided there?** Isaac. He died probably three years later.

**11. JACOB AND HIS SONS (Gen. 37)**

**1. To which son did Jacob show a great partiality?** To Joseph.

**2. Why did Jacob feel this, and how did he show it?** Because Joseph was the son of his old age; the son of his most beloved wife Rachel. By making him a "coat of many colors," a robe of honor, worn by princes and those not expected to work. It was a sign that Jacob intended Joseph to be the head of the family.

**3. Why did the older sons hate Joseph?** Because of their father's partiality to him; and perhaps because his better moral character shamed them.

**4. Had his dreams anything to do with it? What were they?** Yes, most certainly. He dreamed that his brothers' sheaves made obeisance to his, and that the sun, moon, and eleven stars did the same to him.

**5. How did Joseph get into his brothers' power?** On Jacob's sending him to them to see if they were well.

**6. What did they do to him?** They threw him into a pit or dry cistern.

**7. Who proposed this?** Reuben, who intended to restore him to his father.

**8. What other proposal was made, and by whom?** Judah proposed to sell him to a party of Midianite merchants who passed on their way to Egypt.

**9. How old was Joseph at this time?** Seventeen.

**10. What story did they tell to their father?** That they had found his coat bloody, and that he had been killed by a wild beast.

**11. How did Jacob receive the news?** He mourned and refused to be comforted.

**12. JOSEPH IN EGYPT (Gen. 39–41)**

**1. To whom did the Midianites sell Joseph?** To Potiphar, captain of Pharaoh's guard. Gen. 39:1.

**2. To what office did Potiphar appoint Joseph?** Overseer of his house. Gen. 39:2–6.

**3. How was God's favor manifested to Joseph in this situation?** By everything prospering under his care.

**4. What unjust punishment was suffered by Joseph?** He was put in prison. Gen. 39:19–23.

**5. Did the Lord forsake him?** He was with him and showed him mercy.

**6. How did the keeper of the prison behave to Joseph?** He gave him entire charge of the prison.

**7. What happened to two of the prisoners?** Pharaoh's chief butler and chief baker had dreams which troubled them.

**8. How did Joseph help them in their perplexity?** He interpreted their dreams. Gen. 40.

**9. Were his words found true?** Yes, the chief butler was restored and the chief baker was hanged, as Joseph had foretold.

**10. How did Pharaoh's butler behave to Joseph?** He forgot his promise to ask for Joseph's release.

**11. What brought his dream again to his mind?** A dream which Pharaoh had. Gen. 41:1–37.

**12. Did Joseph take the honor of interpretation to himself?** He said, "It is not in me: God shall give Pharaoh an answer of peace."

**13. What position did Pharaoh give Joseph?** He put him over all the land of Egypt, second only to himself, that he might carry out his plans for the famine. Gen. 41:38–57.

**14. How old was Joseph at this time?** Thirty years.

**15. What name did Pharaoh give Joseph, and what is the meaning of it?** Zaphnath-paaneah, "a revealer of secrets," or "the man to whom secrets are revealed."

**16. What were the names of Joseph's wife and sons?** Asenath; Manasseh and Ephraim.

**17. What did Joseph do during the seven years of plenty?** He laid up the food in the cities.

**18. When during the famine the**

**people cried to Pharaoh for food to whom did he send them?** To Joseph.

**19. Did Joseph feed them?** Yes, but in return he took their money, cattle and lands and finally themselves; so that they belonged to Pharaoh. After the famine they gave one-fifth of their incomes to Pharaoh, in return for the use of the land they had thus sold. Gen. 47:14–26.

**20. Was this great famine confined to the land of Egypt?** No, it was over all the face of the earth; or all the part of it them known.

### 13. JACOB AND HIS SONS IN EGYPT (Gen. 42–50)

**1. How did Jacob and his family procure food during the famine?** Ten of Jacob's sons went to buy corn (grain) in Egypt. Gen. 42:1–5.

**2. How did Joseph behave to his brethren when he saw them?** He made himself strange to them and spoke roughly to them; but not from a spirit of revenge. Gen. 42:6–28.

**3. Of what did he accuse them?** Of being spies.

**4. Did he give them food?** Yes, and returned their money.

**5. On what condition did Joseph say he would see them again?** That they should bring Benjamin with them.

**6. How did he make sure they would return?** He kept Simeon a prisoner.

**7. How did Jacob feel when they returned and told him the news?** He felt that all things were against him, and that he should lose Benjamin also.

**8. Did he let Benjamin go?** Yes, there was no other relief from the famine, and Judah promised to be responsible for his

safe return. Gen. 43:1–15.

**9. How did Joseph feel when he saw Benjamin stand among his brethren?** His love was greatly excited, and he retired to weep. Gen. 43:30, 31.

**10. What closer relationship was there between Joseph and his other brothers?** They had the same mother, Rachel. Gen. 30:22–24; 35:16–18.

**11. How old was Benjamin?** He is supposed to have been about seven years younger than Joseph, which would make him thirty-two. He had ten sons at this time. Gen. 46:21.

**12. How did Joseph treat his brothers?** He received them kindly, and made a great feast for them. Gen. 43:25–34.

**13. What was Joseph's intention in all his treatment of his brothers?** To find our whether their character had changed, so to know what was best to be done for them.

**14. What further test did Joseph make of his brothers?** He put a silver cup in Benjamin's sack of grain; then sent his servant to arrest him as a thief and bring him back to slavery in punishment for his crime.

**15. How did Judah behave at this trying time?** He begged that Benjamin might be allowed to go back with the rest, and offered to remain himself as slave in his stead. Gen. 44:18–24.

**16. How was Joseph affected by all this?** He could bear it no longer, but wept aloud, and told them he was Joseph their brother. Gen. 45:1–15.

**17. How did they feel when they knew that this mighty prince was their own brother?** They could not answer him for fear.

**18. What proofs did he give them of it?** He gave proofs of both his love and his power by the rich presents he made them, and the promise of a home and of plenty in Egypt for the whole family. Gen. 45:17–23; 46:29.

**19. How many of Jacob's family lived in Egypt at this time?** Seventy. Gen. 46:25, 27.

**20. Where in the land of Egypt did Jacob and his family dwell?** In the land of Goshen. Gen. 47:1.

**21. How did the Egyptians regard shepherds?** Shepherds were an "abomination" to them, perhaps because the dynasty of the Shepherd Kings had ill-treated them; perhaps because the Egyptians were mainly city-dwellers and despised the country folk.

**22. Was Jacob introduced to Pharaoh?** Yes, and gave him his blessing. Gen. 47:7–10.

**23. How long did Jacob live in Egypt?** Seventeen years. Gen. 47:28.

**24. What peculiar blessing did Jacob give to the sons of Joseph?** He placed his right hand on the younger instead of on the elder, thus giving the birthright to the younger son. Gen. 48.

**25. What was the last recorded act of Jacob?** His blessing his twelve sons just before his death. Gen. 49.

**26. In his prophetical blessing to whom did he give the birthright?** *"For Judah prevailed above his brethren, and of him came the chief ruler; but the birthright was Joseph's." 1 Chron. 5:2.*

**27. What was the special blessing of Judah?** That out of his family the Messiah should come. Gen. 49:10; Heb. 7:14.

**28. Where was Jacob buried?** In the cave of Machpelah, with his ancestors and his wife Leah. Gen. 49:29–32; 50:13.

**29. What fear had Joseph's brethren after Jacob's death?** That Joseph would now ill-treat and punish them; but he comforted them and spoke kindly to them. Gen. 50:15.

**30. When was Joseph buried?** His body was doubtless prepared in the Egyptian way for preservation; but the final interment was not until the Israelites reached Canaan after the Exodus. Gen. 50:26.

*"And the bones of Joseph, which the children of Israel brought up out of Egypt, buried they in Shechem, in a parcel of ground which Jacob bought of the sons of Hamor, the father of Shechem, for an hundred pieces of silver." Josh. 24:32.*

## 14. THE BIRTH AND EDUCATION OF MOSES (Ex. 1–2)

**1. How did the Egyptians behave to the children of Israel after the death of Joseph?** After the death of those who had seen what Joseph did for them they enslaved and oppressed them. Ex. 1:6–14.

**2. Did the children of Israel increase very rapidly?** They did.

**3. Why did this make the Egyptians afraid?** Lest they should join their enemies, because their lands lay between Egypt and their most dreaded enemies.

**4. How were the children of Israel employed by the Egyptians?** In making bricks, in building, and in other service.

**5. What cruel plan did Pharaoh make to lessen the power of the Israelites?** To employ the Hebrew midwives to kill the Hebrew boys at birth. Ex. 1:16.

**6. Who was Moses?** The second son of Amram and Jochebed of the tribe of Levi. Ex. 2:1; 6:20.

**7. What plan did his mother adopt to spare his life?** She hid him in a floating basket among the flags growing by the banks of the river Nile. Ex. 2:3.

**8. How did her plan succeed?** The child was found by Pharaoh's daughter, who took charge of it.

**9. Whom had his mother set to watch the little basket, or ark?** His sister Miriam.

**10. When the princess sought a nurse for the child whom did Miriam bring?** His mother.

**11. What blessing did this ensure to Moses?** The tenderest care, and knowledge of the true God and training in his worship.

**12. What did Moses gain by his adoption by the princess?** First, of course, his life. Second, a splendid education, as the Egyptians had the highest knowledge and culture in the world at the time. Third, training in war, in leadership of men, etc. All just what he would need when the time came to deliver Israel.

**13. With whom did Moses join himself—with the Egyptians or the Hebrews?** Ex. 2:11–14.

*"By faith Moses, when he was come to years, refused to be called the son of Pharaoh's daughter; choosing rather to suffer affliction with the people of God." Heb. 11:24, 25.*

**14. Did they receive him graciously?** No.

*"Who made thee a ruler and a judge over us? Wilt thou kill me, as thou diddest the Egyptian yesterday?" Acts 7:27, 28.*

**15. What was Moses obliged to do?** To leave Egypt and flee to the land of Midian in the Arabian desert. Ex. 2:15–22.

**16. What happened to him there?** He married a daughter of the priest or prince of Midian.

**17. How long did he stay there?** Forty years. Acts 7:30.

**18. Of what value was this experience?** It gave him lessons in self-control; took him away from the corruption of the court; and made him familiar with the country through which Israel must pass on their way to Canaan.

### 15. MOSES' CALL TO DELIVER ISRAEL (Ex. 3–4)

**1. What wondrous sight attracted the attention of Moses while he was keeping his father-in-law's flock in the desert?** A burning bush unconsumed. Ex. 3:2, 3.

**2. Whose voice addressed him from the midst of the fire?** The voice of God. Ex. 3:4–6.

**3. What commission did the Lord give to Moses?** To bring the Israelites out of Egypt. He would first be obliged to ask Pharaoh's permission. Ex. 3:7–22.

**4. Was Moses willing to undertake it?** He said Israel would not believe that God had appeared to him. Ex. 4:1.

**5. What signs did the Lord give him to show that he was God's messenger?** The changing of Moses' rod into a serpent, the making his hand leprous and then restoring it and the transmutation of water to blood. Ex. 4:2–8.

**6. Did this remove Moses' difficulties?** He then said he was too poor a speaker to deliver God's message. Ex. 4:10.

**7. How did God help him here?** He promised to teach him what to say; and told him to take with him his brother Aaron, who could speak well. Ex. 4:11–16, 27.

**8. How did the Israelites receive the message?** They believed and worshiped God, but later they murmured. Ex. 4:31. See 16, 3.

## 16. THE PLAGUES OF EGYPT (Ex. 5–11)

**1. Was the king of Egypt now the same Pharaoh who had ordered the little children to be killed?** No, the word "Pharaoh" was the title, not the name of the ruler. It was now between eighty and eighty-three years after the edict.

**2. How did he receive Moses and Aaron when they went to him?** He abused them for interfering with the people's work. Ex. 5:2–4.

**3. What was the result?** Heavier work was laid upon the people, for which they blamed Moses. Ex. 5:5–21.

**4. When Pharaoh refused to let the people go what happened?** The ten plagues came on the land as a warning and a punishment.

**5. What were the first nine plagues?** (1) The water of the river Nile turned into blood (Ex. 7). (2) A great number of frogs which came into the houses (Ex. 8:1–15). (3) Lice on man and beast (Ex. 8:16–19). (4) Swarms of flies or stinging insects (Ex. 8:20–32). (5) A murrain or sickness on all cattle, etc. (Ex. 9:1–7). (6) Boils and sores on man and beast (Ex. 9:8–12). (7) A storm of hail and lightning which destroyed vegetation and cattle (Ex. 9:13–35). (8) A terrible and destructive swarm of locusts (Ex. 10:1–20). (9) A thick darkness for three days (Ex. 10:21–29).

**6. How was the first plague a peculiar trial to the Egyptians?** Because they used the water for drinking; a large part of their food was fish; the yearly overflowing of the Nile was most valuable for their land; and they worshiped the river as a god.

**7. How far could the magicians imitate Moses and Aaron?** So far as to turn water into blood and to bring frogs; but they could not take the frogs away.

**8. What did they say when they could go no further?** That the miracles of Moses were the finger of God. Ex. 8:19.

**9. When and how did God mark the distinction between the Egyptians and the Israelites?** No plagues after the third affected the land of Goshen, where the Israelites lived.

**10. What merciful provision did God make in the seventh plague for all who would believe his word?** He warned them to remove their cattle to a place of shelter.

**11. Why was it that all these judgments had no effect on Pharaoh?** Because his heart was hardened, or he hardened his own heart, as it is expressed in Ex. 8:15, 32; 9:34, 35, so that God gave him up to his own wicked heart.

**12. Is it not an awful thing when God gives a man over to his own hardened heart?**
*"If we sin wilfully after that we have received the knowledge of the truth, there remaineth no more sacrifice for sins, but a certain fearful looking for of judgment and fiery indignation, which shall devour the adversaries." Heb. 10:26, 27.*

**13. What effect did the ninth plague have on Pharaoh?** Pharaoh bade Moses see his face no more.

**14. What was the tenth plague?** The death of the first-born. See 17 and 18.

**17. THE PASSOVER (Ex. 12:1–28)**

**1. What did God command the Israelites to do before he brought the last plague on the Egyptians?** To have the passover sacrifice and feast.

**2. Of what did it consist?** The passover meal consisted principally of a lamb, to be eaten with bitter herbs and unleavened bread. Later there were religious exercises connected with the rite.

**3. Of whom was the lamb a type?** Of Christ the Lamb of God, slain from the foundation of the world. John 1:29; Rev. 13:8.

**4. In how many ways was the passover lamb a type of Christ?** In its gentleness and unblemished innocence, and in its being slain without one bone being broken; and in many other ways.

**5. How was the bread to be prepared?** Without any leaven, or yeast, to raise it.

**6. Of what does the apostle Paul declare this to be a type?** Of "sincerity and truth." 1 Cor. 5:7, 8.

**7. What did the bitter herbs signify?** The bitterness of Egyptian bondage, of true sorrow for sin, and of Christ's cup of suffering. Ps. 69:20, 21.

**8. How was the passover to be eaten?** The people were to be entirely prepared to start at once on their journey out of Egypt; and they were to eat it standing, to be the more ready. Later passovers were eaten sitting or reclining in the Oriental manner.

**9. What other command was given them?** That they should strike the lintels and doorposts of their houses with the blood of the slain lamb.

**10. Why was this to be done?** As a sign that they were Israelites and worshipers of Jehovah, so that the angel who was to slay the first-born of the Egyptians might not slay their children.

**11. What is the meaning of the word "passover"?** It refers to the destroying angel passing over the blood-sprinkled doors of the children of Israel.

**18. THE EXODUS (Ex. 12:29–14:31)**

**1. What did Pharaoh do when he found the threatened death of his first-born child had come to pass?** He ordered the Israelites to depart quickly. Ex. 12:31, 32.

**2. How did God recompense the Israelites for all they had suffered at the hands of the Egyptians?** By disposing the Egyptians to give them gold and silver and raiment. Ex. 12:35, 36.

**3. Was it honest to "borrow" so much at this time?** The word translated "borrow" should have been rendered "asked." The things were not intended as loans, but as gifts. Besides they had worked for years without wages. And lastly, they left much property in the land which could not be carried away.

**4. In what way did the Israelites obey the king's command?** They hurried away with their flocks and herds and hastily prepared food. Ex. 12:37–39.

**5. Did Pharaoh quietly allow them to go?** After he had recovered from his first fright he sent an army to pursue them and bring them back. Ex. 14.

**6. What did Israel say to Moses when they saw the sea before them and Pharaoh's army behind?** That they had better have remained in Egypt.

**7. What did Moses answer?** He told them to wait and see how God would save them.

**8. What had the Israelites to guide them?** A pillar of cloud and of fire.

**9. How did God keep the hosts separate all the night?** By the pillar of cloud and fire which kept the Egyptians in darkness and prevented them from moving on; but which gave light to the Israelites.

**10. How did God save the Israelites?** By making a way for them through the sea.

**11. How did he keep the Egyptian chariots from overtaking them?** He took off the chariot wheels in the soft mud so "that they drove them heavily."

**12. Ought we ever to doubt a God who can help his people in any difficulty?** "If God be for us, who can be against us?" Rom. 8:31.

**13. What happened as soon as Israel was safely over the sea?** The Egyptians were overwhelmed by the returning waters.

## 19. THEIR JOURNEY BEGUN (Ex. 15)

**1. What was the first thing done after the crossing?** Moses and all Israel sang a song of praise to God for his mercy.

**2. How many days did Israel travel in the wilderness before they found water?** Three.

**3. And when they found water of what kind was it?** Bitter; at Marah.

**4. How did the children of Israel bear this disappointment?** They murmured against Moses.

**5. Where did Israel next encamp?** At Elim.

**6. What blessing had the Lord in store for them there?** Plenty of water, and seventy palm trees; a true desert oasis.

## 20. THE MANNA (Ex. 16)

**1. How were the Israelites fed in the wilderness?** For the most part with manna.

**2. What was manna?** A small round thing, about the size of a frozen drop of dew, miraculously sent by God, and suitable for food.

**3. How often were they to gather it?** Every day except the Sabbath-day.

**4. What provision did the Lord make for sanctifying the Sabbath-day, and resting on it?** A double quantity of manna was given the day before.

**5. Were the Children of Israel obedient to the Lord in this arrangement?** Some of them went out to gather on the Sabbath-day; but they found none.

**6. Of whom is the manna declared to have been the type?** Of Jesus Christ, the Son of God, the "living bread which came down from heaven." John 6:51.

**7. Were the Israelites satisfied with God's provision?** Not all, for they said, once, "Our soul loatheth this light bread." Num. 21:5.

## 21. THE SMITTEN ROCK (Ex. 17:1–7)

**1. How were the Israelites supplied with water in the wilderness when the springs failed them?** From a stream that flowed from a rock in Horeb when Moses struck it with his rod.

**2. Of whom is the smitten rock a beautiful type?** "That Rock was Christ." 1 Cor. 10:4.

**3. What did Jesus say about this?** *"But whosoever drinketh of the water that I shall give him shall never thirst; but the water that I shall give him shall be in him a well of water springing up into everlasting life." John 4:14.*

## 22. THE BATTLE WITH AMALEK (Ex. 17:8–16)

**1. Who were the Amalekites?** Descendants of Esau, living to the south of Palestine, in the Sinai region.

**2. Why did they attack Israel?** Israel had occupied one of their oases, and water was one frequent reason for war then. They thought Israel was weak and that now was their opportunity, but they forgot that God was on Israel's side.

**3. Was not God angry with them for this?** God sentenced them to constant war, and at last to destruction.

**4. Which army now obtained the victory?** The Israelites.

**5. How was this?** By Moses' continued prayer.

**6. What lesson is for us in the story?** First, the importance of prayer in our own difficulties; and also our duty to support and aid and "hold up the hands" of our leaders, so far as we are able. Ex. 17:12.

**7. What is the meaning of Jehovah-nissi?** "The Lord my banner."

## 23. THE LAW FROM SINAI (Ex. 19–24)

**1. What is the Law?** The term here refers to the Ten Commandments, and to other laws which immediately follow.

**2. Under what circumstances did God give the Law?** From the top of Mount Sinai, amidst thunder and lightening, clouds and darkness, trumpetblast and earthquake. Ex. 19.

**3. Where is Sinai?** In the southern part of what is now called the Arabian Peninsula.

**4. Could Israel bear the presence of God?** They could not. They asked that Moses speak to them, "but let not God speak with us, lest we die." Ex. 20:19.

**5. Who went up into the thick darkness where God was?** Moses. Ex. 19:20; 20:21.

**6. When he came forth with God's message to them what did they promise?** To do all the words which God had said. Ex. 24:3.

**7. What are the Ten Commandments?** Learn them by heart and repeat them. They are found in Ex. 20:3–17.

**8. What is the division into the "two tables of the Law"?** Commandments 1–4, "the first table of the Law," are the duties man owes to God; the rest, "the second table of the Law," are the duties man owe to man.

## 24. THE COVENANT BROKEN (Ex. 32)

**1. How long was Moses on the mount with God?** For forty days and forty nights. Ex. 24:18.

**2. What proof of their inability to keep the Law did Israel give while Moses was on the mount?** They made and worshiped a golden calf, probably after some idol in Egypt. It was doubtless intended as an image of Jehovah. But see Ex. 20:4–6.

**3. Who was their leader?** Aaron, who without doubt remonstrated, but being not strong enough to prevent it, did as they asked him.

**4. How was the calf worshiped?** With an idolatrous feast and dancing about the idol.

**5. What did Moses do when he saw this?** He broke the stone tables as they had broken the Law, and he destroyed the golden calf.

**6. How did Aaron excuse himself?** Partly by laying the blame on the people.

**7. How was Israel punished?** The leaders were slain with the sword, and later there was a plague.

**8. Was this not unnecessarily severe?** No, Moses called first for all "who were on the Lord's side" to come to him. All might have come if they had so chosen. Also, as they had no king but God, such an act was treason, and the worse because done so soon after their solemn covenant.

## 25. THE INTERCESSION OF MOSES FOR ISRAEL (Ex. 32:30–35; 33; 34)

**1. Who interceded for Israel at this awful time?** Moses, who returned into the mount.

**2. What proof did the Lord give to Moses that he had accepted him?** Allowing him to see something of his glory and proclaiming to him his name.

**3. How was the Law given the second time?** Moses took two fresh tables of stone up the mount, and God wrote on them the Ten Commandments. Ex. 34:1–28.

**4. How long was Moses in the mount this time?** Forty days and forty nights. Deut. 10:10.

**5. What showed that Moses had talked face to face with God?** His face shone. Ex. 34:29, 30.

*"And there arose not a prophet since in Israel like unto Moses, whom the Lord knew face to face." Deut. 34:10.*

**6. How did the children of Israel feel when they saw this?** They were afraid to come near him. Ex. 34:30.

## 26. THE TABERNACLE (Ex. 35–40)

**1. How did Moses learn how to make the tabernacle?** From God himself, and a pattern shown him on the mount. Ex. 25:9, 40.

**2. Whom did God specially endow with skill for this work?** Bezaleel and Aholiab, and other wise-hearted men. Ex. 36:1.

**3. Where did Moses get the materials?** From the free offerings of the people. Ex. 35:21–29; 36:3–7.

**4. When was the tabernacle finished?** On the first day of the first month of the second year of the sojourn in the wilderness. Ex. 40:17.

**5. Of whom is the tabernacle a type?** Of Jesus Christ, the "true" and "perfect tabernacle." Heb. 8:2; 9:11.

**6. Are our bodies compared to a tabernacle?** Yes, one to be taken down, that we should dwell in enduring mansions in heaven. 2 Cor. 5:1.

**7. What was the furniture in the tabernacle?** That named: (1) the brazen altar of burnt offering, and (2) the laver, in the court of the tabernacle; (3) the table of shewbread, (4) the candlestick, or lampstand, and (5) the golden altar of incense, in the holy place; and (6) the ark of the testimony in the holy of holies.

**8. Who first kindled a fire on the altar of burnt offering?** God himself. Lev. 9:24.

**9. What stood next to the brazen altar in the outer court?** The laver holding the water for the priests to wash. Ex. 40:30–32.

**10. Of what was the laver made?** Of bronze taken from the mirrors—plates of polished metal—which the women used.

**11. What was the shewbread?** Bread offered to the Lord. There were twelve loaves, one for each tribe. It remained in the holy place for one week, and was then eaten by the priests. Lev. 24:5–9.

**12. Of what was the incense a type?** Of the prayers of the people. Rev. 8:3, 4.

**13. Who ministered in the holy place?** The priests, who alone were allowed within it. Heb. 9:6.

**14. Who alone might go into the holy of holies?**

*"But into the second went the high priest alone once every year, not without blood, which he offered for himself, and for the errors of the people." Heb. 9:7.*

**15. Of what was this most holy place a type?** Of the immediate presence of God.

**16. Who has entered there?**

*"Seeing then that we have a great high priest, that is passed into the heavens, Jesus, the Son of God, let us hold fast our profession." Heb. 4:14.*

**17. What was put between the holy place and the holy of holies?** A beautiful veil of rich materials, finely embroidered.

**18. What happened to the beautiful veil of the temple when the Lord Jesus was crucified?** It was rent in twain from the top to the bottom.

**19. What did this show?** That now the way to heaven was open without a human mediating priest. Heb. 10:19–22.

**20. What stood in the most holy place?** The ark of the covenant, or testimony.

**21. Of what was the ark made?** Of shittim wood, overlaid with gold. Ex. 25:10, 11.

**22. How did it represent the glory of God?** By the mercy-seat and the cherubim above it. Ex. 25:17–22.

**23. What was preserved in the ark?** The golden pot filled with manna. Aaron's rod that budded, and the tables of the covenant. Heb. 9:4.

**24. What dreadful thing happened after the first beginning of the services in the tabernacle?** Nadab and Abihu, sons of Aaron, offered incense in a way displeasing to God, and he slew them. Lev. 10.

**25. What probably was the reason?** Lev. 10:9 intimates that they may have been under the influence of strong drink.

## 27. THE SACRIFICES AND OFFERINGS (Lev. 1–17)

**1. Name the four principal offerings.**
The burnt offering (Lev. 1); the sin offering (Lev. 4); the trespass offering (Lev. 5:1–7:7); and the peace offering (Lev. 3).

**The sin offering** referred rather to atonement, and **the burnt offering** to self-dedication.

**The peace offering,** whether from the herd or the flock, was an expression of thankfulness to God for his gifts.

**The meat offering,** or better, meal offering (Lev. 2) of flour, oil and wine, was also a sacrifice of thanksgiving.

**2. Who was prefigured by all these sacrifices?** Jesus Christ, the great Atonement and the self-devoted Sacrifice, who, being once offered, hath for ever taken away sins. Heb. 10:1–18.

**3. Name some of the ceremonies of the great day of atonement.** Aaron the high priest made sin offerings for himself and for the people, and sprinkled the blood upon the mercy seat in the most holy place; confessed the sins of the people over the scapegoat, and sent it away into the wilderness, and offered burnt offerings for himself and for the people. Lev. 16.

**4. What is the meaning of the word "atonement"?** Reconciliation, or setting at one again, by a sacrifice in another's stead: at-one-ment.

**5. Who has atoned for our sins?** Jesus Christ, who suffered in our stead their punishment.

## 28. THE FEASTS (Lev. 23)

**1. Which is the first "feast" spoken of?** The sabbath. Lev. 23:3.

**2. How often was it to be kept?** Every seventh day.

**3. When was the keeping of the sabbath first commanded?** In the garden of Eden, God first sanctified it, or set it apart as holy. See also Ex. 16 and 20.

*"God blessed the seventh day, and sanctified it: because that in it he had rested from all his work which God created and made." Gen. 2:3.*

**4. Why is it here called a "feast"?**

Because it is a day of sacred rest and joyful worship. See Heb. 4:8–11.

**5. Does God always unite happiness and joy with religion?** He does.

*"If thou turn away thy foot from the sabbath, from doing thy pleasure on my holy day; and call the sabbath a delight, the holy of the Lord, honorable; and shalt honor him, not doing thine own ways, nor finding thine own pleasure, no speaking thine own words: then shalt thou delight thyself in the Lord; and I will cause thee to ride upon the high places of the earth, and feed thee with the heritage of Jacob thy father: for the mouth of the Lord hath spoken it." Isa. 58:13, 14.*

**6. Which was the second feast or festival spoken of?** The feast of the passover, or of unleavened bread. Lev. 23:5–8.

**7. When was that kept?** It began on the fifteenth day of the first month, about our March or April.

**8. How was it kept?** By the sacrifice of a lamb; the use of unleavened bread, and of bitter herbs.

**9. When was this instituted?** When the Israelites came out of Egypt. See 17.

**10. What feast or festival came next?** The offering of the first-fruits of the harvest at pentecost, fifty days after the passover. Lev. 23:9–22.

**11. What ceremony were they to perform with the first sheaf?** The priest was to wave it before the Lord.

**12. What did "waving" it mean?** An act of worship of the Lord of the whole earth.

**13. What festival was held on the first day of the seventh month?** The feast of trumpets. Lev. 23:23–25.

**14. How many days after this festival of trumpets was the great day of atonement kept?** Nine days.

**15. What was the day of atonement?** See 27, 3.

**16. How many days after the day of atonement was the feast of tabernacles?** Five days. Lev. 23:34–43

**17. What ceremonies marked this festival?** The offering of sacrifices, and the dwelling in booths for eight days. It was to be held perpetually in memory of their dwelling in tents in the wilderness.

## 29. THE NUMBERING OF THE ISRAELITES, AND THE DEPARTURE FROM SINAI (Num. 1–4; 7–10)

**1. How long had the children of Israel remained at Sinai?** About eleven months.

**2. What were some of the most important events that had taken place there?** The giving of the law; the worship of the golden calf; the making of the tabernacle; and the punishment of Nadab and Abihu.

**3. What rite did they celebrate on the fourteenth of the first month?** The passover. Num. 9:1–5.

**4. What did God command Moses to do on the first of the second month?** To number the people. Num. 1:1–3.

**5. Whom did God accept for his service instead of the firstborn?** The Levites; and since the firstborn were more in number, five shekels (about $3.20) were paid into the tabernacle treasury for each one in excess.

**6. How were the children of Israel to march and to encamp on their journey?** Each tribe by itself in a fixed order and place, the Levites in the midst. Num. 2.

**7. How was it shown that they were to march?** The moving of the cloud from the tabernacle. Num. 9:17–23.

**8. How was the baggage, etc., carried?** In wagons, except the holy things of the tabernacle, which were borne by the sons of Kohath of the tribe of Levi, on their shoulders. Num. 4:2–15; 7:2–9.

**9. What did each of the princes of Israel offer as a gift to the service of the tabernacle?** Gold and silver vessels and animals for sacrifice. Num. 7.

**10. On what day did the cloud first move?** On the twentieth day of the second month of the second year after the Exodus. Num. 10:11.

**11. Whom did Moses entreat to accompany them?** Hobab the son of Raguel the Midianite, his father-in-law. Num. 10:29.

**12. What proofs have we that he afterward went with the Israelites into the promised land?**
*"The children of the Kenite, Moses' father-in-law, went up out of the city of palm trees with the children of Judah into the wilderness of Judah, which lieth in the south of Arad; and they went and dwelt among the people." Judg. 1:16.*

**13. When all was ready for marching what beautiful prayer did Moses offer?**
*"Rise up, Lord, and let thine enemies be scattered; and let them that hate thee flee before thee." Num. 10:35.*

**14. And what when the ark rested again?**
*"Return, O Lord, unto the many thousands of Israel." Num. 10:36.*

## 30. MURMURINGS (Num. 11)

**1. Had the Israelites by this time learned to obey God?** No, as is shown by their repeated rebellions against him. Heb. 3:8–12; Ps. 106:7, 8, 13–46.

**2. On what did the Lord feed Israel at Sinai?** On manna.

**3. Ought they not, then, to have trusted God on their journey?** Yes; but instead they ungratefully and discontentedly desired a change of food. Num. 11:1–6.

**4. Did they obtain this change of food?** Yes, the Lord sent quails into the camp so that they had abundance. But they probably indulged in them to excess, as they produced a disease. Num. 11:19, 20, 31–33.

**5. Did not Moses feel their continuous provocation too much for him?** He complained to God of the burden it was to him. Num. 11:11–15.

**6. How did the Lord assist him?** He appointed seventy elders to assist him. Num. 11:16, 17.

## 31. THE SIN OF AARON AND MIRIAM (Num. 12)

**1. What was the sin of Aaron and Miriam?** They claimed equal authority with Moses.

**2. What special favor had God given Moses?** More friendly conversation with himself, and a near view of his glory.

**3. Who was the leader in this sin?** It seems to have been Miriam, as she had the severer punishment, being afflicted with leprosy.

**4. Who pleaded for Miriam?** Aaron with Moses, and Moses with God.

**5. Did the Lord remove her punishment?** Yes, but she had to obey the law of leprosy, which required one when healed of the leprosy to be isolated for seven days. Num. 12:14, 15; Lev. 13:46.

**6. Of what was her punishment the type?** Of the loathsomeness of her sin in the eyes of God.

## 32. THE REPORT OF THE SPIES (Num. 13:14)

**1. Where were the children of Israel at this time?** In Kadesh in the wilderness of Paran, near the southern boundary of Canaan.

**2. What did God command Moses to do?** To send men to search the land of Canaan. Num. 13:2.

**3. How many were sent?** Twelve, one from each tribe. Num. 13:3–16.

**4. Which of them are otherwise known to us?** Caleb and Joshua.

**5. How long were they in searching the land?** Forty days. Num. 13:25.

**6. What report did they bring back?** That the land was very rich and fertile, flowed "with milk and honey," but that the inhabitants were giants and the cities were great and walled. Num. 13:26–33.

**7. What conclusion did they reach?** Ten of them said, "We are not able to go up and conquer the land." The other two, Caleb and Joshua, said, "The Lord will help us and bring victory over the people of the land." Num. 13:30; 14:6–9.

**8. What effect did this have on the people?** They were in great distress, and proposed returning to Egypt. Num. 14:1–4.

**9. What did Moses and Aaron do?** They fell on their faces in humiliation and prayer. Num. 14:5.

**10. What did the people do when Caleb and Joshua tried to quiet their fears?** They prepared to stone them. Num. 14:10.

**11. Who appeared at the moment when they were about to be stoned?** God himself in the glory on the tabernacle.

**12. What did God propose to Moses?** To disinherit Israel, and to make of Moses a mightier nation than theirs. Num. 14:11, 12.

**13. Did Moses accept this great honor?** No, he pleaded for their pardon instead. Num. 14:13–25.

**14. What punishment came upon the ten spies who discouraged the people?** They died of the plague. Num. 14:36, 37.

**15. What punishment did the Lord lay on the people?** To wander forty years in the wilderness; and to die there, instead of entering the promised land. Num. 14:33.

**16. Was this punishment too arbitrary and severe?** No, they were not yet fitted to resist the temptations of the idolators living there, if they could not trust God better than they had.

**17. What special mercy did God grant to Caleb and Joshua?** That they alone of their generation should enter the land of Canaan. Num. 14:26–38.

**18. Of what foolish act were the people guilty the next day?** They attempted to enter the land; doing against God's command what they had been afraid to do with his help. Num. 14:40–45.

**19. What was the result?** They were attacked, defeated, and driven back to Kadesh.

## 33. THE SABBATH-BREAKER; THE SIN OF KORAH; AND THE BUDDING ROD (Num. 15–17)

**1. Of what sin was a man found guilty about this time?** Of gathering sticks upon the sabbath day. Num. 15:32–36.

**2. How was he punished?** He was stoned to death at God's command.

**3. Was this not too severe?** No, the people had not learned obedience and they had to learn. Also, as God was their only king such disobedience was virtually treason.

**4. Had not God threatened this punishment for the breaking of this command?** *"Ye shall keep the sabbath therefore; for it is holy unto you; every one that defileth it shall surely be put to death; for whosoever doeth any work therein, that soul shall be cut off from among his people." Ex. 31:14.*

**5. What did the Lord order the people to make that they might keep his commandments in remembrance?** A blue fringe on the borders of their garments. Num. 15:38–40.

**6. Who were Korah, Dathan and Abiram?** Korah, a Levite, the others Reubenites, who rebelled against the regulations for the priesthood. Num. 16.

**7. What did Moses propose for these men to do?** That they should come to the tabernacle, burning incense, to see whether or not God would accept them as priests.

**8. In what way did God at once manifest his displeasure?** By commanding Moses and Aaron and the congregation to keep away from the rebellious company and their dwellings, when the earth opened and swallowed them.

**9. How large a company did these men have, and what became of them?** There were two hundred and fifty, and a fire from the Lord consumed them.

**10. Did this still the murmurings of the people?** The people then charged Moses and Aaron with killing the people of the Lord.

**11. How did God again appear to vindicate the honor of his own appointed priesthood?** About fourteen thousand were struck down with the plague.

**12. What did Moses command Aaron to do to avert the judgment he felt was about to fall on the people?** To burn incense and make an atonement.

**13. What was done with the censers of the rebels?** They were beaten into plates to cover the altar as a memorial of their sin.

**14. How did the Lord himself show whom he had chosen?** He commanded that the head of each tribe should take a rod, and place it in the tabernacle. He declared that he would then show his choice of the head of the priesthood by causing one rod to bloom. On the morrow Aaron's rod had bloomed and born fruit. Ex. 17:1–10.

### 34. THE SIN OF MOSES AND AARON (Num. 20)

**1. What trial of their faith did the children of Israel have in the desert of Zin?** The want of water.

**2. How did they behave?** They reproached Moses for it.

**3. What did the Lord command Moses to do?** To speak to the rock before the people, and it should give forth water.

**4. How did Moses in this matter dishonor the Lord?** He spoke as if he and Aaron, by their own power, would bring the water out; and he also struck the rock.

**5. What punishment did he and Aaron thus bring upon themselves?** They were not allowed to enter the promised land.

**6. Where did Aaron die?** On Mount Hor.

**7. What solemnity attended it?** The removal, first, of his priestly robes, and putting them on Eleazar his son.

**8. What mark of respect did the children of Israel pay to the memory of Aaron?** They mourned for him thirty days.

**9. Of whom was Aaron a type?** Of the Lord Jesus our great High Priest.

**10. How does the priesthood of the Lord Jesus excel the priesthood of Aaron?** Jesus Christ is God, and a priest forever.

### 35. THE BRAZEN SERPENT (Num. 21:1–9)

**1. Why were the people now especially discouraged?** They were on their way from Kadesh to the point in Canaan where it was best that they should enter the country; and the Edomites, who lay directly on their route refused them passage. Num. 20:14–21.

**2. From whom were the Edomites descended?** From Esau, who was called Edom, or "red" from the red pottage he got from Jacob. Gen. 25:30; 36:1. See 9. 6.

**3. What other trouble did they have?** A renewed want of food and water.

**4. How did the Lord punish them for their murmuring?** By means of fiery serpents—fiery in their color or in their bite.

**5. What remedy was Moses commanded to prepare?** A serpent of brass upon a pole, that the people might look at it; and all who had faith to look were healed.

**6. Of whom was this a type?** Of Jesus Christ; as the sinner may look at him and live. John 3:14, 15.

## 36. BALAAM (Num. 21:10–25:17; 31:1–8

**1. How far had the children of Israel now got on their journey?** To the wilderness before Moab on the east side of the Jordan.

**2. What two mighty kings did they conquer and slay?** Sihon, king of the Amorites, and Og, king of Bashan. Num. 21:23–35.

**3. What description is given of Og in Deuteronomy?**

*"For only Og king of Bashan remained of the remnant of giants; behold, his bedstead was a bedstead of iron; is it not in Rabbath of the children of Ammon? Nine cubits was the length thereof, and four cubits the breadth of it, after the cubits of a man. Deut. 3:11.*

**4. What was the name of the king of Moab?** Balak. Num. 22:2–4.

**5. Who was Balaam?** A noted soothsayer, or pretended prophet, who lived by the Euphrates in Mesopotamia, and who sometimes received revelations from God. Num. 24:1–2.

**6. Why did Balak desire so much to see him?** To get him to curse the Israelites, so that he might overcome them. Num. 22:5–6.

**7. Did Balaam desire to go?** Yes, as the rewards which were offered him tempted him greatly.

**8. What hindered him?** The command of God. Num. 22:7–21.

**9. Did God permit him to have his own way?** Yes.

**10. Did that show that God was pleased with his errand?** No, but it gave God the opportunity to show his power over Balaam in a more public and striking manner. Num. 23:7–12.

**11. How did God show his disapprobation?** By sending his angel to stop him on the way. Num. 22:22–34.

**12. Did God send Balaam back or allow him to go on?** He let him go on. Num. 22:35.

**13. Had Balaam any power when he got there?** Only to say what God told him. Num. 22:38.

**14. Did he try to accomplish Balak's wish?** Yes, he tried by divination, while Balak offered sacrifices; but God made him utter a blessing instead of a curse. Num. 23:3, 8–10, 15, 20–24; 24:1–9.

**15. How did Balak feel when he found he had brought a blessing instead of a curse on his enemies?** He was angry with Balaam. Num. 24:10.

**16. When Balaam found he could not prevail by enchantment what did he do?** He yielded to the power of God and uttered a beautiful prophecy. Num. 24:13–17.

*"I shall see him, but not now: I shall behold him, but not nigh: there shall come a Star out of Jacob, and a Sceptre shall rise out of Israel."*

**17. How did he show he was a bad man?** By his infamous advice to Balak to tempt the children of Israel to sin. Rev. 2:14.

**18. What was his end?** He was killed by the Israelites in battle with the Midianites. Num. 31:8.

### 37. THE CITIES OF REFUGE
### (Num. 35; Deut. 19; Josh. 20)

**1. How many men were now left of those who came out of Egypt with Moses?** Only two, Caleb and Joshua. Num. 26:65.

**2. How was this?** God had said that all the rest should die in the wilderness. See 32. 15.

**3. What petition did Moses present to the Lord near the close of his life?** That the Lord would provide him a successor. Num. 27:15–23.

**4. Whom did the Lord appoint?** Joshua, of the tribe of Ephraim, who had been one of Israel's greatest men, and with Caleb had been a loyal spy when the rest had brought a bad report.

**5. What tribe was to have no regular home in Palestine?** The Levites, who were to furnish the priests and religious leaders.

**6. How many cities out of the tribes of Israel were to be given to them?** Forty-eight. Num. 35:7.

**7. For what purpose were six of these cities to be separated?** For cities of refuge.

**8. Who had the privilege of fleeing thither?** Any one who had unintentionally killed another.

**9. Was there any protection to be given to the wilful murderer?** No, if he took refuge there he must be given up as soon as his guilt was shown. Num. 35:11; Deut. 19:11, 12.

**10. Who was the "avenger of blood"?** The next of kin to the slain person, whose duty it was to see that the murderer was punished.

**11. How many witnesses were necessary to prove a murderer?** Two. Num. 35:30.

**12. What event released the unintentional manslayer from the city of refuge and permitted him to go at large again without fear of death?** The death of the high priest.

**13. Of whom were those cities of refuge a type?** Of Christ, the sinner's refuge from Satan and the wrath to come.

**14. Where were these cities of refuge?** Three on the east of Jordan, in the tribes of Reuben, Gad and Manasseh; and three on the west, in Naphtali, Manasseh and Judah. There was one on each side of the river in the extreme north of the land, one on each side at about the middle, and one on each side at nearly the extreme south. Deut. 4:41–43; Josh. 20:7, 8.

**15. What about the roads thither?** All the roads which led to these cities were kept in good order, and care was paid that there were no obstacles in the roads, and that there were signposts to show which road to take.

### 38. THE LAST DAYS OF MOSES
### (Deuteronomy)

**1. Of what is the book of Deuteronomy a summary?** Of much of the history and laws in the three foregoing books, in the form of three farewell discourses of Moses to Israel.

**2. Of whom does Moses speak in Deut. 18:15–19 as "the prophet"?** Of Jesus Christ. Acts 3:20–22.

**3. What beautiful ceremony does he bid them perform when they should get into the promised land?** To bring a basket of the first-fruits to the priest as a thank offering to God. Deut. 26:1–11.

**4. What were the names of the two mountains on which the blessings and the curses were to be written?** Ebal and Gerizim. Deut. 27:1–8, 11–26.

**5. What fearful prophecy and warning did Moses utter?** Curses of pestilence, drought, war, famine, and other evils for disobedience of God's law. Deut. 28–30.

**6. In what way did the Lord signally set apart Joshua to the office of leader of the people?** By appearing to him in the tabernacle in the pillar of cloud. Deut. 31:14, 15.

**7. In what way did Moses preserve what he said to them?** By writing it and delivering it to the priests, to be put into the ark of the covenant. Deut. 31:9, 24–26.

**8. What special song was he commanded to write and rehearse before them?** That contained in Deut. 32:1–43; 31:19.

**9. What did the Lord command Moses to do immediately after he had finished this work?** To go up Mount Nebo, where he should die. Deut. 32:48–52.

**10. What splendid vision did the Lord give him before he died?** That of the land of Canaan. Deut. 34:2–4.

**11. In what did Moses differ from any other prophet?**

*"And there arose not a prophet since in Israel like unto Moses, whom the Lord knew face to face." Deut. 34:10.*

**12. How old was Moses when he died?**

*"And Moses was an hundred and twenty years old when he died: his eye was not dim, nor his natural force abated." Deut. 34:7.*

### 39. THE CROSSING OF THE JORDAN (Josh. 1–4)

**1. Who succeeded Moses as leader of Israel?** Joshua, the son of Nun, one of the two faithful ones who had come out of Egypt. John. 1:2.

**2. What command did God give him?**

*"Now therefore arise, go over this Jordan, thou, and all this people, unto the land which I do give to them." Josh. 1:2.*

**3. On which side of the Jordan were the Israelites?** On the eastern side.

**4. What command of God is several times repeated?** "Be strong and of a good courage."

**5. What was the condition of prosperity here given?** Studying and obeying the law, the word of God. Josh. 1:7, 8.

**6. Was the Jordan a large river?** Not usually, but it overflowed in time of harvest. Josh. 3:15.

**7. What made the river difficult to cross?** There were no bridges; and crossing at any of the fords would be too slow a process and impossible for some of the women and children.

**8. What made it necessary for the crossing to be as quick as possible?** Those on the other side were enemies, and could easily destroy them if they crossed in too small bands.

**9. What was the first thing done by Joshua?** He sent two spies to find out about the land and the people; and especially Jericho, the nearest city. Josh. 2.

**10. How were these two men treated in Jericho?** The king of Jericho sent messengers to take them, and would probably have slain them, had they not been sheltered by a woman named Rahab.

**11. What promise did they make to the woman who had sheltered them?** To save the lives and property of herself and such of her family as she had with her in the house when Jericho was taken.

**12. What token was she to give so that the house should be known by the other Israelites?** A red cord was to be fastened in the window.

**13. Was the promise redeemed?** Yes. Josh. 6:23.

*"By faith the harlot Rahab perished not with them that believed not, when she had received the spies with peace." Heb. 11:31.*

**14. What report did the spies bring back?**

*"Truly the Lord hath delivered into our hands all the land; for even all the inhabitants of the country do faint because of us." Josh. 2:24.*

**15. How did Israel cross the Jordan?** The Lord caused the water of the river to pile up above them, and the waters to run out below them, so that the people crossed on dry land. Josh. 3.

**16. How did they know it was safe to cross?** The priests with the ark stood in the middle of the river bed until the people had all-crossed.

**17. What was the first thing done after crossing?** To set up a memorial on the west bank of the Jordan, made of twelve stones from the river bed. Josh. 4:1–9.

**18. What remarkable events happened on the plains of Jericho?** The circumcising of the people; keeping of the passover; the ceasing of the manna; and to Joshua the appearance of the "captain of the host of the Lord." Josh. 5:12–15.

## 40. THE CAPTURE OF JERICHO AND OF AI (Josh. 6–8)

**1. What directions did God give Joshua as to the taking of Jericho?** To march around it once each day for six days, and on the seventh day seven times. Josh. 6:3, 4.

**2. What was especially odd about this?** The people were to march in perfect silence, led by the priests with the ark, blowing the sacred trumpets. When they had finished the last circuit, at a signal all the people were to shout.

**3. What was the result?** When the people shouted the wall of the city fell down, and the city was taken.

**4. What special command was given to the people?** To bring all the silver and gold they found in the city into the treasury of the Lord, and to burn the rest of the spoil. Josh. 6:18, 19.

**5. Why was this command given?** Partly to prevent war for the sake of the spoil.

**6. Who transgressed this command?** Achan, of the tribe of Judah. Josh. 7.

**7. What punishment did this sin bring on all Israel?** A defeat by the men of Ai.

**8. How was the offender discovered?** By drawing lots under the guidance of God.

**9. What punishment was necessary to cleanse Israel from the sin Achan had brought on them?** The destruction of himself and his family by stoning, and of their bodies, and of all Achan's property by fire.

**10. When Achan's sin was wiped away did God again give victory to Israel?** The City of Ai was taken and destroyed. Josh. 8.

**11. After the destruction of Ai what solemn act did Joshua perform?** He wrote the law upon stone, and read its blessings and its curses to the people from mount Gerizim and mount Ebal. Josh. 8:30–35.

**12. Where were these two mountains?** Near Shechem, or Samaria.

### 41. THE CONQUEST OF CANAAN (Josh. 9–11)

**1. What did the Gibeonites do when they saw the victories of the Israelites?** They sent to Joshua messengers who pretended that the Gibeonites did not live in Canaan, so that Joshua might be at liberty to spare them. Josh. 9.

**2. Were they spared?** Yes, Joshua made a league with them, confirmed by oath.

**3. How came Joshua to fail here?** He was so sure of the right course that he did not ask direction from God.

**4. To what service were the Gibeonites appointed?** To be "hewers" of wood and drawers of water.

**5. What did the rest of the kings of Canaan do when they found that the Gibeonites had made peace with Israel?** Five of them joined in war against Gibeon. Josh. 10.

**6. To whom did the Gibeonites appeal for help?** To Joshua.

**7. Did he go to their aid?** Yes, with all his army.

**8. What proof did God give here that he was with them?** He showered heavy hailstones upon their enemies, and miraculously prolonged the light of the sun and of the moon upon the scene of the battle and pursuit.

**9. Is this ever referred to later in Scripture?**
*"The sun and moon stood still in their habitation: at the light of thine arrows they went, and at the shining of thy glittering spear." Hab. 3:11.*

**10. How is the host described that was mustered against Joshua in the last recorded battle?** As being numerous as the sand upon the seashore. Josh. 11:4.

**11. What great advantage had they over Israel?** The possession of chariots and horses.

**12. Yet which conquered?** The Israelites, completely. Josh. 11:8.

**13. What did Joshua do with the city of Hazor, and why?** He burnt it with fire, because it was the head of all the kingdoms he had fought with.

**14. What command had the Lord given with regard to the destruction of the Canaanites?** See Ex. 34:11–13; Deut. 7:1, 2.

**15. Why did the Lord thus deal with these nations?** Their wickedness had reached its height.
*"The iniquity of the Amorites is not yet full." Gen. 15:16.*
*"Thou shalt not learn to do after the abominations of those nations." Deut. 18:9.*

## 42. THE DIVISION OF THE LAND (Josh. 12–24)

**1. What did Joshua begin as soon as the land had rest from war?** Its division among the tribes, by lot, before the Lord. Josh. 18:6.

**2. What portion had Caleb?** At his own request he was given Hebron, the part he had searched out as spy. Josh. 14:12–14.

**3. How many tribes had their inheritance on the east of Jordan?** Reuben, Gad, and half Manasseh. Num. 32:33.

**4. What condition was made in granting this?** That all their armed men should go over Jordan with the rest of the nation, and should not return until the end of the war, and the division of the land.

**5. What was the next thing they did after the division of the land?** The appointment of the six cities of refuge. See 37.

**6. What was the last public act Joshua performed?** He called Israel to a great council at Shechem where he rehearsed all that God had done for them, and exhorted them to renew their covenant with God. Josh. 23, 24.

**7. What solemn covenant did Israel there enter into?** That they would forsake idols, and serve only Jehovah.

**8. What token of remembrance did Joshua set up there?** A stone of witness. Josh. 24:26, 27.

**9. How old was Joshua when he died?** One hundred and ten years.

**10. Where was he buried?** In Mount Ephraim. Josh. 24:30.

## 43. THE JUDGES

**1. Did Israel conquer all the Canaanites?** No, they left a number of their cities. Judg. 3:1–3.

**2. What was the result?** They were often led astray by them. Judg. 2:12–16.

**3. What resulted when they went astray?** God ceased to protect them and their enemies oppressed them.

**4. Did they then repent?** Yes, and God raised up deliverers who were called "judges."

**5. How many of these judges were there?** Fourteen, besides Eli and Samuel.

**6. Did each rule over all Israel?** No, some only ruled over parts of the country.

**7. Which especially should we remember?** Deborah, Barak, Gideon, Samson, Jephthah.

**8. Who was the first deliverer?** Othniel, the younger brother of Caleb, the loyal spy. Judg. 3:8–11.

### A. Deborah and Barak (Judg. 4:5)

**9. Who was Deborah?** A judge and a prophetess, who lived in northern Palestine, in the hill country of Ephraim. Judg. 4:4, 5.

**10. Who was Barak?** A leader of the tribes of Zebulon and Naphtali. Judg. 4:6, 10.

**11. What nation was afflicting northern Israel at this time?** The Canaanites, under their king Jabin, and their great general Sisera.

**12. How was Barak reproved for his faintheartedness?** By being told that the enemy's general would be given into the hands of a woman.

**13. What kind of an army did the Canaanitish general muster?** Nine hundred chariots of iron formed a part of it.

**14. How came it that Israel conquered such a host?** The power of God was with them.

**15. What became of Sisera?** He fled and took refuge in the tent of Jael.

**16. Who was Jael?** The wife of Heber, a Kenite and a descendent of Jethro, Moses' father-in-law.

**17. Why did Sisera take shelter in their tent?** Because they were at peace with Jabin his master.

**18. What did Jael do?** She allowed him to rest in her tent, but when he was asleep she killed him.

### B. Gideon (Judg. 6–9)

**19. How came it after this that Israel got into trouble again?** They did evil in the sight of the Lord, and he allowed them to be oppressed by the Midianites. Judg. 6:1–6.

**20. Was this in the same part of Palestine as that by the Canaanites?** No, that was in the northern part, and this was in the southern part.

**21. To what miserable plight were the Israelites reduced?** They were left without food.

**22. What did they do?** They cried to God.

**23. Did the Lord hear them?** He sent a prophet to them, and afterward a deliverer, Gideon of the tribe of Manasseh. Judg. 6:7–23.

**24. Who appeared to Gideon?** An angel of the Lord.

**25. What was Gideon doing?** Threshing wheat in a retired place where the enemy could not see him.

**26. Did he at first know who addressed him?** No, but he found out when the angel caused fire to come out of the rock to consume the food set before him, and also by what he said.

**27. What did the angel tell Gideon to do?** To save Israel from the Midianites.

**28. Did Gideon at once accept the mission?** No, he felt that he and his family were too poor and insignificant.

**29. What was Gideon's first act of faith?** To throw down the altar of Baal. Judg. 6:25–32.

**30. Was he killed for this?** No, Joash his father prevented it by wisely saying that if Baal were a god he could punish him himself.

**31. What name of honor did Gideon get from this act?** Jerubbaal, or "let Baal plead" against him.

**32. Describe the army that was at this time gathered against Israel.** *"And the Midianites and the Amalekites and all the children of the east lay along in the valley like grasshoppers for multitude; and their camels were without number, as the sand by the sea side for multitude." Judg. 7:12.*

**33. Was Gideon entirely without fear?** No, for he asked God to give him a private token of his power. Judg. 6:36–40.

**34. How did he prove that God was a hearer and answerer of prayer?** By the sign of the wet fleece on the dry ground, and of the dry fleece on the wet ground.

**35. When Gideon blew his trumpet how many came after him against the Midianites?** Thirty-two thousand. Judg. 6:34; 7:3.

**36. What test did Gideon at God's command first give to this army?** He told all that were afraid to go home. Judg. 7:2, 3.

**37. Did any go home?** Twenty-two thousand.

**38. Did all the rest fight in the battle?** Not in the first part, but they were leaders in the pursuit that followed. Judg. 7:4, 23.

**39. What sign did the Lord give to Gideon whereby he should know how many and which he had chosen for the first part of the battle?** Their two different ways of taking or drinking water on a particular occasion. Judg. 7:4–8.

**40. How was this a valuable test?** The place was one where they could be easily ambushed. Those who caught up the water were on their guard, and quicker.

**41. How many remained with Gideon after this selection?** Three hundred men.

**42. What great encouragement did the Lord give Gideon just before he and his three hundred men went down to battle?** He sent him at night to the camp of Midian where he heard a dream of one of the soldiers there. Judg. 7:9–14.

**43. What effect had this man's dream on Gideon?** He praised God, and immediately prepared his men. Judg. 7:15, 16.

**44. What plan was adopted to surprise the enemy?** The three hundred, each with a trumpet and a lighted torch hidden in a pitcher, surrounded the enemy at night. They were, at a signal, to break the pitchers and blow the trumpets. Judg. 7:16–20.

**45. Why was this so effectual?** In the darkness and confusion the Midianites fought each other. Judg. 7:21, 22.

**46. How did the Israelites afterwards desire to honor Gideon?** They wished him to be their king. Judg. 8:22–23.

**47. Would he accept the office?** He declined it as God had not yet appointed that form of government for Israel.

**48. What son of Gideon tried to be king?** Abimelech. Judg. 9:1–6.

**49. What was one of his first acts?** To kill all his brothers except Jotham.

**50. What parable did Jotham utter?** He spoke of the useful trees, as the olive, the fig, and the vine, refusing to be placed over the rest; and of the worthless bramble, as the only one that desired it. Judg. 9:8–20.

**51. What was the meaning of the parable?** The olive, vine and fig tree are types of useful, wise, and humble-minded men; and the bramble of the character, and its fate, of the fate of Abimelech.

**52. Was the parable fulfilled?** Yes, by the foolish choice of Abimelech by the Shechemites, the violent quarrels between them, and the destruction of both.

### C. Jephthah (Judg. 11)

**53. Did Israel sin again?** Yes, many times and other judges delivered them.

**54. What false gods did they worship?** Baalim, Ashtaroth, and other gods of the heathen around them. Judg. 10:6.

**55. How did God punish them?** By delivering them into the hands of the Philistines and Ammonites for eighteen years. Judg. 10:7, 8.

**56. When God had convinced them of their sin, and they were humbled on account of it, did they forsake it?** Yes, they put away their strange gods. Judg. 10:10–18.

**57. Who was Jephthah?** A great warrior of Gilead in Gad. Judg. 11:1.

**58. On which side of Israel was the land of the Ammonites?** On the east.

**59. Why did the men of Gilead choose Jephthah to be their captain?** Because "he was a mighty man of valor" and was likely to lead them to victory over the Ammonites.

**60. On what condition did Jephthah accept the office?** That he should be their head on his return. Judg. 11:9.

**61. What vow did Jephthah make before he went to battle?** That if he were victorious, whatever came forth first out of his house to meet him on his return should be the Lord's, and that he would offer it up for a burnt offering. Judg. 11:30–40.

**62. Who came out first to meet him?** His daughter and only child.

**63. What did Jephthah feel and say when he saw his only child?** He was deeply distressed, and told her of his vow.

**64. What was her beautiful answer?** That as God had given him victory, he must do to her according to his vow.

**65. What law of God was there to regulate what was to be done under these circumstances?** That the subject of the vow might be redeemed by a payment of money. Lev. 27:2–5.

**66. Why do we think he may have redeemed her?** Because her friends went every year to lament her separation from them or to talk with her. Judg. 11:40, margin.

**67. How long did Jephthah hold his honors?** Six years.

**68. What high honor is given to Jephthah in Heb. 11:32?** Of being named with David and Samuel and the prophets in the roll of heroes and martyrs in the cause of God.

### D. Samson (Judg. 13–17)

**69. Who was Samson?** A member of the tribe of Dan.

**70. What remarkable circumstance took place before his birth?** The angel of the Lord appeared to his mother, and told her that she should have a son who should be a Nazarite unto God and who should deliver Israel from the Philistines. Judg. 13:2–5.

**71. What was the name of Samson's father?** Manoah.

**72. Did the angel appear the second time?** He did, to Manoah as well as his wife. Judg. 13:8–21.

**73. How did Manoah and his wife know that their visitor was an angel?** By the words that he spoke, and by his ascent in the flame of the sacrifice.

**74. What was there remarkable about Samson?** His very great strength.

**75. What was a Nazarite?** A person "separated unto the Lord," the outward signs being the wearing of long hair, and the abstaining from strong drink. Num. 6:2–21.

**76. Did Samson ever lose his strength?** Yes, he was induced to tell his secret, and his hair, the sign of his vow, was cut. Judg. 16:17–21.

**77. Was Samson ever restored to the possession of his strength?** Yes, just before his death. Judg. 16:30.

**78. Name all his wonderful feats of strength that are recorded, and say which was the greatest.** He tore a young lion like a kid (Judg. 14:5, 6); he slew thirty Philistines (Judg. 14:19); and afterwards one thousand (Judg. 15:15); he carried away the gates of Gaza (Judg. 16:3);

he broke the green withs and new ropes with which he had been bound (Judg. 16:9, 11); he carried away the beam of a weaving machine to which his hair had been secured (Judg. 16:14); he pulled down a large building by its two pillars on the heads of the Philistines (Judg. 16:29, 30), the last and greatest feat of all.

### E. Ruth (Ruth)

**79. Who was Elimelech?** A man living in Bethlehem in Judah, in the days of the Judges. Ruth 1:1, 2.

**80. What were the names of his wife and of his two sons?** Naomi; and Mahlon and Chilion.

**81. To what place did his family move?** To the country of Moab, because of a famine in Judah.

**82. Whom did the sons marry?** Orpah and Ruth, women of Moab. Ruth 1:4.

**83. Did they prosper and have long life?** Elimelech and both the sons soon died. Ruth 1:5.

**84. What became of Naomi after the death of her husband and sons?** She returned to Judah, as she heard that the famine had ceased. Ruth 1:6, 7.

**85. What difference was there in the behavior of her daughters-in-law toward her?** Both were distressed at the idea of parting with her, and said they would go with her, but only Ruth went.

**86. Did God accept this stranger who determined to forsake her people and her gods and trust in him?** He did, and showed her much favor.

**87. What is the meaning of the name Naomi?** "Pleasant."

**88. To what name did Naomi wish** hers changed, and why? To Mara, or "bitter," because of the sorrows she had suffered.

**89. What rich and noble relative had Naomi in her native place?** Boaz. Ruth 2:1.

**90. What did Ruth do to find food for the family?** She went to glean behind the reapers, and chanced to go to Boaz's field. Ruth 2:2, 3.

**91. Did Boaz notice Ruth?** Yes, and told her to glean his fields until the end of harvest, and gave orders for her refreshment and protection, and for a plentiful gleaning. Ruth 2:4–17, 21.

**92. What description can you give of Boaz besides that he was rich and noble?** He was a kindhearted and a good man who honored God.

**93. What effect did his kindness have on Naomi when she heard of it?** She blessed God for his goodness, and told Ruth how to claim Boaz as her kinsman in the manner which the custom of the country allowed. Ruth 2:19, 20; 3:1–4; Deut. 25:5–10.

**94. Was he the nearest relative that Naomi had?** He was not. Ruth 3:12; 4:1.

**95. Did the nearest kinsman perform his duty to Naomi?** No, he declined doing it. Ruth 4:1–6.

**96. What then happened?** Boaz took his place and married Ruth. Ruth 4:9–17.

**97. Of what great persons was Ruth thus the ancestor?** Of David, and therefore of Jesus Christ, the Saviour, according to the flesh. Ruth 4:17–22.

### 44. ELI AND SAMUEL (1 Sam. 1–7)

**1. Who was Eli?** The high priest of

Israel, who served also as judge. 1 Sam. 1:9; 4:18.

**2. Who was the first high priest?** Aaron.

**3. Which of Aaron's sons was high priest at his father's death?** Eleazar. Num. 20:25, 26.

**4. From whom had Eli descended?** From Ithamar, Aaron's younger son.

**5. Did Eli's sons walk in the way of their father?** No, they were very wicked. 1 Sam. 2:12–17.

**6. Of what sin was Eli guilty that brought upon him God's anger?** Only mildly reproving his wicked sons when he should have restrained them with the authority of a father and high priest in those days. 1 Sam. 2:23–25; 3:13, 14.

**7. Who was Elkanah?** An Ephrathite of mount Ephraim. 1 Sam. 1:1–9.

**8. What were the names of his wives?** Hannah and Peninnah.

**9. Which did he love the more?** Hannah.

**10. What great trial had Hannah?** Not having any child.

**11. To whom did she tell her sorrow?** To God in prayer. 1 Sam. 1:10–12.

**12. What did Eli suppose when he saw her lips moving in silent prayer?** That she was drunken. 1 Sam. 1:13–18.

**13. What did Eli say when he found he was mistaken?** Read 1 Sam. 1:17.

**14. Did Hannah have a child?** Yes, a son, whom she named Samuel, meaning "Asked of God." 1 Sam. 1:19–28.

**15. Why did she not go up with her husband to worship the next year?** She preferred waiting until her child was old enough to remain for ever in the house of the Lord to be his servant, according to her vow.

**16. How old was Samuel when his mother took him and dedicated him to the Lord?** He "was young," perhaps six years old. 1 Sam. 1:24.

**17. What wrong thing did Eli's sons do as priests, and why was it wrong?** They took whatever part of the sacrifices they liked for their own, while God had assigned to the priests a particular part, the breast and the right shoulder. 1 Sam. 2:12–17; Lev. 7:31–34.

**18. Did the Lord warn Eli of his sons' sins?** He sent to him a man of God, a prophet. 1 Sam. 2:27–36.

**19. Did Eli regard this awful message?** Perhaps not sufficiently, as another was sent to him some years afterward; or it may have been too late, and his sons were thoroughly hardened in their sin. 1 Sam. 2:25.

**20. What manifest token did the Lord give that he had accepted the gift of Hannah?** God gave him a special call and message as a prophet. 1 Sam. 3:4–21.

**21. How old was Samuel when this occurred?** Probably about twelve.

**22. Had Eli instructed Samuel in the knowledge of God before this time?** No doubt Eli had made him acquainted with God's law, and had explained to him the tabernacle service; but Samuel had no experience yet of God's special way of making himself or his word or his will known to his prophets.

**23. When God called to Samuel what did he answer?** "Speak; for thy servant heareth."

**24. Have you answered God's call to you?** If not, he is calling to you now as you listen to his word—called you to be his child, and to give him your heart. Ask him, for his dear Son's sake, to help you to obey the call. Give yourself to him now.

**25. What solemn message did God give Samuel concerning Eli?** That he would punish his house, i.e., family, forever.

**26. Who were Israel's greatest enemies at this time?** The Philistines.

**27. What sinful act did Israel resort to when they found themselves being defeated by the enemy, and why?** They brought the ark from its place in Shiloh and carried it into the battle; because it was then, as later, the custom for armies to carry with them the images or emblems of their gods. 1 Sam. 4:3–11.

**28. What effect did it have on the Philistines?** They were afraid at first, but later they roused each other to a greater effort.

**29. What was the fate of the ark and of those who carried it?** The ark was taken, and Eli's sons, who as priests bore the ark, were killed.

**30. Of what was this a proof?** That God was not with Israel, though the ark was.

*"Go not up, for the Lord is not among you; that ye be not smitten before your enemies." Num. 14:42.*

**31. How did Eli bear the tidings?** He fell back off the seat at the gate where he was watching for news, and died. 1 Sam. 4:12–18.

**32. What did the Philistines do with the ark?** They set it beside their idol Dagon. 1 Sam. 5:1, 2.

**33. What happened to their idol?** It

fell on its face before the ark, and was broken.

**34. What calamities did God bring on the Philistines?** A painful disease and a plague of mice, and a deadly destruction besides.

**35. What did they resolve to do?** To send back the ark with a trespass offering. 1 Sam. 6:2–6.

**36. What test did they employ to ascertain if indeed the God of Israel had brought on them all these miseries?** They yoked to the cart that carried the ark two cows, to see if they would go to the land of Israel without their calves. 1 Sam. 6:7–12.

**37. How was the ark received by Israel?** With joy and a sacrifice of thanksgiving to God. 1 Sam. 6:13, 15.

**38. Of what act of impiety were the men of Beth-shemesh guilty?** Of looking into the ark (1 Sam. 6:19), which caused God to slay fifty thousand and seventy men.

**39. Why was this act of theirs inexcusable?** God had said to them, "They shall not go in to see when the holy things are covered, lest they die." Num. 4:20.

**40. Was the ark taken back to Shiloh?** No, it was taken to Kirjath-jearim. 1 Sam. 7:1.

**41. How long did it remain there?** Twenty years. 1 Sam. 7:2.

**42. Who afterward removed it, and where did it go?** About seventy years after it was taken to Kirjath-jearim David removed it to mount Zion in Jerusalem. It is not certain where it was during the fifty years just previous to that removal. 2 Sam. 6:2–17.

**43. What danger to Israel soon**

**presented itself?** The Philistines again prepared to attack Israel. 1 Sam. 7:7.

**44. To whom did Israel cry for help?** To Samuel to pray to God for their delivery. 1 Sam. 7:8–14.

**45. What did Samuel do for them?** He offered a sacrifice and cried unto the Lord.

**46. What proof did the Lord give that he accepted their sacrifice and heard their prayer?** He caused a great thunderstorm and a defeat of the Philistines.

**47. What memorial did Samuel set up in remembrance of this deliverance?** A stone called "Ebenezer," or "the stone of help."

**48. For how long did Samuel judge Israel?** "All the days of his life," probably about twenty years after his victory. 1 Sam. 7:15–17.

**49. Who were appointed to succeed him?** His sons; but they were bad men, and not worthy of the position. So the people demanded of Samuel a king, before his death. 1 Sam. 8:1–5.

### 45. THE UNITED KINGDOM: THE REIGN OF SAUL (1 Sam. 8–31)

**A. Saul (1 Sam. 8–15)**

**1. Who was Saul?** Son of Kish, of the tribe of Benjamin; the first king of Israel. 1 Sam. 9:1.

**2. What was there remarkable about his person?** He was very tall, and very handsome. 1 Sam. 9:2.

**3. How was he made king?** He was selected by God, anointed by Samuel, and finally chosen by lot at a great meeting of the leaders of Israel. 1 Sam. 9:15–17; 10:1, 17–27.

**4. What contradictions appear in Saul's character?** In many things he honored Samuel and honored God, but he mixed his religion with superstition, and was proud, disobedient and self-willed.

**5. Why did Israel wish a king?** See 44. 49. An added reason, probably, was that they might be like other nations of the time.

**6. How did Samuel feel about it?** He was displeased with them for so refusing God, and probably was hurt at their rejection of himself and his family.

**7. How was he comforted?** By prayer and direction from God. 1 Sam. 8:6, 7.

**8. In what spirit did the Lord give them a king?** *"I gave thee a king in mine anger." Hos. 13:11.*

**9. How did God establish the kingdom in Saul's hand?** By a victory over the Ammonites. 1 Sam. 11:11–15.

**10. Did Saul follow up his victory?** He next attacked the Philistines. 1 Sam. 13.

**11. Who was Jonathan?** Saul's oldest son.

**12. What marked difference was there between him and his father?** He was of a modest and affectionate disposition.

**13. Who obtained the victory recorded in 1 Sam. 13:3?** Jonathan.

**14. Who reaped the honor of it?** Saul, as king and commander-in-chief. 1 Sam. 13:3, 4.

**15. What immediately followed?** A gathering of the forces of both Israelites and Philistines for a great struggle. 1 Sam. 13:4–23.

**16. What was to precede the struggle?** A sacrifice to God.

**17. What did Samuel say to Saul when he came?** He reproved him for offering a sacrifice to God without the high priest, and declared that because of disobedience his kingdom should not continue.

**18. What proof does this chapter give of the oppression of the Philistines?** They did not allow Israel arms, or a smith to sharpen their tools. Vs. 19, 20.

**19. What glorious victory does 1 Sam. 14:4–23 record?** Over the Philistines between Michmash and Aijalon, by Jonathan.

**20. How did Saul nearly spoil the victory of that day?** By pledging his people to eat nothing all day until the battle was won. 1 Sam. 14:24–45.

**21. What test of obedience did God require from Saul?** That in fighting with the Amalekites he should destroy their sheep and oxen also; but he spared the best of them. 1 Sam. 15:2–9.

**22. What did Samuel do?** He told Saul that he should be no longer king, and as he turned away Saul took hold of his garment which rent and he told Saul that God had rent his kingdom from him and given it to a better man. 1 Sam. 15:24–35.

**23. How did Saul's real character come out in this transaction?** He showed himself more anxious to please his people for his own honor than for the honor of God.

**B. The Youth of David (1 Sam. 16)**

**24. Whom had the Lord chosen to be king in the place of Saul?** David. 1 Sam. 16:1, 13.

**25. Who was David?** The youngest son of Jesse, a Bethlehemite.

**26. What was David's character?** He was earnest and lovable; a great warrior, a poet; and "a man after God's own heart." Acts 13:22.

**27. Why had the Lord chosen David?** On account of his qualities of mind and heart.

**28. Who was appointed to anoint David?** Samuel.

**29. What occupation was David following at this time?** Keeping sheep.

**30. What evil power took possession of Saul?** An evil spirit, by permission of God.

**31. In what way did he obtain comfort?** By having someone to play to him on the harp.

**32. Who was selected as his minstrel?** David.

**C. David and Goliath (1 Sam. 17)**

**33. Did David continue to live with Saul?** No, not regularly; he returned to his father's sheep. 1 Sam. 17:15.

**34. What war now broke out?** One of the many wars with the Philistines. 1 Sam. 17:1.

**35. Where were David's brothers?** The three eldest went with Saul to battle.

**36. What did Jesse desire David to do?** To take his brothers a present, and see how they fared.

**37. What had the Philistines particularly to encourage them to fight at this time?** The giant Goliath was fighting for them.

**38. What did David do when he got to the camp?** He asked who Goliath was, and what was to be the reward for killing him.

**39. What was the result?** David undertook to fight with the Philistine.

**40. How did Saul wish to prepare David?** With Saul's own armor; but he refused it, because he was unaccustomed to it.

**41. What preparation did David make?** He only took his staff and sling and five stones in a bag.

**42. What was the result of the engagement?** The giant was killed by the first stone slung. 1 Sam. 17:41–58.

**43. Was only the giant slain?** The Philistines fled, and many of them were slain.

**44. What did David do with the head and armor of Goliath?** He brought the head to Saul and to Jerusalem, and put the armor in his tent.

**45. How was it that David had such power?** Because he trusted in the Lord his God.

**D. David and Jonathan (1 Sam. 18–20)**

**46. Which of Saul's sons standing by felt his soul "knit with the soul of David?"** Jonathan his oldest son. 1 Sam. 18:1, 20:17.

**47. What touching proof did he give of his love?** He gave him his robes and some of his arms, although the scarceness of arms had made them especially valuable. 1 Sam. 18:4; 13:22.

**48. What joyful song did the women sing when they went to meet the conquerors after the battle?** "Saul has slain his thousands, and David his ten thousands." 1 Sam. 18:6–16.

**49. What effect did this have on Saul?** It made him jealous and angry.

**50. How did David behave himself?** Wisely.

**51. Did Saul remember his promise to give his daughter in marriage to the man who should slay Goliath?** No, he gave her to another man. 1 Sam. 18:17–19.

**52. What artful design did he form to get David slain?** He required him to kill one hundred Philistines as the price of his daughter Michal, hoping he would be killed himself. 1 Sam. 18:20–30.

**53. Did it succeed?** No, David slew two hundred and was unhurt.

**54. Did Saul's daughter love David?** Yes, and proved it by letting him down from a window, that he might escape her father's rage. 1 Sam. 18:20, 28; 19:8–17.

**55. Whither did David first escape?** To Samuel, in Ramah. 1 Sam. 19:18.

**56. What wonderful power did God exercise over the messengers sent to take David?** The power of his Spirit, causing them to prophesy like Samuel's prophets. 1 Sam. 19:20–24.

**57. How did Jonathan assure himself that his father really desired David's death?** By Saul's own words when Jonathan defended him. 1 Sam. 19:1–7; 20:25–34.

**58. How did he tell David?** By an agreed upon sign. See story in 1 Sam. 20:18–24, 35–40.

**59. What beautiful covenant did they make together?** That Jonathan should warn David, and that David should be kind to Jonathan and his children. 1 Sam. 20:12–17, 23.

**E. David a Fugitive (1 Sam. 21–31)**

**60. Whither did David flee after Jonathan's warning?** To Nob, to the high priest. 1 Sam. 21:1–9.

**61. What did he obtain there?** Some bread, and Goliath's sword.

**62. Did he do this honorably?** No, he pretended he was on the king's business.

**63. Did he feel safe here?** No, he felt he must go from the kingdom of Saul to be safe.

**64. Where did he go?** To Achish, the king of Gath, where he pretended to be mad, that he might escape imprisonment. 1 Sam. 21:10–15.

**65. Where did he go when he left Achish?** To the cave Adullam. 1 Sam. 22:1.

**66. Who came to him there?** Every one who was discontented, or in debt or distress. 1 Sam. 22:2.

**67. What kind care did he take of his father and mother?** He sent them to the protection of the king of Moab, against Saul's revenge. 1 Sam. 22:3, 4.

**68. Is there any description given of David's men?** Three mighty chiefs are mentioned, of whom Joab was first; and thirty other valiant men, among whom Abishai and Benaiah are especially noted for their exploits. 2 Sam. 23; 1 Chron. 11.

**69. What proof of love did his men give him at this time?** Three of them broke through the host of the Philistines to bring him water from a favorite well. 2 Sam. 23:16, 17.

**70. How did he show the tenderness of his heart in return?** By declining to drink what had been obtained at so great a risk of his men's lives, and by pouring it out as a libation to God instead.

**71. Who had seen David while he was at Nob?** Doeg, an Edomite, a servant of Saul. 1 Sam. 21:7; 22:9, 10.

**72. Of what cowardly act was Saul** guilty toward the priests who had helped David? He ordered them all to be slain, and Doeg carried out the order. 1 Sam. 22:17–19.

**73. How did David and his little band of warriors employ themselves?** In fighting with the Philistines, the enemies of their country. 1 Sam. 23:1–5.

**74. What shows Saul's great enmity to David?** He tried several times to capture him. But he failed. 1 Sam. 23:7–28.

**75. In what strong place did David find refuge?** In En-gedi. 1 Sam. 23:29.

**76. Did Saul again go after David here?** Yes. 1 Sam. 24:1–22.

**77. How did David behave when Saul was in his power?** He would not kill him, nor allow his men to do so.

**78. What effect did this have on Saul?** He wept and spoke kindly to David.

**79. What treatment did David meet with at this time from Nabal?** He refused to give food to David and his men, though they had protected his shepherds from the enemy robbers, and had taken nothing from them. 1 Sam. 25:1–31.

**80. What did Nabal's wife do?** She went to David with a supply of food, and asked him not to avenge the insult.

**81. Did Saul again seek after David?** Yes, in the wilderness of Ziph. 1 Sam. 26:1–25.

**82. How did David revenge himself?** By again sparing Saul's life.

**83. With whom did David now join himself?** With the same Achish, king of Gath, with whom he had before taken refuge. 1 Sam. 27. See Q. 64.

**84. What difficulties did David bring upon himself by this alliance?** He was invited by Achish to join him in fighting against Israel. 1 Sam. 28:1, 2.

**85. Where was David when the last decisive battle between Saul and the Philistines was fought?** Fortunately the Philistine princes objected to his presence when they were attacking Israel, and he returned to his home in Ziklag. 1 Sam. 29.

**86. What event happened to him and his men while they were absent from Ziklag?** The Amalekites burnt the city, and carried away the women and children captive. 1 Sam. 30:1–5.

**87. Did they recover their treasures?** Yes, they pursued and slew the Amalekites, and recovered all, after David had laid his trouble before God and obtained direction from him. 1 Sam. 30:6–20.

**88. What did he do with the spoil that they won?** He divided it among all his men who had taken part in the fight, whether they had actually fought, or had guarded the baggage. 1 Sam. 30:21–25.

**89. What tremendous battle was being fought in Israel while David and his men were thus employed?** A battle with the Philistines in Mount Gilboa. 1 Sam. 31.

**90. What was the result?** The Israelites were defeated and Saul and his sons slain. 1 Sam. 31:7; 1 Chron. 10:1, 2.

**46. THE UNITED KINGDOM:
THE REIGN OF DAVID (2 Sam.;
1 Kings 1:1–2:10; Chron. 11–29)**

**A. David King in Hebron (2 Sam. 1–4;
1 Chron. 11:1–3)**

**1. What effect did the death of Saul have on David?** He mourned for him and wept. 2 Sam. 1:12.

**2. What touching record did David leave of his love to Saul and Jonathan?** A song of lamentation. 2 Sam. 1:17–27.

**3. Did David at once go and possess the kingdom?** Yes, after seeking direction from God he went up to Hebron and was there anointed king. 2 Sam. 2:1–4.

**4. Which tribe first acknowledged David's claim?** Judah, his own tribe.

**5. Did the other tribes join at once?** No, they followed Ish-bosheth, the sole remaining son of Saul. 2 Sam. 2:5–10.

**6. What was the result?** A war between the partizans of each. 2 Sam. 2:12–5:1.

**7. How long did this war continue?** About two years.

**8. What event turned the scale on David's side?** Abner's desertion of Ish-bosheth on account of an insult from him, and his offer to make terms with David.

**9. Did David receive Abner?** Yes, with hospitality and honor.

**10. How did Joab like this?** He blamed David for it, and killed Abner in revenge for the death of Asahel, whom Abner had killed during the war.

**11. Did David approve of Joab's conduct?** No, for Abner was no longer an enemy, and Joab had killed him deceitfully and revengefully while he was enjoying the hospitality of the king, and was therefore under his protection. David called upon all the people to mourn with him for Abner.

**12. Why did he not punish Joab?** He was not yet strong enough on his throne to have the power; and Joab had always been devotedly loyal to him.

**13. Of what act of treachery were**

the servants of Ish-bosheth guilty? They killed their master.

**14. Did not the death of Ish-bosheth clear the way for David to ascend the throne of all Israel?** Yes, as no one else was seeking to be king.

**15. Did David on this account reward the murderers?** So far from rewarding them for their treachery, he ordered them to be slain.

**B. David and the Ark of God (2 Sam. 5; 6; 1 Chron. 14; 15; 16)**

**16. What was David's first conquest as king of all Israel?** The stronghold of Mt. Zion. 2 Sam. 5:6–9.

**17. What king made presents to David?** Hiram, king of Tyre. 2 Sam. 5:11.

**18. Where was Tyre?** To the north of Canaan, on the borders of the Mediterranean Sea.

**19. For what was Tyre remarkable?** For its manufacture of purple dye and for its commerce.

**20. Did the Philistines treat David as Hiram did?** No, they went to fight against him, but were conquered. 2 Sam. 5:18–25.

**21. What was David's next act?** To bring the ark from Baale of Judah (another name for Kirjathjearim). 2 Sam. 6. See Josh. 15:9, 60; 44, 27–42.

**22. In what way did they bring it?** In a new cart, with singing of praises.

**23. How ought it to have been brought?** By hand, with staves. Num. 4:15.

**24. What happened to Uzzah, the driver of the cart?** He died by the hand of God for thoughtlessly taking hold of the ark.

**25. How did David feel?** He was displeased, and afraid to go further.

**26. What did he do with the ark then?** He placed it in the house of Obed-edom the Gittite.

**27. How many months passed before David had courage again to try to fetch the ark?** Three.

**28. What induced him to do it then?** The blessing that rested on those who had the charge of it.

**29. Why was Michal, David's wife, offended with him?** Because of his dancing to the music before the ark.

**30. What did David's manner really express?** Religious joy and humble thankfulness.

**31. Where did David place the ark?** In a tent on Mt. Zion, in the city of David. 2 Sam. 7:2, 7.

**32. Was he satisfied with this?** No, he wanted to build for the ark a house of cedar.

**33. Did the Lord permit him to do it?** No.

**34. How did the Lord make his will known to David?** Through Nathan the prophet. 2 Sam. 7:3–15.

**35. What did David feel, and what did he say?** He felt deeply humble, and unworthy of God's promised blessings, and prayed to God to confirm his word. 2 Sam. 7:16–27.

**36. In whom was David's house to be confirmed for ever?** In Jesus Christ, as Zacharias declared in Luke 1:68–70.

**C. David's Conquest; His Sin (2 Sam. 8–12; 1 Chron. 18–20)**

**37. What had God's promise been of**

the boundary of Israel's possession?
"From the river of Egypt unto the river
Euphrates."

**38. What conquests did David make
which fulfilled this?** The conquests of
the Philistines, Moabites, Ammonites
and Syrians. 2 Sam. 8:6, 12–14; 10:19.

**39. What did David do with the spoil
he took in battle?** He gave the gold and
silver and brass (or bronze) for the orna-
menting and service of the tabernacle, or
for the temple which his son was to
build. 2 Sam. 8:10, 11.

**40. Did he forget his friend Jonathan
in his prosperity? What proof did he
give?** No, he inquired after the family of
Saul, and gave Saul's land and a place at
his own table to Mephibosheth, son of
Jonathan. 2 Sam. 9.

**41. Whom did David send to besiege
Rabbah?** Joab. 2 Sam. 11:1.

**42. Where was David?** At Jerusalem.

**43. Why did David send Uriah with
a letter to Joab, telling him to put him
in the front of the battle?** In order that
he might be killed. 2 Sam. 11:15.

**44. Why did David wish the brave
Uriah to die?** That he might get possession of his wife.

**45. Whom did the Lord send to con-
vince David of his sin?** Nathan the
prophet. 2 Sam. 12:1–12.

**46. Did the Lord pardon David?** Yes,
but he was punished by the death of his
child. 2 Sam. 12:13–23.

**47. How did David feel?** It is believed
that his deep sorrow for his sin is expressed in the fifty-first Psalm; and his
joy in God's forgiveness in the thirty-
second Psalm.

**48. What signal proof did the Lord**

give to David of his full and free forgiveness? By giving him another child.
2 Sam. 12:24.

**49. What was the name of this child?**
Solomon, meaning "Peaceable."

**50. What name did the Lord through
Nathan the prophet, add to this?**
Jedidiah, meaning "Beloved of the Lord."
2 Sam. 12:25.

### D.  David and Absalom (2 Sam. 13–20)

**51. Who was Absalom?** A son of
David; perhaps the oldest living son, and
the natural heir. 2 Sam. 13:1.

**52. Why did he flee away to Geshur?**
Because he had killed his half-brother
Amnon for outraging his sister Tamar.
2 Sam. 13:24–38.

**53. Who brought him back again?**
Joab, who by a contrivance had gotten
David's leave, after three years. 2 Sam.
14:1–23.

**54. How did he repay his father's
kindness?** By making a conspiracy
against him, to make sure of the kingdom,
as he was not David's favorite son, and at
that time the successor might be chosen
among any of the heirs. 2 Sam. 15.

**55. How did Absalom steal away the
affection of the people from David?** By
artful speeches, promises and civilities.

**56. When David heard of the con-
spiracy what did he do?** He fled from
Jerusalem.

**57. Who went with him?** All his household, and six hundred men from Gath.

**58. What famous counsellor fol-
lowed Absalom?** Ahithophel.

**59. Who managed by an artifice to
set his counsel aside?** Hushai, David's
friend. 2 Sam. 15:32–37; 17:1–14.

**60. What effect did this have on Ahithophel?** He hanged himself. 2 Sam. 17:23.

**61. Why did Hushai give this advice?** That he might secure David's escape, and time to muster his army.

**62. Who won the battle?** David's men. 2 Sam. 18.

**63. Who slew Absalom?** Joab.

**64. How was it done?** As Absalom hung from an oak tree by his head, which had become caught as he rode under it. (There is no indication that the popular belief that he hung by his hair has any foundation in fact.)

**65. What command had David given to his captains in regard to Absalom?** That they should deal gently with him for his sake.

**66. How did David feel when Absalom was slain, and what did he say?** He was deeply distressed, and said, *"Would God I had died for thee. O Absalom, my son, my son." 2 Sam. 18:33, 19:1–4.*

**67. Was Absalom's death just?** Yes, he was a rebel against his father and his king. Any other man would have been slain, at David's command.

**68. What sort of a man was Absalom?** He was the handsomest man in the country, and especially remarkable for his long and beautiful hair. He was suave and conciliatory among the people, and a great favorite.

**69. What Psalm of David is supposed to refer to these events?** Psalm 3.

**70. Did David do anything to Joab for killing Absalom?** He deposed him from being commander-in-chief of his army, and put Amasa in his place. 2 Sam. 19:13.

**71. What did Joab do on hearing this?** He killed Amasa. 2 Sam. 20:9, 10.

**72. What relation was Amasa to David?** Nephew, as son of his sister Abigail.

**73. Did David again spare Joab from punishment?** Yes, he continued to be commander-in-chief, as whatever his faults, he was the ablest man for the place, and thoroughly loyal to David as king.

**74. What is the twenty-second chapter of 2 Samuel about?** It is David's Psalm of thanksgiving for deliverance from his enemies.

**E. David's Last Days (2 Sam. 24; 1 Kings 1; 2; 1 Chron. 21–29)**

**75. By whom was David tempted to number Israel?** By Satan. 1 Chron. 21:1.

**76. Who remonstrated with him?** Joab. 2 Sam. 24:3.

**77. Did not David's heart smite him after he had done it?** Yes, he said he had sinned greatly and done very foolishly. 2 Sam. 24:10.

**78. Whom did the Lord commission to reprove David?** The prophet Gad. 2 Sam. 24:11–25.

**79. What did he offer him?** The choice of three punishments.

**80. Which did David choose, and why?** Famine or pestilence rather than war; the immediate hand of God, rather than the hand of man.

**81. At what point did the destroying angel stop?** At the threshing-floor of Araunah.

**82. How did David know that the Lord had accepted his offering?** By the plague being stayed.

**83. What preparations did David make for the future building of the temple?** Hewn stone, silver and gold, iron, brass (bronze) and cedar. 1 Chron. 22:2–5, 14–16.

**84. What solemn charge did David give to Solomon concerning the temple?** To build it as David himself had desired to do. 1 Chron. 22:6–16.

**85. What other arrangements did David make?** He divided the priests and Levites and other officers into orders, and fixed their duties. 1 Chron. 23–27.

**86. Did anyone besides David contribute toward the future glory of the temple?** The chiefs and the people. 1 Chron. 29:6–9.

**87. Whom did David make king over Israel before he died?** Solomon, to whom he had promised it. 1 Chron. 23:1.

**88. Why was this done?** Because Adonijah, David's oldest living son, had conspired to seize the throne. 1 Kings 1.

**89. How old was David when he died?** Seventy.

**90. How many years had he reigned?**
*"David was thirty years old when he began to reign and he reigned forty years. In Hebron he reigned over Judah seven years and six months; and in Jerusalem he reigned thirty and three years over all Israel and Judah."* 2 Sam. 5:4, 5.

**91. In what respect was David "a man after God's own heart"?** In the general character of his life; and in his sorrow and true repentance after his sins.

**92. Of whom is David a type?** Of Jesus Christ, whose reign forever over David's kingdom was prophesied.

**47. THE UNITED KINGDOM: THE REIGN OF SOLOMON (1 Kings 1–11; 1 Chron. 29; 2 Chron. 1–9)**

**1. What was the character of Solomon's reign?** It was generally peaceful.

**2. What alliance did he make with Egypt, and why?** He married the daughter of the Pharaoh, probably as a political measure, as Egypt was still almost the most powerful nation in the world. 1 Kings 3:1.

**3. What remarkable appearance in a dream did Solomon see soon after his father's death?** God asked him what he should give him. 1 Kings 3:2–15.

**4. What did he choose?** Wisdom to govern his people well.

**5. What did God promise to give him that he had not asked for?** Riches and honor.

**6. By whose command did Solomon build the temple?** By God's. 1 Kings 5:5.

**7. Who had prepared greatly for this before him?** David. 1 Chron. 22. See 46. 83–86.

**8. Why was not David permitted to build the temple?** Because he had been "a man of war." 1 Chron. 28:3.

**9. To whom had the pattern been shown?** To David, by "the Spirit" of God. 1 Chron. 28:11, 12.

**10. Who selected the place on which the temple was to be built?** David. 1 Chron. 21:28–22:2.

**11. On what mountain was it built?** On Mount Moriah, in Jerusalem. 2 Chron. 3:1.

**12. What is on that mountain now?** The Mohammedan mosque of Omar.

**13. Who provided Solomon with timber and stone for the buildings?** Hiram, king of Tyre. 1 Kings 5.

**14. Was this a gift to Solomon, or did he pay for it?** Solomon paid wages and supplied food to Hiram's men; and gave him twenty cities in what was later Galilee. See 1 Kings 9:11.

**15. Was there anything peculiar about the preparation of the stone?** It was entirely prepared before being brought to the temple site.

*"And the house . . . was built of stone made ready before it was brought thither: so that there was neither hammer nor ax, nor any tool of iron heard in the house, while it was in building." 1 Kings 6:7.*

**16. How was Solomon's temple dedicated?** There was a solemn feast, the bringing in of the ark, Solomon's prayer and blessing, and a sacrifice of peace-offerings. 1 Kings 8.

**17. Describe Solomon's grandeur.** He had an immense daily provision for this household, and thousands of chariot-horses and riders. 1 Kings 4.

**18. For what is Solomon especially noted?** For his wisdom in deciding difficult questions. See 1 Kings 4:29–31; 3:12, 16–28.

**19. What queen, having heard of it from afar, came to visit Solomon?** The queen of Sheba, probably in Arabia. 1 Kings 10.

**20 Was she disappointed?** No, she said the half had not been told her.

**21. Of what is this story often used as a type?**

*"Eye hath not seen, nor ear heard, neither have entered into the heart of man, the things which God hath prepared for them that love him. But God hath revealed them unto us by his Spirit." 1 Cor. 2:9, 10.*

**22. How did our Lord Jesus speak of this incident?**

*"The queen of the south shall rise up in the judgment with this generation, and shall condemn it: for she came from the uttermost parts of the earth to hear the wisdom of Solomon; and, behold, a greater than Solomon is here." Matt. 12:42.*

**23. Of what great sin was Solomon guilty in his latter days?** Idolatry, through the influence of his wives. 1 Kings 11:1–10.

**24. What did the Lord say to Solomon about this?** That he would take away the greater part of his kingdom from his family. 1 Kings 11:11–13.

**25. To what "covenant" did the Lord refer?**

*"When thy days be fulfilled, and thou shalt sleep with thy fathers, I will set up thy seed after thee . . . and I will establish his kingdom. He shall build an house for my name, and I will establish the throne of his kingdom for ever. I will be his father and he shall be my son." 2 Sam. 7:12–14.*

**26. Had Solomon broken this covenant?** Yes, by his idolatry.

**27. What were the consequences?** The stirring up of enemies after a long reign of peace.

**28. How long did Solomon reign?** Forty years.

**48. REHOBOAM (1 Kings 12:1–20)**

**1. Who succeeded Solomon as king?** His son Rehoboam. 1 Kings 11:43.

**2. Was he a wise or a foolish king?**
A foolish one.

**3. What is the proof?** He followed the advice of the young courtiers, the "court gallants," instead of that of the older men who had been the advisers of his wise father Solomon.

**4. What exactly was the point at issue between Rehoboam and his people?** Solomon's reign of splendor had been very hard for the common people, who were forced to labor on the great buildings, and were heavily taxed. They asked that their burdens should be made lighter.

**5. What was Rehoboam's answer?** A harsh one, that he would rather increase than reduce their burdens.

**6. What was the result?** Ten of the tribes revolted under the leadership of Jeroboam, leaving Rehoboam but two.

(For the later history of Rehoboam see 55.)

**49. THE KINGS OF ISRAEL: JEROBOAM'S DYNASTY (1 Kings 11:26–40; 12:15–14:20; 15:25–28)**

**1. Who was Jeroboam?** Son of Nebat, and servant of Solomon who "lifted up his hand against the king," and had been forced to take refuge in Egypt. 1 Kings 11:26, 40.

**2. What prophecy was spoken about him?** The prophet Ahijah said that he should rule over ten of the tribes of Israel. 1 Kings 11:29–39.

**3. How did he do this?** By tearing Jeroboam's outer garment into twelve pieces and giving him ten.

**4. When was this prophecy fulfilled?** At the revolt of the ten tribes. See 48.

**5. What wicked means did he use to keep the ten tribes under this rule?** Setting up for worship two calves in Bethel in the tribe of Benjamin, and in Dan, in the extreme north. 1 Kings 12:28, 29.

**6. Were they intended as images of false gods?** No, he intended them as images of Jehovah; but he broke the second commandment in setting them up; and their worship easily became that of false gods.

**7. What other fault was there in the worship from the first?** The priests were not from the Levites; and later were from the lowest of the people, and the worship degenerated into real idolatry. 1 Kings 12:30–33; 13:33, 34.

**8. Did God suffer the sinful idolatry of Israel to go unrebuked?** No, he sent a prophet to rebuke Jeroboam. 1 Kings 13:1–6.

**9. When the king heard the prophet's message what did he do?** He put out his hand to seize him.

**10. How was this punished?** His arm was stiffened and dried up.

**11. How was the king's arm recovered?** By the prophet's prayer.

**12. How long did Jeroboam reign?** Twenty-two years. 1 Kings 14:20.

**13. How many of Jeroboam's family came to the throne?** Only Nadab his son, who ruled parts of two years, and was killed by Baasha. 1 Kings 14:20.

**50. THE KINGS OF ISRAEL: BAASHA, ELAH, ZIMRI (1 Kings 15:27–16:20)**

**1. How did Baasha take the throne?** By a conspiracy in a time of war, when he killed king Nadab.

**2. What was his first act as king?**
To strengthen himself in the kingdom in Oriental fashion by killing all the family of Jeroboam.

**3. What sort of king was Baasha?**
*"He did evil in the sight of the Lord."*
*1 Kings 15:34.*

**4. How long did he reign?** Twenty-four years. 1 Kings 15:33.

**5. Who succeeded him?** His son Elah who reigned parts of two years. 1 Kings 16:8–10.

**6. Who was Zimri?** One of the captains of Elah, who conspired against the king, slew him and took the throne. 1 Kings 16:9–12.

**7. How long did Zimri reign?** About seven days. 1 Kings 16:15–20.

**8. What was his end?** He burnt himself in his house when surrounded by his enemies with no chance of escape.

**51. THE KINGS OF ISRAEL: THE DYNASTY OF OMRI (1 Kings 16:21–22:40; 2 Kings 1:1–9:26)**

**A. Omri (1 Kings 16:16–28)**

**1. Who reigned over Israel next?** Omri, "the captain of the host," chosen by the people to be king.

**2. How long did he reign?** Twelve years.

**3. What city did he purchase and make the chief city of Israel?** Samaria.

**4. Was he a good king?** He enlarged and strengthened his kingdom, but "wrought evil in the eyes of the Lord."

**B. Ahab (1 Kings 16:29–22:40)**

**5. Who was Ahab?** The son of Omri.

**6. What was his character?** He was a strong king, politically, but morally and spiritually the worst that Israel ever had. 1 Kings 16:30–33.

**7. What was the name of his wife?** Jezebel, daughter of the king of Zidon, or Sidon. 1 Kings 16:31.

**8. What new idol-worship was she the means of bringing in?** The worship of Baal.

**9. What great prophet appeared during this reign?** Elijah.

(For further account of Ahab, see under **C. Elijah;** and **D. Ahab's Later History.**)

**C. Elijah (1 Kings 17–19; 2 Kings 2:1–18)**

**10. Who was Elijah?** A prophet of Gilead, and one of the greatest prophets that either Israel or Judah ever had.

**11. What was his appearance?** He was rugged and unkempt looking, dressed in skins, with a leathern girdle and long sheep-skin cape or "mantle."

**12. What was Elijah commissioned to tell Ahab?** That there should be neither dew nor rain; which of course would bring a famine over the land. 1 Kings 17:1.

**13. Why did God send a famine?** On account of the sins of the people, as Moses had prophesied in Deut. 28:15–18.

**14. Where did God promise to provide for Elijah? and how?** Beside the brook Cherith; and by ravens.

**15. When the brook dried up where did the Lord command Elijah to go?** To Zarephath, where a widow would support him.

**16. In what sorrowful employment did Elijah find the woman engaged?**

In gathering sticks to prepare her last meal.

**17. What resulted from Elijah's coming to her?** *"She, and he, and her house, did eat many days. And the barrel of meal wasted not, neither did the cruse of oil fail." 1 Kings 17:15, 16.*

**18. What miracle did Elijah perform here?** He raised to life the son of the widow with whom he lived.

**19. Were the people of Israel at this time idolaters, or worshippers of the true God?** Idolaters; worshippers of Baal.

**20. Were all worshippers of Baal?** No, seven thousand of them were not.

**21. Who was Obadiah?** Governor or steward of Ahab's house.

**22. What kind act had he performed?** When Jezebel, the wicked queen slew the Lord's prophets, he hid and fed them. 1 Kings 18:4.

**23. How many years had the famine lasted when Elijah next stood before Ahab?** "Above two years."

**24. What accusation did Ahab make against Elijah?** Of being the cause of Israel's trouble.

**25. Who was really to blame?** Ahab himself, and the other idolaters.

**26. How did Elijah propose to decide the point as to who was the true God?** By a contest with the priests of Baal, and observing upon whose sacrifice the fire came down from heaven. 1 Kings 18:19–46.

**27. How many contestants were there on each side?** Four hundred and fifty priest of Baal on one side; and Elijah—with God—on the other.

**28. How did Elijah mock the priests of Baal?** By telling them to cry aloud, as their god might be asleep.

**29. Did he give them time enough to make a fair trial?** Yes, from morning till evening.

**30. What did Elijah then do?** He built an altar and prepared the sacrifice; then drenched the sacrifice and wood and altar with water; and then offered a quiet prayer to God.

**31. How could so much water be found at such a dry time?** There is on Mount Carmel a never failing spring; a fact proved by the sort of life found in it.

**32. How was the power of God manifested?** By the fire drying up the water, and burning the wet bullock and the wood and stones.

**33. What effect did it have upon the people?** They fell on their faces and cried out that Jehovah was the true God.

**34. What became of Baal's priests?** They were taken out and slain.

**35. What did Elijah venture to promise Ahab even before there was any appearance of it?** Abundance of rain.

**36. On what did Elijah's faith rest?** On the promise of God.

**37. What did Jezebel say when she heard of the death of her priests?** She threatened Elijah with immediate death. 1 Kings 19:1, 2.

**38. To what place did he flee?** To Beer-sheba, and thence to the wilderness.

**39. Why was he so much discouraged?** Reaction from excitement; disappointment that the people were not more ready to follow him; weariness after a long and hurried journey.

**40. What kind care did the Lord take of him?** An angel twice brought him bread and water.

**41. For how long did that food sustain him?** Forty days.

**42. When he was revived to what place did he go?** To mount Horeb.

**43. How did the Lord speak to Elijah?** First there was a wind, then an earthquake, then a fire; but the Lord himself spoke in a still, small voice. 1 Kings 19:11, 12.

**44. What is God's way of speaking to his people now?** He sometimes speaks in the voice of suffering and distress, but more frequently in the gentler one of his Spirit's whisper to the heart.

**45. What further work did the Lord give Elijah to do?** To anoint two kings and a prophet.

**46. What effect did the casting of Elijah's mantle on Elisha have?** It made him leave his work and his home for the service to which God had called him.

**47. What was the strange manner of Elijah's departure from this world?** He did not die, but was taken to heaven by a whirlwind, with a chariot and horses of fire. 2 Kings 2:1–12.

**48. What did Elijah ask Elisha ere he was parted from him?** He asked what he should do for him.

**49. What did Elisha request?** A double portion of Elijah's spirit; that is, not twice as much as Elijah, but the inheritance of the first-born, the successor; twice as much as others who might inherit.

**50. Was it granted?** Yes.

**51. What was left by Elijah?** His long sheep-skin mantle.

**52. How did Elisha use it?** To divide the waters of Jordan, so that he could pass over.

**53. How did the other prophets recognize the superiority of Elisha?** By the spirit of Elijah resting on him. 2 Kings 2:15.

**54. How did they manifest their unbelief?** By proposing to send men to search for Elijah.

**55. Did Elisha yield to this?** He did, at last.

(For the history of Elisha see 52.)

**D. Ahab's Later History (1 Kings 20–22; 2 Chron. 18)**

**56. Who were Israel's greatest enemies at this time?** The Syrians, under their king Ben-hadad.

**57. What was the capital city of Syria?** Damascus.

**58. What did Ben-hadad propose to do to Israel?** He made greater and greater demands until he virtually demanded the entire kingdom. 1 Kings 20:1–10.

**59. Did Ahab yield?** At first, but was goaded into resistance.

**60. What proverb did Ahab quote?** *"Let not him that girdeth on his harness [armor] boast himself as he that putteth it off." 1 Kings 20:11.*

**61. What was the result?** A small company surprised the Syrians while their leaders were drinking, and put them into confusion; then a larger band followed and finished their defeat. 1 Kings 20:13–21.

**62. Was this a permanent defeat?** No, the war was continued later. 1 Kings 20:22–43.

**63. Who was Naboth?** The owner of a vineyard near Ahab's palace at Jezreel. 1 Kings 21.

**64. Why did he refuse to let Ahab have his vineyard?** Because he was forbidden by the Mosaic law to part permanently with the land which had come to him from his fathers. *"The land shall not be sold for ever: for the land is mine; for ye are strangers and sojourners with me. And in all the land of your possession ye shall grant a redemption for the land." Lev. 25:23, 24.*

**65. What wicked act did Jezebel stir up Ahab to do?** To kill Naboth and take his vineyard.

**66. Did God suffer this to go unpunished?** No, Elijah was sent to Ahab to tell him that God would destroy Ahab's family, and that the dogs should eat the flesh of Jezebel, and lick his own blood.

**67. How did Ahab receive the tidings?** He showed the outward signs of penitence and humbled himself before God.

**68. What enemies again fought against Israel?** The Syrians. 1 Kings 22:1–40.

**69. What place did they take?** Ramoth-gilead, east of the Jordan, in Gad.

**70. With whom did Ahab make an alliance?** With Jehoshaphat, king of Judah. See 56.

**71. What did Jehoshaphat require before he would go up to fight?** That the will of God should be known.

**72. What did Ahab's prophets say?** That he might go, and God would be with him.

**73. Did all agree in this?** All but one, Micaiah.

**74. What wonderful vision did Micaiah describe?** Of God upon his throne, and the host of heaven around him and of an evil spirit going forth to entice Ahab to his fall.

**75. What did Ahab do to prevent this prediction from coming true?** He disguised himself that he might not be known to the enemy.

**76. Was Ahab killed?** Yes, he was killed by an arrow shot at random.

**77. How was Elijah's prediction in 1 Kings 21:19 fulfilled?** The dogs licked up his blood in his chariot.

**E. Ahaziah (1 Kings 22:51–53; 2 Kings 1)**

**78. Which of Ahab's sons succeeded his father?** Ahaziah.

**79. What character did he bear?** He was wicked and idolatrous.

**80. What accident befell him?** He fell from a lattice, or window, in an upper room. 2 Kings 1:2.

**81. What means did he take for his recovery?** He sent to an idol-god.

**82. What did Elijah tell him?** That he should not recover, since he had not applied to God or to his prophet.

**83. What course did Ahaziah take?** He sent soldiers to take Elijah.

**84. What befell his messengers?** Two companies were consumed by fire from heaven, but the third was spared in answer to their leader's prayer.

**F. Jehoram (2 Kings 3:1–27; 8:28, 29; 9:16–26)**

**85. Who reigned in Israel after Ahaziah?** Jehoram, his brother, as he had no son. 2 Kings 1:17; 3:1.

**86. What was the character of Jehoram?** He put away Baal, but was otherwise very wicked. 2 Kings 3:2, 3.

**87. Did he continue the alliance with Jehoshaphat?** Yes, 2 Kings 3:7.

**88. Whom did they go to fight?** The Moabites.

**89. Why was Elisha sent for?** To know from him whether the Moabites would be defeated or not. 2 Kings 3:11–20.

**90. How did the Lord appear for them?** He deceived the Moabites, by the miraculous appearance of reddened water, with the belief that the armies of their enemies had destroyed each other. 2 Kings 3:20–27.

**91. What frightful sacrifice did the king of Moab offer to propitiate his gods?** His eldest son as a burnt offering. 2 Kings 3:27.

**92. How did the king of Moab soon after try to avenge this defeat?** By making war against Jehoshaphat. 2 Chron. 20:1.

**93. For how long did Jehoram reign?** Twelve years. 2 Kings 3:1.

**94. What was his end?** He was slain by Jehu when the latter took the throne. 2 Kings 9:16–20. See 53.

**52. ELISHA THE PROPHET (2 Kings 2:19–25; 3:11–19; 4:1–8:15; 9:1; 13:14–21)**

**1. To what city did Elisha return from Jordan?** To Jericho. 2 Kings 2:15, 18.

**2. What great trouble did the people of the city have?** There was no good water in the place. 2 Kings 2:19–22.

**3. How did Elisha make the water good?** By casting a little salt in it, accompanied by the healing power of God.

**4. Who mocked Elisha as he came to Bethel?** "Little children," or more

correctly, young lads. (The word is often used for boys from sixteen to eighteen years old, and is the word used by Solomon in 1 Kings 3:7.) 2 Kings 2:23–25.

**5. How were they punished?** They were "torn" by two she-bears. (They are not said to have been killed.)

**6. Who cried to Elisha for help?** The widow of one of the "sons of the prophets" or students at the school of the prophets. 2 Kings 4:1–7.

**7. What was her trouble?** A creditor of her late husband had taken her two sons as bondmen for the debt.

**8. What did Elisha command her to do?** To borrow empty vessels and fill them from her pot of oil, the only valuable property she had.

**9. When did the oil stop running?** Only when she provided no more vessels to be filled.

**10. Of what may this oil be a type?** Of the Holy Spirit, which is given to us according to our capacity. There is no limit to God's provision, but only in ourselves.

**11. How was Elisha entertained by a rich woman in Shunem?** She and her husband built and set apart a room, to be for his use whenever he came that way, because she knew him for a holy man of God. 2 Kings 4:8–37.

**12. What kind gift did the Lord bestow upon her for Elisha's sake?** A son, when she had no child.

**13. What happened to this child later?** He died by a sunstroke.

**14. What did the poor mother do?** She set off quickly for Mt. Carmel, to Elisha.

**15. What means did Elisha first use to recover the child?** His servant went ahead and laid Elisha's staff upon the child; but it was not effectual.

**16. What did Elisha then do?** Elisha prayed and then stretched himself upon the child, and he revived.

**17. Who was Naaman?** The Commander-in-chief of the army of the king of Syria; and he was afflicted with leprosy. 2 Kings 5.

**18. What did the little captive maid do for her master?** She said she wished that he was with Elisha, who would cure him.

**19. Did he go to Israel?** Yes, with letters from the king of Syria to the king of Israel, whose servant they supposed Elisha was.

**20. How did Elisha receive him?** He sent a message to him to wash in the Jordan and be clean.

**21. What had Naaman expected?** That Elisha, impressed by his dignity, would come to him and in a solemn manner call upon God to heal him.

**22. Was he induced to try the remedy?** Yes, his pride and anger yielded to the wise advice of those about him, and he was perfectly cured.

**23. Is there any lesson for us in this history?** Yes, humbleness of mind before God and his ministers.

**24. Of what is leprosy a type in the Scriptures?** Of the uncleanness of sin.

**25. If a little captive maid could do so much for her master is there not something we can do for others?** Yes, we can give ourselves, and a portion of our time and money, for the spreading of the knowledge of our Saviour in the world. And we can all give our prayers.

**26. What dreadful sins did covetousness lead Gehazi, Elisha's servant, to**

**commit in this connection?** Lying and tempting God's Spirit.

**27. What was his punishment?** He became a leper, thus being required to live apart. See the law in Lev. 13:45, 46.

**28. What did Elisha do for his country?** He learned from God the plans of the Syrians who were invading Israel, and warned the king of Israel. 2 Kings 6:8–12.

**29. How was the king of Syria affected by this?** He was much troubled, and at first suspected some of his own people of betraying him.

**30. What means did he use to prevent it?** He sent a host of men to take Elisha. 2 Kings 6:13–23.

**31. How did Elisha's servant feel when he saw the host of Syrians?** He was greatly afraid.

**32. Why was not Elisha equally frightened?** Because he had more confidence in God.

**33. How did Elisha give his servant confidence?** He asked God to open his eyes that he might see their heavenly defenders.

*"The angel of the Lord encampeth round about them that fear him, and delivereth them." Ps. 34:7.*

**34. What was the result?** The soldiers were blinded and Elisha led them to the camp of the king in Samaria.

**35. Did it save Israel from them?** Yes, they came no more for some time.

**36. What happened when they again fought Israel?** They besieged Samaria and caused a terrible famine there. 2 Kings 6:24; 7:20.

**37. What did the King of Israel do?** He threatened Elisha.

**38. What did Elisha tell the king?**

That within twenty-four hours there would be plenty to eat.

**39. What unbelieving answer was made to this?** One of the lords who accompanied the king said that unless God were to make windows in heaven the promise could not be fulfilled.

**40. What was Elisha's answer?** That he should see it, but should not eat of it.

**41. How was the wondrous change of events brought about?** By making the Syrians fancy they heard the noise of a great host coming to relieve the city, God caused them to fly for their lives, and leave all their provisions and other supplies behind.

**42. How was the prediction concerning the nobleman fulfilled?** He was placed in charge of the city gate, and was trodden to death by the crowd as they rushed out of the city for the food.

**43. Do we know any more about the deeds of Elisha?** He prophesied to Hazael of Damascus that he should murder his master to take his throne (2 Kings 8:7–15); and sent one of the young prophetical students to anoint a captain of Israel named Jehu to be king in place of Jehoram (2 Kings 9:1, 2). Then there is a silence of perhaps of fifty years, until his last illness. For this see 53. C.

**53. THE KINGS OF ISRAEL: THE DYNASTY OF JEHU (2 Kings 9:1–10:36; 13:1–25; 14:8–16, 23–29; 15:8–12)**

**A. Jehu (2 Kings 9:1–10:36)**

**1. Who was Jehu?** A captain in the Israelite army, stationed at Ramoth-gilead.

**2. What messenger came to him?** A young prophet sent by Elisha anointed him to be king. 2 Kings 9:1–14.

**3. Where was Joram, or Jehoram, king of Israel?** At Jezreel. 2 Kings 9:15.

**4. Who was visiting him?** His nephew, Ahaziah king of Judah. 2 Kings 9:16; 8:16–18, 29. See 57. B.

**5. What did Jehu do?** He at once rode to Jezreel, killed Jehoram and Ahaziah, and entered the city. 2 Kings 9:13–30.

**6. How was Jezebel slain?** She was thrown from a window and killed. 2 Kings 9:30–33; 1 Kings 21:23.

**7. Of whom is Jezebel a type?** Of any wicked church or people who have cast off the true love and worship of God, and led men astray. Rev. 2:20–22; 17; 18; 19:1–3.

**8. What did Jehu do next?** He killed all the rest of Ahab's family in Israel, and later by a great deceit gathered together and slaughtered all the worshippers of Baal. 2 Kings 10:1–28.

**9. What was Jehu's character?** He destroyed Baal-worship, but he left the calves in Bethel and Dan. 2 Kings 10:31.

**10. What promise did the Lord make to Jehu?** That his children for four generations should sit on the throne of Israel. 2 Kings 10:30.

**11. How long did Jehu reign?** Twenty-eight years. 2 Kings 10:36.

**B. Jehoahaz (2 Kings 13:1–9)**

**12. Who succeeded Jehu?** His son Jehoahaz.

**13. What character did he bear?** He was a wicked man.

**14. How did the Lord punish Israel?** By delivering them into the hands of Hazael the king of Syria.

**15. What effect did this have upon the king?** He prayed to God for relief, and was heard; but idolatry still continued in the land.

**16. How long did he reign?** Seventeen years.

### C. Jehoash or Joash
### (2 Kings 13:10–25; 14:8–16)

**17. Who succeeded Jehoahaz?** Joash his son (also called Jehoash). 2 Kings 13:10, 25; 14:1.

**18. Was he a better king?** He was no better, but walked, like his father, in Jeroboam's sins.

**19. What sorrowful event happened in this reign?** The death of Elisha.

**20. When Joash heard of the prophet's illness what did he do?** He came and wept over him and praised him.

**21. What symbolical prophecy was given at this interview?** Joash was told to strike the ground with arrows as a token of success against the Syrians. He struck three times only.

**22. Was Elisha's prophecy fulfilled?** Joash defeated the Syrians three times as Elisha had said.

**23. How came Israel and Judah to go to war in this reign?** Because the king of Judah challenged Joash. 2 Kings 14:8–14.

**24. What answer did Joash make to Judah?** He replied that he would crush him as a wild beast does a thistle.

**25. On which side did victory turn?** On Israel's side.

**26. How long did Joash reign over Israel?** Sixteen years. 2 Kings 13:10.

### D. Jeroboam II (2 Kings 14:16, 23–29)

**27. Who succeeded Joash on the throne of Israel?** Jeroboam his son.

**28. How many years did he reign?** Forty-one.

**29. Of what character was he?** He did evil in the sight of the Lord.

**30. What kind of a king was he?** He was successful in war, and recovered some border lands which Israel had lost. He was for some time, apparently, in virtual control of Judah also. 2 Kings 14:25–28.

**31. How many prophets prophesied in this reign?** Probably Jonah, Hosea, and Amos.

**32. Who succeeded Jeroboam II?** Zachariah his son, for six months; making the four generations which God had promised to Jehu. 2 Kings 10:30; 15:8–11.

### 54.  THE LAST KINGS OF ISRAEL
### (2 Kings 15:10–31; 17)

**1. Who slew Zachariah, the last of Jehu's dynasty?** Shallum. 2 Kings 15:10.

**2. How long did he reign?** A month. 2 Kings 15:13–15.

**3. Who destroyed him?** Menahem.

**4. How long did Menahem reign?** Ten years. 2 Kings 15:17–22.

**5. What kind of a King was he?** A wicked one.

**6. Who fought against him?** Pul, King of Assyria.

**7. Who succeeded Menahem?** Pekahiah, his son.

**8. How long did he reign?** Parts of two years. 2 Kings 15:23–26.

**9. Who slew him?** Pekah, on of his captains.

**10. How long did Pekah reign?** Twenty years. 2 Kings 15:25–31.

**11. Which was the last King of Israel?**
Hoshea, who slew Pekah and became king. 2 Kings 15:30.

**12. How long did he reign?** Nine years. 2 Kings 17:1.

**13. Who conquered Israel in his reign?** Shalmanezer, King of Assyria.

**14. How was this?**
*"The Lord shall bring thee, and thy king which thou shalt set over thee, unto a nation which neither thou nor thy fathers have known; and there shalt thou serve other gods, wood and stone. . . . Moreover all these curses shall come upon thee, and shall pursue thee, and overtake thee, till thou be destroyed; because thou hearkenedst not unto the voice of the Lord thy God, to keep his commandments and his statutes which he commanded thee." Deut. 28:36, 45.*

**15. To what places was Israel carried captive?** To places in Media and Mesopotamia.

**16. Who were brought in to fill the depopulated cities?** People from Babylon and the regions round it. 2 Kings 17:24.

**17. What was the result?** A mixture of worship of God and of idols. 2 Kings 17:33.

**55. THE KINGS OF JUDAH: REHOBOAM; ABIJAH, ASA (1 Kings 12:1–24; 14:21–31; 15:1–24; 2 Chron. 10:1–16:14)**

**A. Rehoboam (1 Kings 12:1–24; 14:21–31; 2 Chron. 10:1–12:16)**

**1. Who was Rehoboam?** The son and successor of Solomon.

**2. What was the first important event in his reign?** The revolt of the ten tribes. See 48.

**3. Did Rehoboam try to win back the people?** Yes, by war; but God commanded him not to fight. 1 Kings 12:18–24; 2 Chron. 11:1–4.

**4. How long did Rehoboam worship God truly?** Three years. 2 Chron. 11:17.

**5. When he forsook God what happened?** He was attacked and defeated by Shishak, king of Egypt. 1 Kings 14:25–28; 2 Chron. 12:1–10.

**B. Abijah (1 Kings 14:31–15:8; 2 Chron. 13:1–22)**

**6. Who succeeded Rehoboam as king of Judah?** Abijah his son.

**7. With whom did Abijah make war?** With Israel.

**8. What appeal did they make to Jeroboam?** "Fight ye not against the Lord God of your fathers."

**9. How did Jeroboam receive the appeal?** He sent soldiers to ambush the king of Judah.

**10. To whom did the army of Judah cry when they were in danger?** To God; and they gained the battle because they relied upon God.

**C. Asa (1 Kings 15:8–24; 2 Chron. 14:1–16:14)**

**11. Who followed Abijah upon the throne of Judah?** Asa his son.

**12. What was Asa's character in God's estimation?** He did what was good and right.

**13. What proof did he give of his heart being right with God when he first came to the throne?** He destroyed the idols and their places of worship. 1 Kings 15; 2 Chron. 14.

**14. Was his early reign prosperous?**
Yes, his land was at peace.

**15. How did he behave when the vast army from Ethiopia came up against him?** He prayed to God and fought in his name; and the Ethiopians fled. 2 Chron. 14.

**16. What encouragement did the Lord give Asa by the mouth of Azariah, the prophet?** That God would be with him as long as he was obedient. 2 Chron. 15:1–7.

**17. What effect did it have on the king and people?** He put down idolatry, and the people made a covenant to seek God with all their heart (2 Chron. 15:8–15), and the Lord gave them peace.

**18. Did this happy state of things continue to the end of Asa's reign?** It continued to the thirty-fifth year of his reign.

**19. What happened then?** Baasha, king of Israel, came against him, and instead of going for help to God Asa made an alliance with the king of Syria. 1 Kings 15:16–21; 2 Chron. 16:1–6.

**20. What did the prophet Hanani then say to Asa?** He reminded him of God's readiness to help his people, and told him that henceforth he should have wars. 2 Chron. 16:7–10.

**21. How did Asa receive the reproof?** He was enraged, and put the prophet in prison.

**56. THE KINGS OF JUDAH: JEHOSHAPHAT (1 Kings 15:24; 22:1–20; 2 Kings 3; 2 Chron. 17:1–21:1)**

**1. Who succeeded Asa as King of Judah?** His son Jehoshaphat. 2 Chron. 17:1.

**2. What was his character?** He sought the God of his father and walked in his commandments.

**3. Did he have a prosperous reign?** Yes, he was long without war, and became a great king, with riches and honor in abundance.

**4. With whom did Jehoshaphat made an alliance? With what result?** With Ahab of Israel. See 51. D. 68–77; 2 Chron. 18.

**5. How did the Lord show his displeasure when Jehoshaphat joined Ahaziah, Ahab's son, in sending ships to go to Tarshish?** The ships were wrecked. 1 Kings 22:48; 2 Chron. 20:35–37.

**6. With what other King of Israel did Jehoshaphat ally himself?** With Jehoram, son of Ahab, successor of Ahaziah. 2 Kings 3. See 51. F.

**7. Whom did they go to fight?** The Moabites.

**8. How did the king of Moab soon after try to avenge this defeat?** By making war against Jehoshaphat. 2 Chron. 20:1–30.

**9. What kings joined with him?** The Ammonites and others.

**10. How did Jehoshaphat feel?** He was afraid, proclaimed a fast and prayed to God before the people.

**11. What gracious message did the Lord send to him?** That he would destroy their enemies without a battle.

**12. Did Jehoshaphat and his people believe the message that thus came to them from God?** Yes, and united together immediately in praising God.

**13. What spoils did they gain?** Abundance of riches and jewels.

**14. What effect did this great conquest have on the nations around?** The fear of God was upon them, and they troubled Jehoshaphat no more.

**15. Did Jehoshaphat rid the land of all the abominations of idolatry?** He left the high places of the heathen gods.

**16. Which of Jehoshaphat's sons ruled jointly with his father for a time?** Jehoram, for about four years. Compare 2 Kings 1:17 with 2 Kings 3:1; 8:16.

**17. How old was Jehoshaphat when he died?** Sixty years old, having reigned twenty-five years. 2 Chron. 20:31.

**57. THE KINGS OF JUDAH: JORAM (OR JEHORAM) TO AMAZIAH (2 Kings 8:16–29; 9:16–29; 11; 12; 14:1–20; 2 Chron. 21–25)**

**A. Joram (2 Kings 8:16–24; 2 Chron. 21:1–20)**

**1. Whose son was Joram (Jehoram) king of Judah?** Son of Jehoshaphat. 2 Chron. 21:1.

**2. Which of Israel's kings reigned at the same time?** Ahaziah, and afterward Jehoram. 2 Kings 1:17, 18.

**3. Whose daughter was Joram's wife?** Ahab's daughter Athaliah. 2 Chron. 21:6.

**4. What effect did this alliance have on the king?** It led him into the sins of Ahab's house.

**5. What message came to him from God by the hand of Elijah the prophet?** Of a great plague or affliction for his family and people, and a mortal disease for himself.

**6. How long did he reign?** Eight years; probably including the four years

he was associated with his father. See 56. 16.

**7. Who succeeded him?** Ahaziah his son.

**B. Ahaziah (2 Kings 8:25–29; 9:16–29; 2 Chron. 22:1–9)**

**8. By what three names is this king called?** Ahaziah, Jehoahaz and Azariah; but he is most generally known as Ahaziah. 2 Kings 9.

**9. Which of Joram's sons was he?** The youngest; the rest had been captured in war. 2 Chron. 21:16, 17.

**10. To what untimely end did this King of Judah come?** He was killed, with Joram of Israel, by order of Jehu. 2 Kings 9:27; 2 Chron. 22:7, 8. See 53. A.

**C. Athaliah (2 Kings 11; 2 Chron. 22:10–12)**

**11. What was the name of Ahaziah's mother?** Athaliah, daughter of Ahab and Jezebel, of Israel.

**12. When she saw that her son was dead what did she do?** She ordered all the king's sons, her own grandsons, killed; and she usurped the throne. 2 Chron. 22:10.

**13. How was one grandson unexpectedly preserved?** He was hid by his aunt Jehoshabeath, who was the wife of Jehoiada the high priest. 2 Chron. 22:11.

**14. How long did the wicked Athaliah keep the throne?** Six years.

**15. What was her end?** She was slain when Joash, the lawful king, who had been preserved when the others were slain, was raised to the throne.

**D. Joash (2 Kings 12; 2 Chron. 23; 24)**

**16. How old was the young king**

**when he began to reign?** Seven years old.

**17. How long did he continue to do well?** During the life of the high priest Jehoiada, about twenty-eight years.

**18. What good service did he do the temple of God during Jehoiada's life?** He repaired and refitted it. 2 Chron. 24:4–14.

**19. How old was the good Jehoiada when he died?** One hundred and thirty years. 2 Chron. 24:15.

**20. What honor did they show him?** They buried him among the kings.

**21. How did Joash behave after his uncle's death?** He worshipped idols.

**22. Whom did the Lord send to warn him of his sins?** Zechariah the son of Jehoiada.

**23. What did Joash cause to be done to him?** To be stoned to death. 2 Chron. 24:21.

**24. How did the Lord punish Judah for their idolatry?** By the Syrian army.

**25. How did he punish the king?** By great diseases.

**26. In what way did he die?** He was killed by his own servants.

**27. How long did he reign?** Forty years. 2 Chron. 24:1.

**28. Who succeeded him?** Amaziah his son.

**E. Amaziah (2 Kings 14; 1–20; 2 Chron. 25)**

**29. Was Amaziah a better man than his father?** Probably not, as his heart was not right toward God, and as, after reigning well for some time, he fell into idolatry.

**30. What new idolatry did he introduce?** The gods of Edom. 2 Chron. 25:14, 20; 2 Kings 14:19, 20.

**31. How was he punished for this?** By defeat in war with Joash of Israel; and by conspiracy at home. 2 Chron. 25:17–24; 2 Kings 14:19, 20.

**32. How did he die?** He was killed by his own people.

**33. How long did he reign?** Twenty-nine years.

**58.  THE KINGS OF JUDAH: UZZIAH, JOTHAM AND AHAZ (2 Chron. 26–32; 2 Kings 14:21, 22; 15:1–7, 32–38)**

**A.  Uzziah (2 Chron. 26; 2 Kings 14:21, 22; 15:1–7)**

**1. Who was Uzziah?** Amaziah's son.

**2. How old was he when he began to reign?** Sixteen.

**3. By what other name is he called?** Azariah. 2 Kings 15:1.

**4. What king was reigning in Israel at this time?** Jeroboam II.

**5. What prophets prophesied in the reign of Uzziah?** Amos, Hosea and Isaiah.

**6. What is said of Uzziah in 2 Chron. 26:5?** That while he sought the Lord he prospered.

**7. How was this manifested in the early part of his reign?** By great success in war. 2 Chron. 26:6–15.

**8. By whose influence was he kept in the right way?** By the influence of Zechariah, a man of God.

**9. What effect did prosperity have on him?** It "lifted up his heart," that is, he became proud and presumptuous.

**10. To what act of impiety did Uzziah's pride prompt him?** To burn incense like a priest.

**11. How was it punished?** By Uzziah's being smitten with leprosy.

**12. What great deprivations did Uzziah suffer on account of his malady?** He was cut off from the house of the Lord, from the honors of a king and from all human society.

**13. What were Uzziah's main occupations?** War, the building of cities and towers, the digging of wells, and the keeping of much cattle; also the cultivation of fruitful fields.

**14. How many years did he reign?** Fifty-two years.

**15. Who shared the government with him when he was laid aside, and succeeded him on the throne?** Jotham his son.

**B. Jotham (2 Kings 15:5, 32–38; 2 Chron. 26:21; 27)**

**16. How old was Jotham when he began to reign?** Twenty-five. 2 Chron. 27:1. (This probably means when he was made regent during his father's life.)

**17. How is his character described?** "He did that which was right in the sight of the Lord."

**18. How long did he reign?** Sixteen years as king, in addition to his regency during his father's life.

**C. Ahaz (2 Kings 16; 2 Chron. 28)**

**19. Who followed Jotham?** Ahaz his son, a man who "did not right in the sight of the Lord."

**20. Did Ahaz go on in this sad career without warning?** No, he was warned by the prophets.

**21. Which of the prophets prophesied in his reign?** Isaiah and Micah.

**22. What idol-worship did Ahaz again introduce?** Of Baal and of the gods of Syria. 2 Chron. 28:2, 23.

**23. What cruel heathen practice did he exercise on his son?** He burnt his children in sacrifice. 2 Chron. 28:3.

**24. What enemies came against Judah as a punishment for their sins?** Pekah, king of Israel, and Rezin, king of Syria.

**25. Of whom did Ahaz ask aid?** Of Assyria.

**26. How did he strip the temple of God to pay the Assyrian king?** He took away much of its brass (or rather bronze) work. 2 Kings 16:17, 18.

**27. Did he after all, obtain the help he desired?** He did not.

**28. What effect had chastisement on him?** He sinned yet more against the Lord. 2 Chron. 28:23.

**29. How many years did he reign?** Sixteen years.

**59. THE KINGS OF JUDAH: HEZEKIAH (2 Kings 18–20; 2 Chron. 29–32; Isaiah 36–39)**

**1. Who reigned after Ahaz?** His son Hezekiah.

**2. How old was Hezekiah when he began to reign?** Twenty-five.

**3. What was the condition of the temple?** It was in great disrepair. 2 Chron. 29:3–7.

**4. What did Hezekiah do to set up the worship of God again?** He called upon the priests and Levites to assist in cleansing the temple, and the people. 2 Chron. 29:12–17, 28–35.

**5. Was his reformation confined to Judah, or did he desire to extend it to all Israel?** He invited all Israel and Judah to join in a solemn passover.

**6. How were Hezekiah's messengers received?** They were laughed at and mocked by the majority, but some came from Asher, Manasseh, and Zebulun. 2 Chron. 30:10, 11.

**7. What beautiful prayer did Hezekiah offer for these?** That the good Lord would pardon every one who had prepared his heart to seek him, although he was not clean according to the temple laws.

**8. How long had it been since there had been such a passover as this?** Not since the time of Solomon, nearly three hundred years before.

**9. What effect did this joy in the Lord have on the people with regard to the idols of the land?** They destroyed them all. 2 Chron. 31:1.

**10. What was the next proof the people gave that their hearts were right with God?** The abundance of their offerings for the service of God. 2 Chron. 31:5–7.

**11. Who came against Jerusalem?** Sennacherib, king of Assyria. 2 Chron. 32:1; Isa. 36:1.

**12. What did Hezekiah do?** He fortified Jerusalem, and cut off the water from the enemy's camp.

**13. On whom did he depend for succor?** On God alone. 2 Chron. 32:8.

**14. How did the people feel when Hezekiah cheered them?** They "rested on his words."

**15. What did Sennacherib do to endeavor to shake their confidence in God?** He sent his officer, the Rabshakeh, to read to the people themselves letters which boasted of his victories in other lands.

**16. Did he succeed?** No, the people held their peace, and their confidence in God. 2 Kings 18:36.

**17. To whom did Hezekiah send? and what did he himself do?** He sent for Isaiah, and went into the temple for prayer to God. 2 Kings 19:1, 2; Isa. 37:2.

**18. How did the Lord appear for his people at this time?** He promised them the departure and death of Sennacherib. 2 Kings 19:6, 7.

**19. Did the King of Assyria make another attempt on Jerusalem?** Yes, and sent another threatening letter.

**20. What did Hezekiah do with the letter?** He spread it before God in prayer.

**21. What was Hezekiah's prayer?** That God would save them for his own glory. 2 Kings 19:15–19.

**22. How was this wonderful deliverance effected?** By means of the angel, or literally, "messenger" of God, who struck the Assyrian army with death.

**23. What was Sennacherib's own end?** He was killed by his own sons.

**24. What mighty city was the capital of the Assyrian empire?** Nineveh.

**25. Are there any proofs at the present day of this Assyrian king's conquests and final defeat?** The ruins of Nineveh have been exposed to view, and letters and figures been found, carved upon slabs of stone, or on bricks of clay, which thoroughly confirm the Bible account.

**26. What is next recorded of Hezekiah?** That he was "sick unto death." 2 Kings 20:1–7; Isa. 38:1.

**27. Did he die of this illness?** He was restored to health in answer to prayer and by God's blessing on the means which Isaiah ordered to be used.

**28. Was there any part of Hezekiah's history that was dishonorable to him?** Yes, he made a display to the king of Babylon's messengers of all his treasures.

**29. What fearful prediction was Isaiah commissioned to take to him?** That at some future time all his treasures should be carried away to Babylon. 2 Kings 20:17, 18; Isa. 39:6.

**30. Name the benefits that Hezekiah conferred upon Jerusalem.** He erected various public buildings, and brought water from a distance to the city.

**31. How long did he reign?** Twenty-nine years. 2 Kings 18:2.

**60. THE KINGS OF JUDAH: MANASSEH, AMON AND JOSIAH (2 Kings 21:1–23:30; 2 Chron. 33–35)**

**A. Manasseh (2 Kings 21:1–18; 2 Chron. 33:1–20)**

**1. Whose son was Manasseh?** Hezekiah's.

**2. Was he a good king like his father?** No, he restored idolatry and witchcraft, and set up idols even in the temple itself. He is said to have slain the prophet Isaiah.

**3. How was he punished by the Lord for this?** He was carried captive to Babylon.

**4. What effect did captivity have upon him?** It brought him, by the grace of God, to penitence and prayer.

**5. Did the Lord hear and answer his prayer?** Yes, he restored him to his kingdom.

**6. How did Manasseh act on his** return to his kingdom? He put away idolatry throughout all Judah.

**7. How long did Manasseh reign?** Fifty-five years.

**B. Amon (2 Kings 21:19–25; 2 Chron. 33:20–25)**

**8. Who succeeded Manasseh?** Amon his son; who, had he lived, would have undone all the reformation of his father.

**9. How long did Amon reign?** Two years.

**10. What was his melancholy end?** He was killed by his own servants.

**C. Josiah (2 Kings 22:1–23:30; 2 Chron. 34; 35)**

**11. How old was Josiah when he came to the throne of Judah?** Eight years.

**12. Whose son was he?** Amon's.

**13. What character did he bear?** "He did that which was right in the sight of the Lord."

**14. How soon did he begin to manifest his love of God?** At the age of fifteen or sixteen. 2 Chron. 34:3.

**15. What was the first reformation he effected?** The removal of everything connected with idol-worship.

**16. What wonderful discovery was made in cleansing the temple?** A book of the law which had been forgotten. Probably it was all or part of Deuteronomy.

**17. What effect did the reading of God's word have on the young king?** He was shocked and alarmed by the national guilt and danger.

**18. To whom did he send to inquire the will of God concerning his people?** To Huldah the prophetess.

**19. How did God comfort Josiah?** By promising that his judgments should not take place during Josiah's life.

**20. What effect did this message have on Josiah?** He caused the book of the law to be publicly read, and induced the people to renew their covenant with God.

**21. What idolatries does 2 Kings 23 show had gained footing in Judah at this time?** The worship of Baal, and the abominations of Sidon, Moab and Ammon.

**22. How did Josiah deal with them all?** He destroyed them, and defiled the altars.

**23. What remarkable prophecy had gone before of this young king?**

*"And, behold, there came a man of God out of Judah by the word of the Lord unto Beth-eli: and Jeroboam stood by the altar to burn incense. And he cried against the altar to burn incense. And he cried against the altar in the word of the Lord, and said, O altar, altar, thus saith the Lord; Behold, a child shall be born unto the house of David; Josiah by name; and upon thee shall he offer the priests of the high places that burn incense upon thee, and men's bones shall be burnt upon thee." 1 Kings 13:1, 2.*

**24. Did he fulfill it?** Yes, exactly. 2 Chron. 34:5.

**25. What was Josiah's end?** He was killed in battle at Megiddo.

**26. How did this come about?** He had attacked the king of Egypt as he was going against the king of Assyria.

**27. How was the news of his death received by his people?** With deep and universal mourning.

**28. Which famous prophet is named as mourning for him?** Jeremiah. 2 Chron. 35:25.

*"The breath of our nostrils, the anointed of the Lord, was taken in their pits, of whom we said, Under his shadow we shall live among the heathen." Lam. 4:20.*

**29. How long had this good king reigned?** Thirty-one years.

**61. THE LAST KINGS OF JUDAH (2 Kings 23–25; 2 Chron. 36; Jeremiah)**

**1. Which of Josiah's sons succeeded him on the throne?** Jehoahaz.

**2. How old was he when he began to reign, and how long did he reign?** He was twenty-three years old, and reigned three months.

**3. How was it that his reign was so short?** He was put down from his throne by the King of Egypt, and carried away into Egypt; where he died. Jer. 22:11, 12.

**4. Who reigned next?** Eliakim, another son of Josiah.

**5. To what did the king of Egypt change Eliakim's name?** Jehoiakim.

**6. How old was he when he began to reign, and how long did he reign?** he was twenty-five years old, and reigned eleven years.

**7. Who succeeded Jehoiakim?** His son.

**8. By how many names is this son called?** Three; Jehoiachin (2 Kings 24:8), Jeconiah (1 Chron. 3:16), and Coniah (Jer. 22:24).

**9. How old was he when his father died?** Eight years.

**10. How soon after was he carried to Babylon?** About three months. 2 Chron. 36:9, 10.

**11. Who was made king in his place?** The King of Babylon, Nebuchadnezzar, set on the throne his uncle Mattaniah, whose name he changed to Zedekiah.

**12. What relation was Zedekiah to the good King Josiah?** Son.

**13. What did Nebuchadnezzar carry to Babylon from Jerusalem, with the king?** The treasures and ornaments from the temple.

**14. What character did Zedekiah bear?** He did evil in the sight of the Lord. 2 Chron. 36:12.

**15. What prophet was very prominent in these times?** Jeremiah.

**16. What did Zedekiah ask of Jeremiah?** What would be the result of an attack on Jerusalem by Nebuchadnezzar.

**17. What message did the Lord send to Zedekiah on this subject?** That those who escaped the pestilence and famine should fall by the sword of the king of Babylon.

**18. What army did Zedekiah get to help him against the Chaldeans?** The Egyptians. Jer. 37.

**19. Did their alliance prosper?** They drove away the enemy for a time.

**20. What was the fate of Jerusalem?** It was captured by the Chaldeans, and the people taken into captivity.

**21. How did Nebuchadnezzar treat Zedekiah?** He had him brought before him at Riblah, and put out his eyes after killing his sons and his nobles in his sight, and then imprisoned him in Babylon for the rest of his life. Jer. 52:10, 11.

**22. What two apparently conflicting prophecies are reconciled by this?** That in Jer. 34:3–5 that he should be carried captive to Babylon and die there; and that in Ezek. 12:12, that he should never see the city.

**23. By what prophet had this captivity of the Jews been foretold?** By Jeremiah (25:11). "These nations shall serve the king of Babylon seventy years."

**24. Why had that exact time been fixed?** See 2 Chron. 36:20, 21; Lev. 26:33–35.

*"Them that had escaped from the sword carried he away to Babylon; where they were servants to him and his sons until the reign of the kingdom of Persia: to fulfill the word of the Lord by the mouth of Jeremiah, until the land had enjoyed her sabbaths: for as long as she lay desolate she kept sabbath to fulfill threescore and ten years."*

**25. Were all the people of Judah carried away?** No, the poorer people were left there to care for the land. Jer. 39:10.

**26. Did they yield quietly to the rule of Babylon?** Some tried to revolt, killed the Babylonian governor, and fled to Egypt, carrying Jeremiah with them, against his will. Jer. 41; 42.

## 62. EZRA

**1. In whose reign did the Israelites return from this seventy years' captivity?** In the reign of Cyrus, king of Persia, who had conquered Babylon.

**2. Which prophet had spoken of this king Cyrus by name?** Isaiah.

*"Thus saith the Lord to his anointed, to Cyrus, whose right hand I have holden, to subdue nations before him." Isa. 45:1.*

**3. How long had that been uttered before the event?** About one hundred and seventy years before the taking of

Babylon by Cyrus; the Return was perhaps a year later.

**4. What edict concerning the captive Jews did Cyrus issue?** That they might return to Judea, and rebuild the temple.

**5. Who was at this time prince of Judah?** Sheshbazzar.

**6. Who was the head of the tribe of Levi, and thus by birth the high priest?** Jeshua, or Joshua. Ezra 2:40; 3:2.

**7. How many returned to Judea when this decree was published?** 42,360, beside 7,337 servants. Ezra 2:1, 64, 65.

**8. What did they take with them?** The gold and silver vessels of the temple.

**9. How long a journey was it?** Probably about four or five months at that time with such a company.

**10. In which month of the year did they reach Jerusalem?** The seventh, our modern October. Ezra 3:1.

**11. What feast fell on the fifteenth day of that month?** The feast of tabernacles.

**12. How far did they get in building the temple before they were interrupted?** The foundation was laid. Ezra 3:11; 4:4.

**13. What enemies interrupted them, and for how long?** The Samaritans, or mixed races which occupied the land which had belonged to the northern kingdom; for fifteen years.

**14. By what means did the Lord rouse them to their duty?** By Haggai and Zechariah, the prophets. Ezra. 5:1.

**15. How does Haggai's first chapter show us that the Jews were more anxious to build their own houses than the temple of the Lord?**
*"Is it time for you, O ye, to dwell in your cieled houses, and this house lie waste?" Hag. 1:4.*

**16. What effect did it have on Zerubbabel the prince of Judah, and Joshua the high priest?**
*"The Lord stirred up the spirit of Zerubbabel the son of Shealtiel, governor of Judah, and the spirit of Joshua the son of Josedech, the high priest, and the spirit of all the remnant of the people: and they came and did work in the house of the Lord of hosts, their God." Hag. 1:14.*

**17. What promises did the Lord give to the Jews in connection with the building of his house?** That he would be with them, and give them glory and peace. Hag. 2:4, 9. See also 83.

**18. What effect did these promises have on the Jews?** They began to build the house of the Lord, and prospered, and finished it. Ezra. 5:2; 6:12.

**19. How did they withstand their adversaries?** Through "the eye of their God" upon them. Ezra. 5:5.

**20. What new edict did they obtain from the king?** That the Persian governors should furnish them supplies for the building and the sacrifices. Ezra. 6:6–14.

**21. How had this been brought about?** Through the discovery of the former decree of Cyrus. Ezra. 5:3; 6:2, 3.

**22. When was the temple finished?** In the sixth year of king Darius, in the year 516 B.C.

**23. How was it dedicated?** With special sacrifices, and the keeping of the passover. Ezra. 6:16–22.

**24. Who is the Artaxerxes mentioned in Ezra?** He is thought to have been Artaxerxes Longimanus, son of the Xerxes who is connected with Grecian history.

**25. Who was Ezra?** A priestly descendant of Aaron, and a writer of the law. Ezra. 7:1–5, 11.

**26. What was his object in going to Jerusalem?** He wished to take back a number of volunteers, and to aid in restoring the worship and knowledge of God.

**27. What kind letter and munificent gift did he bear from the Persian king?** A letter empowering the Jews to return to Jerusalem, and exempting many of them from tribute and custom, and a gift of silver and gold, and other needful things. Ezra. 7:11–25; 8:26, 27.

**28. How does Ezra describe his journey from Babylon to Judea?** That they set out with fasting and prayer, and arrived in safety through the protection of God alone. Ezra. 8:21–23, 31, 32.

**29. What act of worship did they perform when they arrived in Judea?** They offered a burnt offering. Ezra. 8:35.

**30. What sinful act was Ezra told about by the princes of Judah?** That the Jews had intermarried with the people of the land. Ezra. 9.

**31. Did he justify these acts before the Lord, or confess the sin to him?** He confessed it with the deepest humiliation.

**32. What effect did his faithfulness have on the people?** They were truly penitent and distressed and put away their heathen wives. Ezra. 10:1, 19.

**33. How did they bring about the desired reformation?** They made a covenant with God and with each other, and a public proclamation.

## 63. NEHEMIAH

**1. What office did Nehemiah hold in the Persian court?** That of king's cup-bearer. Neh. 1:11.

**2. What king of Persia was this?** It is thought to have been Artaxerxes Longimanus. 62. 24.

**3. Was this a high office?** Yes, it meant that he was a royal favorite, and had access to the king when others were excluded.

**4. Why did he wish to give up so high an appointment?** That he might return to Jerusalem to assist in the rebuilding of the temple and city.

**5. What means did he adopt to obtain his desire?** Prayer to God. Neh. 1:11; 2:4.

**6. Did the king grant his request?** He did. Neh. 2:6.

**7. What was Nehemiah's particular request to the king?** That he would send him to Judea to rebuild his city. Neh. 2:5.

**8. How was he sent?** With a large retinue, as royal governor.

**9. How did the Jews' enemies feel when they understood Nehemiah's errand?** They were much displeased. Neh. 2:10, 19; 4:1, 7.

**10. What was Nehemiah's first act after he got to Jerusalem?** He privately examined the ruins by night. Neh. 2:12–15.

**11. In what state did he find the wall?** Everywhere broken down.

**12. What was his first public act?** To urge the people to rebuild the walls. Neh. 2:17, 18.

**13. How was his urging received?** The people said, "Let us rise up and build." Neh. 2:18.

**14. Who did the work of rebuilding?** The citizens themselves.

**15. When the enemies of the Jews saw the walls of Jerusalem progressing, what did they wish to do?** To stop the work. Neh. 4:11.

**16. What reproachful thing did they say of the work?** "If a fox go up, he shall even break down their stone wall." Neh. 4:3.

**17. How did Nehemiah meet the danger?** By prayer and faith, and by being armed and watchful both day and night. Neh. 4:9–23.

**18. What great abuse did Nehemiah set himself to rectify?** The requiring of usury, or excessive interest, for the loan of money to the famished and distressed. Neh. 5.

**19. Were the people willing to do as he said?** Yes, and did it at once.

**20. What example did Nehemiah himself set them?** He declined receiving his own allowance as royal governor, in order to spare the poor.

**21. What wicked device did Sanballat and his companions next try to put the good Nehemiah in fear?** They invited him to a conference, in order to get him into their hands, and they sent him a false prophet to induce him to leave his work. Neh. 6.

**22. How long was the wall in building?** Fifty-two days. Neh. 6:15.

**23. Whom did Nehemiah appoint to the charge of Jerusalem, and why?** *"I gave my brother Hanani, and Hananiah the ruler of the palace, charge over Jerusalem: for he was a faithful man, and feared God above many." Neh. 7:2.*

**24. What did God put into the heart of Nehemiah to do after this?** To make a register of the families that returned from Babylon. Neh. 7:5.

**25. Why was the preservation of the genealogies of the children of Israel so important?** To show the fulfillment in Christ of the promise to Abraham, that in his seed should all the nations of the earth be blessed (Gen. 22:18), and of the promise to David, that God would raise up a king to sit forever on his throne. Acts 2:29, 30; Luke 1:30–33.

**26. What further arrangement was completed by the seventh month?** The settling of the Israelites in their cites throughout the land. Neh. 7:73.

**27. What special feast was to be kept in that month?** The feast of tabernacles. Neh. 8:14–18.

**28. Of what was it symbolical?** The tabernacles, or booths, were in remembrance of the tents in the wilderness. Lev. 23:43.

**29. What great gathering was held?** All the people gathered in an open space where a pulpit was erected and the law was read and explained. Neh. 8.

**30. Why was the law read thus?** Books were very costly and rare; few could own a copy for themselves.

**31. Who read the law to Israel?** Ezra himself, and a company of Levites.

**32. What effect did the reading of the law have on the people?** They wept from mingled feelings of sorrow and of joy.

**33. How did Ezra encourage the people?** He said the joy of the Lord was their strength.

**34. What followed shortly after the feast of tabernacles?** A solemn fast with reading of the law and confession of sin. Neh. 9:1–37.

**35. What was the result of these?** The chiefs of the people made and signed a covenant to keep God's law. Neh. 9:38–10:27.

**36. How was the wall dedicated?** With music, and thanksgiving and great joy. Neh. 12:27–30.

**37. How long did this reformation last?** During the days of Zerubbabel and Nehemiah. Neh. 12:47.

**38. When did Nehemiah return to the king of Persia, his master?** In the thirty-second year of Artaxerxes' reign. Neh. 5:14.

**39. When he returned to Jerusalem again did he find the government going on prosperously?** No.

**40. What evils did he discover?** Abuse and neglect of the house of God, Sabbath breaking, and heathen marriages. Neh. 13.

**41. Had not the sabbath day been the great token of the covenant between the Lord and Israel?** It had. Isa. 58:13, 14; Ezek. 20:12–20.

**42. What command did the Lord give about marrying heathen wives?** *"Thou shalt make no covenant with them, nor show mercy unto them: neither shalt thou make marriages with them: thy daughter thou shalt not give unto his son, nor his daughter shalt thou take unto thy son. For they will turn away thy son from following me, that they may serve other gods." Deut. 7:2–4.*

**43. Did Nehemiah not vigorously root out this evil?** He did. Neh. 13:25–28, 30.

**44. Where is Nehemiah supposed to have ended his days?** At Babylon as cup-bearer to the king.

## 64. ESTHER

**1. Who was Ahasuerus?** He is usually thought to have been Xerxes the Great of Persia, known in secular history for his invasion of Greece.

**2. Who was Esther?** A Jewish maiden dwelling in Persia, who became the queen of Persia.

**3. How did this happen?** Ahasuerus' former wife had been divorced, and Esther was chosen in her place from many who had been taken to the king by his command. Est. 1:9; 2:1–17.

**4. Who was Mordecai?** A cousin of Esther, who took her for his daughter at the death of her parents. He had some office in the palace. Est. 2:5–7.

**5. Where was the Persian court held at this time?** At Shushan (or Susa) in Persia.

**6. Who was the Jews' great enemy in Persia now?** Haman, traditionally said to have been descended from Agag, King of Amalek.

**7. Why did Haman hate the Jews?** Because Mordecai was the only man in Susa who failed to do him reverence. Est. 3:2, 5, 6.

**8. How did Haman attempt to wreak vengeance on them?** By destroying all of them throughout the kingdom.

**9. Who learned of the plot?** Mordecai, who urged Esther to plead with the king for her people. Est. 4:1–14.

**10. Why was this a dangerous task?** No one was allowed to approach the king, unsummoned, under penalty of death, unless the king remitted the punishment.

**11. What did the king command to be read before him? Why?** The history of his reign to amuse him while wakeful at night. Est. 6:1.

**12. What did he find there?** That

Mordecai had discovered a plot and so saved the king's life, but had received no reward.

**13. How did Esther obtain the deliverance of her kindred?** By petitioning the king to deliver them from Haman.

**14. What was the king's answer?** Haman was executed, and the Jews were given the right to defend themselves. Est. 8:9–11.

**15. What feast was ever after celebrated among the Jews to commemorate this deliverance?** The feast of Purim. Est. 9:26.

**16. Why was it so called?** Because their enemies had cast Pur, or the lot, as to the time of destroying them. Est. 9:24; 3:6, 7.

**17. To what dignity was Mordecai raised at the Persian court?** The highest dignity under the king. Est. 10:3.

## 65. JOB

**1. Who was Job?** A very rich man in the north of Arabia who worshipped the true God. Job. 1:3.

**2. When is he supposed to have lived?** Probably in the age of the patriarchs, some 2,000 years before Christ.

**3. Who wrote the book of Job?** No one knows.

**4. What is the character of the book?** It is almost entirely in poetry; the first and last chapters, and an occasional verse, only, being in prose.

**5. Where does the scene of the poem open?** In heaven, where Satan comes in with the servants of God, and talks over the things done on the earth.

**6. What high terms of praise did the Lord use when speaking of Job to Satan?** Read Job 1:8.

**7. And how did the Lord, afterward, to Ezekiel mention him?** He classed him with Noah and Daniel as a righteous man. Ezek. 14:12–21.

**8. In what way did the Lord first try this good man?** By suffering him to be deprived in one day of his children, his servants, and his property. Job. 1.

**9. Did Job fail?** He submitted to God's will, and blessed him in memorable words. Read Job 1:21.

**10. Did Satan again have permission to hurt him?** Yes, by bodily suffering. Job 2:4–8.

**11. Did he continue steadfast?** He seems to have uttered no complaint against God, even when urged thereto by his wife.

**12. Who came to comfort him?** His three principal friends. Job. 2:11.

**13. Did not his friends suppose that all his misfortunes had come upon him in consequence of sin?** They did, and almost the whole of the poem consists in their arguments for their belief, and Job's defense of himself as righteous.

**14. How did Job feel when God himself spoke to him at last?** Deeply humbled.

**15. What did Job say?** *"Then Job answered the Lord, and said, Behold, I am vile; what shall I answer thee? I will lay mine hand upon my mouth." Job 40:3, 4.*

**16. Did the Lord condemn him?** No, he accepted him. Job. 42:9.

**17. How did the Lord pass over the error of Job's three friends in their condemnation of Job?** In consideration of their sacrifice and Job's prayer. Job 42:7–9.

**18. What was the later history of Job?** He was healed of his sickness, and he prospered so greatly that he had twice as much property as before his testing. He also had seven sons and three daughters, in place of the children he had lost. Job 42:10–17.

## 66. THE PSALMS

**1. What are the Psalms?** The Hebrew hymnal, the Book of Praises; the hymns being designed to be set to music, and used in worship.

**2. How many Psalms are there?** One hundred and fifty; divided into five books, ending respectively with Pss. 41, 72, 89, 106, and 150; each of which closes with some form of the benediction.

**3. Who wrote the Psalms?** David wrote the greater number, though many were written by other authors at different periods, both earlier and later.

**4. What are the titles, etc., given before some of the Psalms?** The titles ascribing them to certain authors and circumstances, although very ancient, are not an original part of the Psalms, and may or may not be true. The other inscriptions mean directions as to the music, such as "Alamoth"—for soprano voices; "Sheminith"—for bass voices; "Nehiloth"—with flute accompaniment. There are also a few which are the names of the popular melody to which the Psalm was to be sung, for example, Psalm 9 is set to the tune, "Death of the Son"; Psalm 45, to the tune, "The Lilies."

**5. Are these hymns equally valuable for our times?** Yes, they nearly all voice the inner feelings of the human heart in all ages.

**6. What Psalms may be cited as** among the most valuable for us? It would be easier to select a few which are among the least valuable; but we may at least name Pss. 1, 19, 23, 24, 32, 46, 51, 84, 90, 91, 103, 119, 121.

**7. Are there some Psalms which foreshadow the Messiah?** Yes, the whole or parts of Pss. 2, 16, 22, 40, 110 among others.

**8. Are there some historical Psalms?** Yes, for example, Pss. 78, 105, 106.

**9. What is the longest Psalm, and its subject?** Ps. 119, on the Word of God.

**10. What is the best-known verse in this Psalm?** Probably verse 105.

*"Thy word is a lamp unto my feet, and a light unto my path."*

## 67. PROVERBS

**1. What is the Book of Proverbs?** "A Miscellany of Wisdom in five books, being 375 brief literary compositions, wholly unconnected."

**2. Who wrote the Book of Proverbs?** Solomon is said to have written two of these five books; another was collected by men of Hezekiah's time, very probably from the common sayings of their time, some of which might well have dated back to Solomon's time, if not to that king himself; and the author or authors of the other two books are unknown.

**3. What is the beginning of wisdom?** The fear of the Lord. Prov. 1:7.

**4. What is an ornament of grace to the neck of a child?** Obedience to the instruction of his father and mother. Prov. 1:8, 9; 6:20, etc.

**5. What reward is promised those who seek diligently after Wisdom?** That they shall find.

**6. From what will Wisdom preserve them?** True wisdom preserves from the ways and society of the wicked, from all folly and sin, and from all real evil.

**7. What is the value of Wisdom?** Above all the wealth of this world. Prov. 3:13–18; 8:11, 19.

**8. Have those anything to fear who put their trust in the Lord? Why not?** No, because the Lord has promised it. Prov. 3:5, 6, 21–26.

**9. What proverb teaches the evil of laziness?** "Go to the ant, thou sluggard," etc. Prov. 6:6–11.

**10. What verses teach the evil of strong drink?** Prov. 20:1; 23:29–35.

**11. What chapter teaches the qualities of the virtuous woman?** Chapter 31.

## 68. ECCLESIASTES

**1. By whom was Ecclesiastes written?** Solomon has generally been considered the author.

**2. What is the meaning of the name?** "The Preacher."

**3. What is the general subject?** The confession of a man of great knowledge and wide experience, who has sinned and paid the penalty, and through it learned the lesson God would teach him.

**4. What was the result of his great knowledge, taken by itself?** That all is vanity under the sun. Eccl. 1:2, 3.

**5. What does the twelfth chapter teach as to the lesson he finally learned?** That to fear God and keep his commandments brings the truest life.

**6. What arguments does he use to urge the beginning of this service of God in youth?** The certainty of old age and death. Eccl. 12:1–7.

**7. Does the Apostle Paul agree with this author?** *"I reckon that the sufferings of this present time are not worthy to be compared with the glory which shall be revealed in us."* Rom. 8:18. See also 2 Cor. 4:17, 18.

## 69. THE SONG OF SOLOMON

**1. What is this book?** Perhaps a wedding song about Solomon. It is a poem.

**2. What is its religious interpretation?** It symbolizes the love of Christ for his Church, "his bride" (Rev. 21:2; 22:17); and the love of the Church for Christ.

## 70. ISAIAH

**1. Who was Isaiah?** One of the greatest of the Hebrew prophets, and the author of the book which bears his name.

**2. In whose reign did he prophesy?** In those of "Uzziah, Jotham, Ahaz, and Hezekiah, kings of Judah." See 58; 59.

**3. Is any part of his book historical?** Yes, chapters 1–39 are chiefly so, although interspersed with songs, poems and prophecies; and much historical matter is given in symbolic language.

**4. What great and glorious person was he privileged to announce?** The Messiah; especially in Isa. 7:14; 9:1–7; 11:1–10; 53.

*"Unto us a child is born, unto us a son is given: and the government shall be upon his shoulder: and his name shall be called Wonderful, Counsellor, The mighty God, The everlasting Father, The Prince of Peace. Of the increase of his government and peace there shall be no end, upon the throne of David, and upon his kingdom, to order it, and to establish*

*it with judgment and with justice from henceforth even for ever." Isa. 9:6, 7.*

**5. What prophecy of Isaiah's is quoted in Matt. 1:23?**
*"Therefore the Lord himself shall give you a sign; Behold, a virgin shall conceive, and bear a son, and shall call his name Immanuel." Isa. 7:14.*

**6. Under what name is the Lord Jesus spoken of in Isa. 11:1?** "A rod out of the stem of Jesse, and a Branch out of his roots."

**7. Who was Jesse?** The father of David.

**8. Where does the Lord Jesus call himself "the root and the offspring of David"?** Rev. 22:16.

**9. What is the Lord Jesus called in Rev. 5:5?** "The Lion of the tribe of Juda, the Root of David."

**10. How does Isaiah describe the kingly power of the Lord Jesus?** "Behold, a king shall reign in righteousness." Isa. 32:1.

**11. Under what character does he represent the Lord Jesus in the second verse of that chapter?**
*"A man shall be as an hiding place from the wind, and a covert from the tempest; as rivers of water in a dry place, as the shadow of a great rock in a weary land."*

**12. What part of Isaiah did the Lord Jesus read and use on one occasion as a text while he was on earth?** Isa. 61:1, 2.
*"The Spirit of the Lord is upon me, because he hath anointed me to preach the gospel to the poor; he hath sent me to heal the broken-hearted, to preach deliverance to the captives, and recovering of sight to the blind, to set at liberty them that are bruised, to preach the acceptable year of the Lord." Luke 4:18, 19.*

**13. What did he say when he closed the book?** "This day is this scripture fulfilled in your ears." Luke 4:21.

**14. What part of Isaiah's prophecy was the Ethiopian reading when Philip overtook him?** Isa. 53:7, 8.

**15. Apply the prophecy in Isaiah 53 to the earthly life of Christ Jesus.**
*Ver. 1. "Though he had done so many miracles before them, yet they believed not on him." John 12:37.*

*Ver. 2. He "made himself of no reputation, and took upon him the form of a servant, and was made in the likeness of men." Phil 2:7.*

*Ver. 3. "Is not this the carpenter, the son of Mary?" Mark 6:3.*

*"Out of Galilee ariseth no prophet." John 7:52.*

*Ver. 4. "He cast out the spirits with his word, and healed all that were sick." Matt. 8:16.*

*Ver. 5, 6. "Christ died for our sins according to the scriptures." 1 Cor. 15:3.*

*Ver. 7. "When he was accused of the chief priests and elders, he answered nothing." Matt. 27:12.*

*Ver. 8. "And when they had bound him, they led him away, and delivered him to Pontius Pilate the governor . . . and when he had scourged Jesus, he delivered him to be crucified." Matt. 27:2, 26.*

*Ver. 9. "There were also two other, malefactors, led with him to be put to death." Luke 23:32.*

*"There came a rich man of Arimathaea, named Joseph . . . He went to Pilate, and begged the body of Jesus. Then Pilate commanded the body to be delivered." Matt. 27:57, 58.*

**16. Where in the New Testament are verses 10–12 applied?** *Vers. 10, 11.* "*Lo, a Lamb stood on the mount Sion, and with him an hundred forty and four thousand, having his Father's name written in their foreheads . . . These were redeemed from among men, being the first fruits unto God and to the Lamb. And in their mouth was found no guilt: for they are without fault before the throne of God." Rev. 14:1, 4, 5.* Ver. 12. "*Forasmuch then as the children are partakers of flesh and blood, he also himself likewise took part of the same; that through death he might destroy him that had the power of death, that is, the devil." Heb. 2:14.*

**17. Are there not many gracious invitations to sinners throughout the book of Isaiah?** Yes, Two of the best known are:
"*Come now, and let us reason together, saith the Lord: though your sins be as scarlet, they shall be as white as snow; though they be red like crimson, they shall be as wool." Isa. 1:18.*
"*Ho, every one that thirsteth, come ye to the waters, and he that hath no money; come ye, buy, and eat; yea, come, buy wine and milk without money and without price." Isa. 55:1.*

**18. Were there not many special promises to Gentiles?** Yes, as in chapters 9, 11, 35, 42, 49, 60 and 65.

**19. Who are the Gentiles?** All who are not Jews.

**20. To whom are the principal prophecies in this book addressed?** To the Jews.

**21. What glorious promises are addressed to God's favored people?** More than we can quote. Among them:

"*As for me, this is my covenant with them, saith the Lord; my spirit that is upon thee, and my words which I have put in thy mouth, shall not depart out of thy mouth, nor out of the mouth of thy seed, nor out of the mouth of thy seed's seed, saith the Lord, from henceforth and for ever." Isa. 59:21.*
"*The Lord shall comfort Zion: he will comfort all her waste places; and he will make her wilderness like Eden, and her desert like the garden of the Lord." Isa. 51:3.*
"*Awake, awake; put on thy strength, O Zion; put on thy beautiful garments, O Jerusalem, the holy city: for henceforth there shall no more come into thee the uncircumcised and the unclean." Isa. 52:1.*

**22. Under what beautiful symbol does he describe God's care of Israel in chapter 5?** A husband-man's care of his vineyard.
"*What could have been done more to my vineyard, that I have not done in it? wherefore, when I looked that it should bring forth grapes, brought it forth wild grapes?"*

**23. Are there not many fearful denunciations against the wicked in this prophecy?** There are, as in 1:28, 31.
"*The destruction of the transgressors and of the sinners shall be together, and they that forsake the Lord shall be consumed . . . and the strong shall be as tow, and the maker of it as a spark, and they shall both burn together, and non shall quench them."*

**24. Against what nations did Isaiah especially prophesy?** Arabia, Assyria, Babylon, Egypt, Ethiopia, Israel, Judah, Moab, Tyre.

**25. How were the prophecies fulfilled?** For centuries these lands were in a wretched condition under the yoke of strangers who oppressed them. Some were destroyed. Gradually however, some others have been rising from their ashes, and there may yet be a strong Hebrew nation in those countries.

**26. How was Isaiah set apart for service?**

*"In the year that king Uzziah died I saw also the Lord sitting upon a throne, high and lifted up, and his train filled the temple. Above it stood the seraphims: . . . Then flew one of the seraphims unto me, having a live coal in his hand, which he had taken with the tongs from off the altar; and he laid it upon my mouth, and said, Lo, this hath touched thy lips; and thine iniquity is taken away, and thy sin purged. Also I heard the voice of the Lord, saying, whom shall I send, and who will go for us? Then said I, here am I; send me." Isa. 6:1–8.*

**27. Do you find anything similar to this vision in the book of Revelation?** Yes, in Rev. 4:2.

**28. What effect did the sight of God's glory have on Isaiah?** He deeply felt his sinfulness.

**29. What alone can remove the terror which all men as sinners must feel in the presence of God?**

*"The blood of Jesus Christ his Son, cleanseth us from all sin." 1 John 1:7.*

## 71. JEREMIAH

**1. Who was Jeremiah?** The great prophet who lived and prophesied during the sad days at the time of the conquest and captivity of Judah.

**2. When is the first mention of Jeremiah?** In the thirteenth year of Josiah's reign.

**3. How did Jeremiah at first feel when he realized that God had appointed him as a prophet?** Timid, and unfitted, like a child. He was, probably, very young.

**4. What office did Jeremiah hold by birthright? and what was his native city?** He was a priest, and was born at Anathoth, in Benjamin. Jer. 1:1.

**5. How does Jeremiah compare the worship of God and idolatry?**

*"My people have committed two evils; they have forsaken me, the fountain of living waters, and hewed them out cisterns, broken cisterns, that can hold no water." Jer. 2:13.*

**6. Compare Jer. 2:21 with Isa. 5 and Ps. 80, and describe God's people under this figure.** Like a vineyard, or a vine, they are tenderly sheltered, nourished, and trained, are wisely instructed and restrained, and bear rich and abundant fruit.

**7. What evils did Jeremiah prophesy as a judgment on the people for their sins?** That a mighty and ancient nation should come upon them and conquer them. Jer. 5:15.

**8. Did this warning leave them utterly without hope?** No, Jeremiah gave them still other invitations to repent and obey. For example, Jer. 17:19–27.

**9. Was Jeremiah the only prophet whom the Lord had sent to warn Israel?** No, they had constantly had warning prophets in the past. Jer. 7:25, 26.

**10. What special charge was given to Jeremiah as to his mission?** He was to stand in the court of the Lord's house, and to speak to all who came thither from all parts of Judah to worship. Jer. 26.

**11. How did the people receive the message?** They gathered together against Jeremiah.

**12. What bitter lamentation does the prophet utter in chapter 8:20?** *"The harvest is past, the summer is ended, and we are not saved."*

**13. What beautiful prayer is there for us in Jer. 17?** *"Heal me, O Lord, and I shall be healed; save me and I shall be saved."* Ver. 14.

**14. To what does the Lord compare himself and Israel in chapter 18?** To a potter moulding clay, and dealing with it as he wills.

**15. What sign did the Lord bid Jeremiah show the people? and what was the meaning of it?** The breaking of a potter's vessel, as a token of the ruin of Israel. Jer. 19.

**16. What misery did Jeremiah bring upon himself by thus faithfully proclaiming God's word?** He was put in the stocks. Jer. 20.

**17. Was not the good Jeremiah sometimes tempted to keep back God's word?** Yes, when he saw it was so badly received. Jer. 20:8, 9.

**18. Was there not a mighty power over him that he could not withstand?** Yes, God was stronger than he.

**19. Of whom does Jeremiah speak in chapter 23:5, 6?** Of Jesus Christ.

**20. How many other prophets spoke of Christ as a "Branch"?** Two. *"There shall come forth a rod out of the stem of Jesse, and a branch shall grow out of his roots."* Isa. 11.

**21. Who did Jeremiah say was to come up against Jerusalem and take it?** Nebuchadnezzar, king of Babylon. Jer. 25:9.

**22. How long was the Captivity to last?** Seventy years. Jer. 25:12.

**23. What was to happen at the end of it?** Babylon was to be destroyed. Jer. 25:12–14.

**24. After Jeremiah had spoken these words what did the Lord command him to do?** To write them in a book, or roll, and read the book to the princes. Jer. 36.

**25. Who was Jeremiah's assistant in these duties?** Baruch.

**26. What prophecies were in the roll?** Probably the greater, or perhaps, all, of Jer. 1–35 as we now have it. It prophesied the Captivity. (See Questions 21–23.)

**27. When the princes heard it to whom did they wish it to be read?** To the king.

**28. Why did they tell Jeremiah and Baruch to go hide themselves?** Lest the king should at once seize them.

**29. How did King Jehoiakim receive the message?** With anger and contempt. Probably only three or four leaves were read.

**30. What did he do with it?** He cut it and burnt it.

**31. What was Jeremiah commanded to do?** To write the words in another roll.

**32. What punishment did the king bring on himself by this act?** His dead body was cast out unburied and his family ceased to reign on the throne of Judah. Jer. 36:30; 22:30.

**33. What prediction did Jeremiah utter to King Zedekiah of the com-**

plete and entire destruction of Jerusalem? That by sword, famine and pestilence its people should be consumed. Jer. 24.

**34. Is the book of Jeremiah really historical?** Yes. See LX1.

**35. How did Jeremiah picture the conquest by Babylon?** By bonds and yokes upon his own person. Jer. 27.

**36. Who prophesied in opposition to Jeremiah?** Hananiah. Jer. 28.

**37. What symbol did he make with the yoke which was on the neck of Jeremiah?** He broke it, as if God would break Nebuchadnezzar's yoke.

**38. Did the Lord allow such impiety to pass?** No, he sent Hananiah a message by Jeremiah that he should die the same year.

**39. What object lesson was Jeremiah commanded to give the Israelites in Jer. 35?** To try to give the Rechabites wine to drink.

**40. Who were the Rechabites?** Descendants of Rechab, who belonged to the Kenites. 1 Chron. 2:55.

**41. Who were the Kenites?** Descendants of Abraham through his wife Keturah, being a branch of the Midianites. Gen. 25:2; Ex. 2:15–21; Judg. 1:16.

**42. What sort of people were the Rechabites?** They were a nomad people, living in tents in the desert.

**43. Why had they come to Jerusalem?** They were afraid of Nebuchadnezzar's army, and had come to take refuge in the walled city, as a safer place.

**44. Did Jeremiah succeed in persuading the Rechabites to drink wine?** No.

**45. Why not?** Their ancestor, Jonadab, the son of Rechab, had commanded them not to build houses, nor live in villages, nor drink any wine; and they had always obeyed his command.

**46. What great reward did the Lord give to the Rechabites because of their obedience?** That the family should always have a representative, and not die out.

**47. What other references are there in the Bible as to drinking and drunkards?** Prov. 23:19–21, 29–32; 1 Cor. 6:10; Rom. 13:13; Gal. 5:21; Eph. 5:18, etc.

**48. Was Judah won to obedience by this object lesson?** No, they still refused to serve God alone.

**49. What army did the king of Judah get to help him against Babylon?** Egypt. Jer. 37.

**50. Did this give any relief?** Only for a time.

**51. While the Chaldeans were away what did Jeremiah desire to do?** To return to his own home at Anathoth. Jer. 37:12.

**52. What did the princes do to him, and why?** They put him in prison, because they thought he was deserting to the Chaldeans.

**53. Did he remain in prison?** He was released by order of King Zedekiah, but was soon after put into a still worse dungeon. Jer. 38.

**54. Who stood up and spoke for Jeremiah?** Ebed-melech.

**55. How did he rescue him?** He raised him by cords from the dungeon pit.

**56. What did Jeremiah tell the king soon after this?** That if he stayed in the city it would be taken and burnt. Jer. 38:18.

**57. Did the king believe him and obey the word of the Lord?** No, he stayed until it was too late. Jer. 39:2, 4, 8.

**58. Where was Jeremiah when the city was taken?** In the court of the prison. Jer. 38:28.

**59. How did the Chaldeans treat Jeremiah?** By order of the king he was kindly sent back, according to his wish, to his own land. Jer. 39; 40.

**60. What comforting promises did the Lord give his people before they were carried away captive?** Of their return to their own land, and of the coming of the Messiah, the Lord our Righteousness. Jer. 32; 33.

**61. Did Jeremiah prophesy against any other nations besides Judah?** Yes, against at least ten others. See Jer. 50; 51.

**62. What other book did Jeremiah write besides his prophecy?** The Lamentations, when the city had finally fallen.

**63. Where is it supposed Jeremiah died?** In Egypt, by the hands of the Jews, who had fled there, and had forced Jeremiah to go with them. See Jer. 40–44.

## 72. EZEKIEL

**1. Who was Ezekiel?** A priest and prophet.

**2. Where was he when he saw his wonderful vision?** By the river Chebar, in Mesopotamia.

**3. How came he there?** With the Jews carried captive to Babylon by Nebuchadnezzar.

**4. How old was he at this time?** In his thirtieth year, as it is understood from chapter 1:1.

**5. How long had he been in captivity?** Above four years. Ezek. 1:2.

**6. Who was the Jehoiachin whose captivity is here spoken of?** King of Judah. See 61. 7–10.

**7. Was he the last king of Judah?** No, there was one more, Zedekiah.

**8. How long before the destruction of Jerusalem was this prophecy written?** About seven years; since the city was taken eleven years after the captivity of this king, and the vision is said to have been four years after his captivity. Ezek. 1:2.

**9. How does the Lord describe the children of Israel to Ezekiel?** As "most rebellious." Ezek. 2.

**10. How did the Lord prepare the prophet for his mission?** By encouraging and warning him not to fear. Ezek. 3.

**11. How was the coming destruction of Jerusalem described by Ezekiel?** Under the figure of a siege, with tokens of severe famine. Ezek. 4.

**12. To what does the Lord compare the inhabitants of Jerusalem?** To a useless vine-branch, and to a neglected infant. Ezek. 15; 16.

**13. To what is Nebuchadnezzar compared?** To a great eagle. Ezek 17.

**14. What merciful provision is given in Ezek. 18:19, 20?** "The son shall not bear the iniquity of the father, neither shall the father bear the iniquity of the son."

**15. What does Ezekiel give as the duty of the watchman?** To warn the wicked to turn from his evil way. Ezek. 33:8.

**16. What is the duty of those who hear the alarm?** To at once turn from their evil ways.

**17. Against whom is the prophecy in Ezek. 34 uttered?** Against the priests, prophets, and religious leaders, who were misleading the people.

**18. Who is the Good Shepherd?** Jesus Christ. Ezek. 34:23; John 10:11.

**19. Are there any promises of future blessing in Ezekiel's prophecy?** Yes, of the restoration of Israel to their own land, and of great spiritual and temporal blessings, like a resurrection from the dead. Ezek. 36; 37.

**20. What remarkable vision did the prophet see?** A valley of dry bones revived into an army of living men.

**21. What vision did Ezekiel see in the twenty-fifth year of the captivity of Judah?** Of a glorious temple, and of healing waters issuing from it. Ezek. 40–48.

**22. What great similarity is there between Ezek. 47 and Rev. 22?** The waters issuing from the temple are like the "pure river of water of life, clear as crystal, proceeding out of the throne of God." And in both visions there were on the bank of the river fruitful and healing trees.

## 73. DANIEL

**1. Who was Daniel?** One of Judah's choicest young men, who were trained in Babylon to be officers of the king. He is thought by some to have been of the royal family of Judah. Dan. 1:3–5.

**2. When was Daniel taken to Babylon?** With Jehoiakim, king of Judah, by Nebuchadnezzar while still "crown prince" under his father Nabopolassar.

**3. Where was Babylon?** On the Euphrates, in Chaldea.

**4. How old was Daniel when taken to Babylon?** Somewhere between fourteen and seventeen years old, probably.

**5. Why did Daniel object to eating the king's food?** Mainly because such food would doubtless include articles forbidden by Jewish law.

**6. What was the result of the experiment suggested by Daniel?** Those who ate the simple food looked better than those who ate the king's food. Dan. 1:15.

**7. What astonishing proof did Daniel give Nebuchadnezzar that God had endowed him with divine knowledge?** By telling him the dream that he had forgotten. Dan. 2.

**8. What was the dream?** That he had seen a great and composite metal image, with a golden head, struck and destroyed by a stone, which became a great mountain.

**9. How did Daniel interpret this dream?** Nebuchadnezzar was "the head of gold," as he was a king of kings in glory and power. The silver, brass and iron, represented three other kingdoms, which should each possess the earth.

**10. What power was to be greater than all these kingdoms?** The kingdom of Christ, a kingdom which the God of heaven should set up, and which should never be destroyed.

**11. What does it mean by "cut out without hands?"** That it was formed by the power of God, without the help of man. Isa. 63:1–6.

**12. What effect did this wonderful interpretation have on Nebuchadnezzar?** He worshipped Daniel as the messenger of God.

**13. To what position was Daniel promoted?** To be ruler over the whole province of Babylon.

**14. For whom did he request promotion also?** For Shadrach, Meshach and Abed-nego, his especial friends.

**15. How was the faith of these three friends of Daniel tried?** They refused to fall down at the king's command and worship a golden image which he had set up. Dan. 3.

**16. What was the consequence of their refusal?** They were cast into a burning, fiery furnace.

**17. Were they injured?** No, there walked with them the Son of God, who protected them from all harm.

**18. What happened to the men who threw them into the furnace?** They were killed by the flames.

**19. What effect did this wonderful deliverance have on Nebuchadnezzar?** He blessed and honored God, and promoted his three faithful servants.

**20. Was the heart of Nebuchadnezzar humbled by what he saw of the power of God?** No, it was full of pride.

**21. What dream did God send to him to warn him?** A vision of a lofty and flourishing tree hewn down, with its stump left for seven years among the grass and beasts of the field. Dan. 4.

**22. Who interpreted this dream to the king?** Daniel.

**23. How was it fulfilled?** Nebuchadnezzar was deprived of reason and made a companion of beasts. Dan. 4:33.

**24. What was the final result?** At the end of seven years his reason returned, and he acknowledged and praised God.

**25. How did the Babylonian kingdom end?** By the conquest of the city by Cyrus, king of the Medes and Persians (or by Cyrus' generals in his name).

**26. Who was the king of Babylon at this time?** Belshazzar is called "the king" (Dan. 5). It has been proved by the cuneiform inscriptions that Nabonidus was the last king of Babylon, but that his eldest son Belshazzar was regent during his absence; a fact that would account for the use of the word "king."

**27. Of what impious act was Belshazzar guilty?** On the night in which the city was taken he was drinking out of the gold and silver vessels of the temple, at a feast given to his lords.

**28. How was it that he did not know that destruction was so near?** Perhaps he was bent on sinful pleasures and refused to understand; and perhaps he was too young to appreciate thoroughly the danger, since his father, with the army, was opposing Cyrus' advance.

**29. How was the city taken?** By turning the river into another channel, and so entering the city by surprise along its bed.

**30. How did God reveal to Belshazzar his impending fate just before it fell upon him?** By an awful handwriting on the wall.

**31. What did the mystic handwriting predict?**
*"Mene; God hath numbered thy kingdom, and finished it. Tekel; thou art weighed in the balances, and art found wanting. Peres; Thy kingdom is divided, and given to the Medes and Persians."* Dan. 5:26–28.

**32. How soon after this was Belshazzar slain?** The same night.

**33. How long before this had Cyrus been mentioned by the prophet Isaiah?** About one hundred and seventy years. Isa. 44:27, 28; 45:1.

**34. Of what spiritual power is Babylon the type?** Of that which is apostate and contrary to God.

**35. What is the present state of the city of Babylon?** It is a huge mound, unnoticed for centuries; but now being explored and giving proofs of many Bible statements.

**36. Who was ruler over Babylon?** Darius, the Mede. It is said in Dan. 5:31 that he "took the kingdom"; in the Revisions, "received the kingdom." He seems to have been civil ruler while Cyrus was completing his conquest of the kingdom; a period of from one to two years.

**37. What did Darius do for Daniel?** He made him the chief, next to himself, of the 120 princes among whom the care of the government was divided. Dan. 6.

**38. How old was Daniel at this time?** Not far from eighty years old.

**39. What feelings did Daniel's prosperity excite in the minds of the other princes?** Jealousy, envy and malice.

**40. How did they try first to find an occasion against him?** Out of his manner of performing the duties of his office.

**41. What unwilling testimony did they bear to his excellence of character and uprightness?** That they could find in him no error or fault.

**42. What trap did they lay for him?** They obtained from Darius a decree that no one should offer a petition or prayer for thirty days to any one but himself, under penalty of being thrown into the den of lions, which was a part of the royal estate.

**43. Did Daniel forsake the worship of his God when he knew the consequences?** No.

**44. How did Darius feel when he found what his edict involved?** He was much displeased with himself.

**45. Why could not the king alter the decree?** Because of a law of the Medes and Persians that no decrees of the king could be altered. Dan. 6:15.

**46. Could he not have evaded it in some way?** Most certainly, if he had been a really great king he would have done so; as Xerxes later issued an edict that the Jews could defend themselves, to counteract the edict giving Haman and his followers the right to attack the Jews. See 64.

**47. What became of Daniel in the den?** He was not hurt.

**48. Was it because the lions were not hungry?** No.

**49. How do you prove this?** By the fury with which they devoured those who immediately after were cast into the den.

**50. How were Daniel's enemies punished by Darius?** By the same dreadful punishment they had intended for him.

**51. What effect had this wonderful deliverance on Darius?** He ordered reverence to be paid to the God of Daniel throughout his kingdom.

**52. Of what does the rest of the book of Daniel consist?** Of prophecies, some of which are clear, but most of which are obscure.

**53. Who is meant by "the Ancient of Days" named in Dan. 7?** The eternal God.

**54. When will his throne of judgment be set?** When God puts down the power of his enemies.

**55. What glorious Person is introduced into this chapter under the name of the "Son of Man"?** Jesus Christ.

**56. What "kingdom" is spoken of that "the saints of God" are to take and possess for ever and for ever?** The kingdom of Christ, to the end of time.

**57. Of what glorious Person does chapter nine speak?** Of the Messiah, Christ.

**58. What is the meaning of these names?** They both mean "Anointed."

**59. How is the death of Christ set forth in this prophecy?** He was to be cut off, not for himself, but for sinful man. Dan. 9:26.

**60. What blessed promise is given in Dan. 12:3?**

*"They that be wise shall shine as the brightness of the firmament; and they that turn many to righteousness as the stars for ever and ever."*

## 74. HOSEA

**1. Who was Hosea?** A prophet, son of Beeri; who prophesied in Israel during the reign of Jeroboam II, and the succeeding king. See 53. D.

**2. What touching words does the Lord address to Israel in Hosea 11:8?**

*"How shall I give thee up, Ephraim? How shall I make thee as Admah? How shall I set thee as Zeboim? Mine heart is turned within me, my repentings are kindled together."*

**3. Why is the name Ephraim given to Israel here?** Because the tribe of Ephraim was the most powerful in the kingdom of Israel.

**4. What is meant by Admah and Zeboim?** They were among the "cities of the plain" destroyed with Sodom. See Gen. 10:19; 14:8; Deut. 29:23.

**5. What idolatries of Israel are alluded to in Hos. 13?** The worship of Baal and of the golden calves.

**6. What beautiful invitation is given in Hos. 14:1, 2?**

*"O Israel, return unto the Lord thy God; for thou hast fallen by thy iniquity. Take with you words, and turn to the Lord: say unto him, take away all iniquity and receive us graciously."*

**7. Does the Lord address such gracious words only to Israel as a nation, or may we believe them spoken to us as well?** "For our sakes, no doubt, this is written," as sinners in every age and in every country need the same mercy and the same invitation. See 1 Cor. 9:9, 10.

## 75. JOEL

**1. Is it known when Joel prophesied?** No, he prophesied in Judah, but his date is uncertain.

**2. What can we gather from it as to the time of its writing?** He probably wrote it in a time of famine, as he speaks of the devourings by locust and of the want of pasture, corn, wine, and figs. 1:4–20.

**3. What does he call upon the people to do?** To fast, repent and pray.

**4. In what part of the book of Acts does the apostle Peter quote a prophecy of Joel?** In Acts 2:16–21 he quotes Joel 2:28–32.

**5. With what glorious and consoling prophecies does the prophecy close?** That war shall be done away with, and that finally Jerusalem and Judah shall be restored.

## 76. AMOS

**1. At what time did Amos live?** In the time of Uzziah of Judah and Jeroboam II, of Israel. See 53. D. and 58. A.

**2. Where was his home?** At Tekoa, in Judah.

**3. What was his occupation?** That of a shepherd, and a dresser of sycamore trees.

**4. Into what two sins of Israel does Amos give us an insight in 2:12?** Drunkenness and rejection of God's word and prophets.

**5. How does Amos 3:2 show us that man's punishment will be according to his privileges?** *"You only have I known of all the families of the earth: therefore I will punish you for all your iniquities."*

**6. What prophecy of Amos does Stephen quote?** In Acts 7:42, 43 he quotes Amos 5:25–27.

**7. What sins of Israel does Amos 8 set forth?** Dishonesty, oppression, and neglect of God's word. Vs. 5, 6, 11, 12.

**8. After the fearful denunciation of chapters 8 and 9 what prediction of after glory is given at the close of the last chapter?** The restoration of Israel to their own land in plenty and peace.

## 77. JONAH

**1. Is there any mention of Jonah besides the book called by his name?** He prophesied the reconquest by Jeroboam II, recorded in 2 Kings 14:25.

**2. What does the book of Jonah describe?** His commission to preach at Nineveh, and his attempt to evade it.

**3. Where was Nineveh?** On the river Tigris, in ancient Assyria, not far from modern Bagdad.

**4. How is Nineveh described in Scripture?** An "exceeding great city," of three days journey (or sixty miles) round; though this may have included the outlying suburbs.

**5. Do the vast ruins lately discovered confirm or contradict this Scripture testimony?** They strongly confirm it.

**6. Why did Jonah shrink from his errand?** From fear of being killed; or of seeming to be a false prophet if God's threatenings were mercifully unfulfilled; or perhaps from a dislike to prophesy to a mere heathen nation.

**7. Where did he try to go?** By ship to Tarshish; probably Tartessus, in Spain.

**8. How did the Lord overtake Jonah in his rebellion?** By a storm at sea.

**9. What did the mariners strive to do?** To save their lives by calling on their gods, and lightening the ship, and rowing hard to reach the land.

**10. How did Jonah own God's righteous dealings?** By telling them of his flight, and that the storm was on his account.

**11. When thrown overboard, how did God preserve him?** By means of a great fish he had prepared.

(The popular idea of its being what we know as **a whale** is not necessary from the Bible accounts; as the Hebrew word in Jonah, and the Greek word in Matthew both denote, literally, "sea-monster.")

**12. When the Lord again commanded Jonah to go to Nineveh, did he obey?** He did. Jonah 3.

**13. What was the result of his preaching?** The king and people believed God, and repented, and turned from their evil way.

**14. How did Jonah like this?** He was very angry that his threatening was not fulfilled, fearing, perhaps, that he would not be considered a true prophet, and that the Israelites would not repent if they saw that the Ninevites were spared.

**15. How did the Lord comfort and reprove Jonah?** By giving him a shelter from the heat, and by rebuking his anger at its loss.

## 78. MICAH

**1. In whose reigns did Micah prophesy?** In the reigns of Jotham, Ahaz and Hezekiah, kings of Judah. See 58. B. and C.; and 59.

**2. What prophecy of his is referred to in Jeremiah?**
*"Micah the Morasthite prophesied in the days of Hezekiah, king of Judah, and spake to all the people of Judah, saying, Thus saith the Lord of hosts; Zion shall be ploughed like a field, and Jerusalem shall become heaps, and the mountain of the house as the high places of a forest."* Jer. 26:18.

**3. Where is it found in his book? and how has it been fulfilled?** Mic. 3:12. The site of the temple was really ploughed over by a Roman emperor, and Jerusalem has at different times been made heaps in the various sieges it has sustained.

**4. In what state does he declare Samaria will be?** "As an heap of the field." Mic. 1:6.

**5. What sins of Israel are enumerated in Mic. 2:3, 8, 9?** Cruelty, oppression and idolatry.

**6. What promises for the latter days does Mic. 4:1–4 record?** The restoration of Zion; the reign of peace; and the coming of the Gentiles to the knowledge of the true God.

**7. What glorious Person is prophesied of in Mic. 5:2?** Jesus Christ.

**8. Where was Jesus born?** In Bethlehem, of Judah.

## 79. NAHUM

**1. Who was Nahum?** Nothing is known of him except that he wrote the book bearing his name.

**2. What is the subject of this book?** The downfall of Nineveh.

**3. Have we any idea of its date?** From the facts that Nahum speaks of the destruction of No-Ammon (Nah. 3:8) which took place in 664 B.C.; and of Nineveh as still powerful; proves that it was written between 664 B.C. and 606 B.C., the date of the capture of Nineveh.

## 80. HABAKKUK

**1. What proof have we that Habakkuk wrote before the Captivity?** The fact that in chapter 1:6 he prophesies its coming.

**2. Who were the Chaldeans?** The inhabitants of Babylon and the surrounding country.

**3. What prediction does Habakkuk make with regard to the Chaldeans?** That in due time God would destroy Chaldean power. Hab. 2.

**4. What promise that affects us is given in this chapter?**
*"The earth shall be filled with the knowledge of the glory of the Lord, as the waters cover the sea."* Hab. 2:14.

**5. What emphatic verse in Habakkuk is quoted three times in the New Testament? and where is it quoted?** Hab. 2:4. "The just shall live by his faith." It is quoted in Rom. 1:17; Gal 3:11; Heb. 10:38.

**6. What great reformer was converted to God by it?** Martin Luther.

**7. What is found in Hab. 3?** A magnificent psalm of praise to God for his great deeds for the people of Israel.

**8. How does the prophet express his confidence in God?** In the beautiful words of Vs. 17 and 18 of this chapter.

## 81. ZEPHANIAH

**1. In whose reign did Zephaniah prophesy?** In that of Josiah. See 60. C.

**2. How does the first chapter show the abominations of the land before Josiah's reformation?** It speaks of the idolatry and indifference to God that prevailed.

**3. What proof is there in this book that Nahum's prophecy against Nineveh had not yet been fulfilled?** Its desolation is spoken of as yet to come. Zeph. 2:13.

**4. With what glorious promises of Israel's restoration does the prophecy close?**

*"Sing, O daughter of Zion; shout, O Israel; be glad and rejoice with all the heart, O daughter of Jerusalem. The Lord hath taken away thy judgments, he hath cast out thine enemy: the king of Israel, even the Lord, is in the midst of thee: thou shalt not see evil any more."*

## 82. HAGGAI

**1. Who was Haggai?** A prophet of the Return who prophesied in Jerusalem about 520 B.C. See 62. 12–18.

**2. Do we know anything more about him?** Only an inference that he was an old man at the time of his prophesy. Hag. 2:3.

**3. What was the great effect of Haggai's prophecy?** The rousing of the people of the Return to stop the building

of their own houses in order to complete the temple.

**4. To whom did the prophet refer in chapter 2:6, 7?** To Christ, as the "desire of all nations."

## 83. ZECHARIAH

**1. What do we know of Zechariah?** He prophesied at the same time as Haggai; but was much younger, and lived until about 479 B.C. See 62.

**2. About what did he prophesy?** Like Haggai he tried to rouse the people to the building of the temple.

**3. What further prophecy of the Lord Jesus is there in Zech. 9:9?**

*"Rejoice greatly, O daughter of Zion; shout, O daughter of Jerusalem: behold, thy King cometh unto thee: he is just, and having salvation; lowly, and riding upon an ass, and upon a colt the foal of an ass."*

**4. When was this fulfilled?** On the Sunday preceding the crucifixion of our Lord, when he entered Jerusalem riding on an ass. John 12:12–16.

**5. To what fountain does Zech. 13 refer?** To the blood of Jesus Christ that cleanseth from all sin.

**6. What other phrases in Zechariah are frequently quoted?**

*"Not by might, not by power, but by my Spirit, saith the Lord."*

*"A brand plucked out of the fire."*

*"Who hath despised the day of small things?"*

*"My Servant the Branch."*

**7. What prophecy of Jesus Christ is found in Zech. 13:7?**

*"Awake, O sword, against my shepherd, and against the man that is my fellow."*

**8. When was this prophecy fulfilled?** When Jesus was crucified and the disciples fled.

**9. What prophecy is there in Zech. 14:4 of the second coming of the Lord Jesus?** "His feet shall stand in that day upon the Mount of Olives."

**10. In Zech. 14:8, living waters are spoken of; where else in Scripture are these described?** In Ezek. 47:1–12, as issuing "out of the sanctuary"; in Joel 3:18, as "coming forth out of the house of the Lord"; in Rev. 22:1, as "proceeding out of the throne of God and of the Lamb."

**11. What glorious promises does this prophecy contain of future blessings in store for Israel?** That God would bring them again to their own land (Zech. 10:6–12), and would dwell among them (Zech. 2:10–12), and pour his spirit upon them (Zech. 12:6–14), and that they should be holiness unto the Lord (Zech. 14:16–21), and be a blessing (Zech. 8:3–23).

**12. Must these not have been peculiarly comforting to the poor Jews in their impoverished state?** They must indeed.

**13. What effect did they have on them?** They began to build the house of God, and prospered, and finished it. Ezra 5:2; 6:14.

## 84. MALACHI

**1. When and where did Malachi live?** Nothing is known about him save from the book itself. It seems, however, to belong to about the time of Nehemiah's second visit to Jerusalem, which was about 432 B.C.

**2. What evils does he record?** Scanty and mean sacrifices and offerings to God. Mal. 1.

**3. What especially does he record in the second chapter?** He reproves the priests for neglecting their duties, and the people generally for idolatry and neglect of God.

**4. Where does Malachi prophesy of John the Baptist?** In Mal. 3:1; 4:5, 6.

**5. How is he described?** As the messenger of the Lord, the Messiah, sent to prepare his way.

**6. What urgent appeal does Malachi make?**
*"Bring ye all the tithes into the storehouse, that there may be meat in mine house, and prove me now herewith, saith the Lord of hosts, if I will not open you the windows of heaven, and pour you out a blessing, that there shall not be room enough to receive it." Mal. 3:10.*

**7. Were there any faithful ones left among this general corruption?** Yes, some that feared God, and met together to speak about him for their mutual comfort and help, and who were all written down in his book of remembrance. Mal. 3:16, 17.
*"And they shall be mine, saith the Lord of hosts, in that day when I make up my jewels."*

**8. Of what awful day does the prophet speak in chapter 4?** The great and dreadful day of judgment; the "second coming" of our Lord Jesus Christ.

**9. Is this "day" mentioned in any other part of Scripture?** Yes, in Joel 2:31 as "the great and terrible day of the Lord."

**10. Who is spoken of under the figure of "the Sun of righteousness"?** Our Lord and Saviour Jesus Christ.

*(The Life and Teachings of Jesus Christ as recorded in the Four Gospels will be taken up in chronological order. References to all the Gospels will be given with the heading, but the detailed references with the questions will be to that Gospel where the account is the longest or clearest.)*

## 85. THE FOUR GOSPELS

**1. What are the names of the four Gospels?** Matthew, Mark, Luke, and John.

**2. What is the subject of these four books?** The life and ministry of Jesus Christ.

**3. Who was the evangelist Matthew?** A "publican" who became one of the twelve apostles. (See 91. 34.)

**4. What are the characteristics of his Gospel?** It is not strictly chronological; he wrote for the Jews to prove Jesus the Messiah, and for that reason groups teachings and events.

**5. Who was the evangelist Mark?** One of those who believed in Jesus during his life, and afterwards became prominent in the church.

**6. What are the characteristics of his Gospel?** It was the earliest Christian writing; is the most nearly chronological of the four; but he omits a considerable portion of Jesus' life.

**7. Who was the evangelist Luke?** A Greek physician, said to have been born in Antioch, Syria. He was a great friend of the Apostle Paul, and wrote also the Acts, partly from his own experiences.

**8. What are the characteristics of his Gospel?** His is the only Gospel which describes the infancy of Jesus; in many places it shows the influence of his medical training; and it is very accurate historically.

**9. Who was the evangelist John?** Another of the twelve apostles, called "the disciple whom Jesus loved."

**10. What are the characteristics of his Gospel?** It is the only one which records the doings of the first year of Jesus' ministry in detail; has in general fuller reports of Jesus' words; and is the only one recording the teachings of Christ to his disciples at the last supper.

## 86. THE THIRTY YEARS OF JESUS' PRIVATE LIFE (Matt. 1:2; Luke 1:2; John 1:1–18)

**1. What may we call John 1:1–18?** The prologue of John's Gospel.

**2. Why is our Lord called "The Word"?** Because he is the revelation of God; his Word, which expresses him and his character.

**3. What proofs of his divinity are there in John 1:1–3?** He is stated to be "God," and to have been "in the beginning" and to have "made all things."

**4. What else is Jesus called in John's prologue?** The light of men. John 1:4. See also John 3:19; 8:12.

**5. How do we know the gospel is free to all?** Because Jesus Christ, like the light, reaches all, "that all through him might believe." John 1:7, 9.

**6. Who are here meant by "his own"?** The Jews.

**7. What great change takes place in us when we truly believe?** We become new creatures in Christ, even "sons of God."

**8. What is referred to in John 1:14?** The incarnation: God in human form, living on this earth, among men.

**9. Who is the John referred to in John 1:15?** John the Baptist. See 87.

**10. Which Herod is referred to in Luke 1:5?** Herod the Great, King of Judea.

**11. What temple is meant in Luke 1:9?** The temple at Jerusalem built by Herod the Great. It replaced the temple built by the returned captives under Zerubbabel. (See 62. 18). The holy house, or temple proper, was completed a few years before the birth of Jesus.

**12. What is meant by "the courses of the priests"?** The priests were divided by lot in the time of David, and each lot, or "course," had its regular and stated time of service in the temple.

**13. What message came to Zacharias the priest while in the temple?** The promise that he should have a son, whose name should be called John. Luke 1:13.

**14. Who was this son?** He was afterwards called John the Baptist.

**15. What was his work to be?** To prepare the way for Jesus, the Christ. Luke 1:17.

**16. Did Zacharias believe at once?** No; and the angel messenger told him therefore that he should be dumb until the promise was fulfilled. Luke 1:18–20.

**17. What wonderful song did Zacharias sing after the birth of John?** "The Benedictus." Luke 1:68–79.

**18. To what other person was the same angel sent?** To Mary of Nazareth. Luke 1:26. Compare Luke 1:19.

**19. What message was brought to her?** That she should have a son whom she should name Jesus; that he should save his people from their sins, and rule over the kingdom of David forever. Luke 1:30–33; Matt. 1:21.

**20. What wonderful song did Mary sing?** "The Magnificat." Luke 1:46–55.

**21. Who was Caesar Augustus?** The first emperor of Rome.

**22. What does the term "all the world" in this account include?** The Roman empire, which then included nearly all the known or civilized world.

**23. What is meant by the "taxing" of Luke 2:1?** More exactly, enrolment, or census; but probably made for some purpose of taxation.

**24. Where was Jesus born?** In Bethlehem of Judea, where Joseph and Mary had gone for the enrolment, as they were descended from David. Luke 2:3, 4.

**25. Where in Bethlehem was he born?** In a stable, or a cave used for cattle, "because there was no room for them in the inn." Luke 2:7.

**26. What was Jesus' cradle?** A manger in the stable.

**27. What are "swaddling clothes"?** Long pieces of cloth which were wrapped closely around the child, to keep it straight.

**28. To whom was Jesus' coming first announced, and by whom?** To shepherds in the fields by Bethlehem, by angels. Luke 2:8–20.

**29. What was the angel's message?** *"Fear not; for, behold, I bring you good tidings of great joy, which shall be to all people. For unto you is born this day in the city of David a Saviour, which is Christ the Lord." Luke 2:10, 11.*

**30. What was the "song of the angels" at this time?**
*"Glory to God in the highest, and on earth peace, good will toward men." Luke 2:14.*

**31. What did the shepherds do?** They went to Bethlehem, and found all as the angel had said. Luke 2:16.

**32. What was done for Jesus when he was forty days old?** He was presented in the temple, according to the Jewish law. See Lev. 12:6–8.

**33. What sign of the poverty of Joseph and Mary was there in this service?** They brought two young pigeons, the offering of the poorest. Luke 2:24.

**34. Whom did they meet in the temple?** Simeon and Anna, both of whom had for years been watching for the coming of the Christ. Luke 2:25–38.

**35. What song did Simeon sing?** That called "Nunc Dimittis" and found in Luke 2:29–32.

**36. Who were the "wise men" of Matt. 2?** Some learned men from the East, who studied the stars and their supposed influence upon human affairs. They were called magi, from a word meaning wise.

**37. What journey did they make and why?** To Jerusalem, to find the newborn king of the Jews.

**38. Why was all Jerusalem troubled?** Many were afraid lest he should overthrow the reigning king, or lest they should suffer for welcoming him.

**39. Who was especially troubled?** Herod the king, who feared lest he should be overthrown.

**40. What did Herod do in this emergency?** After finding out from the prophets where the Messiah was to be born, he sent the magi there with the request that they return and tell him where to find him. Matt. 2:3–8.

**41. What did the wise men give Jesus?** Rich gifts of gold, frankincense and myrrh.

**42. What vision came to Joseph?** He was told to flee to Egypt with Jesus and his mother, because Herod would seek him to destroy him. Matt. 2:13.

**43. What did Herod do?** He ordered all the boys of Bethlehem under two years to be slain. Matt. 2:16–18.

**44. Where did Jesus live after his return from Egypt?** In Nazareth, in Galilee.

**45. Do we know anything about his childhood?** Before he was twelve years old, only that
*He "grew and waxed strong in spirit, filled with wisdom: and the grace of God was upon him." Luke 2:40.*

**46. What happened when he was twelve years old?** He made his first visit to Jerusalem for the passover.

**47. What happened there?** When Mary and Joseph started for home they missed Jesus, and returning to Jerusalem hunted for him three days, and finally found him in the temple "sitting in the midst of the doctors [teachers], both hearing them, and asking them questions."

**48. What did Jesus say when they found him?**
*"How is it that ye sought me? wist ye not that I must be about my Father's business?"*

**49. When next do we hear of Jesus?** Not for eighteen years, when he began his ministry.

### 87. THE MINISTRY OF JOHN THE BAPTIST (Mark 3:1–2; Mark 1:1–8; Luke 3:1–18)

**1. Who was Tiberius?** The second emperor of Rome.

**2. Who was John the Baptist?** The forerunner, sent to prepare the way for Christ. See 76. 13–17.

**3. What prophecy had been spoken concerning him?** *"Behold, I will send you Elijah the prophet before the coming of the great and dreadful day of the Lord: and he shall turn the heart of the fathers to the children, and the heart of the children to the fathers, lest I come and smite the earth with a curse." Mal. 4:5, 6.*

**4. What were the special features of John's preaching?** Repentance; and forgiveness of sin through the coming Messiah; and baptism as the outward sign of this repentance.

**5. What is repentance?** A sorrow for sin which produces a change in mind and heart.

**6. Was John's preaching successful?** Yes, people from all parts of Judea confessed their sins and were baptized. Matt. 3:5, 6; Mark 1:5.

**7. What especial virtues did John recommend to those who came to him?** Generosity, honesty, kindness and contentment.

**8. What is the fruit of true repentance?** Ceasing to do evil willfully and habitually. Isa. 1:16.

**9. What were the publicans?** Jewish collectors of Roman taxes.

**10. Why were they so odious to their countrymen?** Because although Jews they aided their Roman masters to oppress them. Some also were dishonest, and worked for their own gain.

**11. What is the meaning of the word "Christ"?** "Anointed." Luke 4:18.

**12. What was the difference between John's baptism and our Lord's?** John's was "the baptism of repentance"; the symbol of a desire to live a new life, that should show the fruits of repentance. Our Lord's was "the baptism of the Holy Spirit."

**13. What is the meaning of "baptism with fire"?** The purifying force of the Holy Spirit, or some searching and exposing power. 1 Cor. 3:13.

**14. What is the allusion to the use of the fan?** The final separation by Christ of the righteous and the wicked, as the winnowing-fan divides the chaff from the wheat.

### 88. THE PREPARATION OF JESUS FOR HIS MINISTRY (Matt. 3:13–4:11; Mark 1:9–13; Luke 3:21–4:13)

**1. Why did Jesus come to be baptized by John?** As a seal of consecration to God's work.

**2. What wonderful thing happened at his baptism?** *"The heaven was opened, and the Holy Ghost [Spirit] descended in a bodily shape like a dove upon him, and a voice came from heaven which said, Thou art my beloved Son; in thee I am well pleased." Luke 3:22.*

**3. What may be the reason for the "temptation" of Jesus?** That "he might be in all points tempted like as we are, yet without sin." Heb. 4:15.

**4. Where did these temptations occur?** In the wild country called "the wilderness of Judea."

**5. What is the devil called in Mark?**
Satan.

**6. What is the meaning of the two terms?** Satan means "adversary" or "enemy," and devil means "accuser."

**7. What were the three temptations?** (1) To make from the stones of the place bread to satisfy his personal hunger. (2) To throw himself down from a high point on the temple, trusting that God would work a miracle to save him. (3) To offer homage to Satan and receive through him power over the world.

**8. What was the real temptation in the last two?** They seemed to offer Jesus at once, without toil or suffering, the very things he had come to earth to win.

**9. How did Jesus conquer?** By the use of the Word of God in direct answer to Satan's proposals.

**10. Can we conquer in the same way?** Yes, and we have besides the help of our Lord Jesus.

**11. What does living "by every word of God" (Matt. 4:4) signify?** Trusting all his promises, and keeping all his commands.

**12. What is the meaning of the word "tempt" in Luke 4:12?** Presumptuously try or provoke.

**13. Was it an empty boast of the devil in Luke 4:6?** Not altogether, as he is called "the god of this world" (2 Cor. 4:4), and "the prince of the power of the air" (Eph. 2:2).

## 89. THE BEGINNING OF JESUS' MINISTRY (John 1:19–2:12)

**1. What was the difference between priests and Levites?** The priests were descendants of Aaron, and were the chief officers of the temple; the Levites were descendants of the other families of the tribe, and the assistants of the priests.

**2. Who was Elias?** "Elijah the prophet."

**3. Why was he expected to reappear?** It was so prophesied in Mal. 4:5, 6.

**4. Who was meant by "that prophet"?**
*"The Lord thy God will raise up unto thee a Prophet from the midst of thee, of thy brethren, like unto me." Deut. 18:15.*

**5. Why did John call Jesus "the Lamb of God"?** Because he was the spotless sacrifice and gift of God.

**6. What further proof of the freeness of the gospel is there in John 1:29?** He "taketh away the sin of the world."

**7. Who were Jesus' first three disciples?** Andrew, John and Simon (Peter).

**8. Who came to him next?** Probably James the brother of John. Then Philip and Nathanael.

**9. What were Nathanael's first words about Jesus?** "Can there any good thing come out of Nazareth?" John 1:46.

**10. What was Nathanael's confession when he talked with Jesus?**
*"Rabbi, thou art the Son of God; thou art the King of Israel." John 1:49.*

**11. What was the first miracle performed by Jesus?** The making of water into wine at the wedding feast at Cana of Galilee. John 2:1–11.

## 90. THE EARLY JUDEAN MINISTRY (John 2:13–4:42)

**1. What did Jesus find when he visited the temple?**
*He "found in the temple those that*

*sold oxen and sheep and doves, and the changers of money sitting." John 2:14.*

**2. For what purpose were the animals brought to the temple?** To be sold as offerings and sacrifices to God, and for the food of the priests and people.

**3. What did Jesus do?** *"When he had made a scourge of small cords, he drove them all out of the temple." John 2:15.*

**4. What temple did our Lord refer to in John 2:19?** The temple of his own body.

**5. What important man came to see Jesus?** Nicodemus, a Pharisee, and a "ruler of the Jews."

**6. Who were the Pharisees?** A sect of the Jews who "trusted in themselves that they were righteous, and despised others." Luke 18:9, 10.

**7. Why did he come at night?** He came secretly, so that his visit might not be known to the Jews.

**8. To what recent miracles does Nicodemus refer?** Probably to those related or referred to in John 2.

**9. Is there any exception to the necessity for the new birth?** None.

**10. By whom are we born again?** By the Holy Spirit.

**11. What fresh proof of the freeness of the gospel is there in John 3:15, 16?** Jesus says there that "whosoever believeth in him," shall "have everlasting life."

**12. Where did Jesus now go?** To Galilee, John 4:1–3.

**13. Why must Jesus "needs go through Samaria"?** It was the nearest and most natural route.

**14. When was the parcel of ground sold to Jacob?** Jacob bought it on his return from Laban. Josh. 24:32.

**15. Why had the Jews no dealings with the Samaritans?** In part because of their origin, and in part because they would not go up to Jerusalem to worship.

**16. What was their origin?** They were colonists from Assyria who were mixed with the Jews still remaining in the country. They worshipped God, but not like the Jews, and their worship was somewhat mixed with heathen customs. 54. 16, 17.

**17. What are the soul-satisfying effects of faith?** The grace and comfort of the Holy Spirit. John 4:13, 14.

**18. What is the true worship which alone is acceptable to God?** The worship of the heart. John 4:23, 24.

**91. THE FIRST PERIOD OF THE GALILEAN MINISTRY (Matt. 4:12–23; 8:1–4; 9:1–17; 12:1–14; 14:3–5; Mark 6:17, 18; 1:14–3:6; Luke 3:19, 20; 4:14–6:11; John 4:43–5:47)**

**1. Why was John imprisoned?** Because of his faithful boldness in reproving Herod's unlawful marriage with his brother's wife. Mark 6:17, 18.

**2. Did not Herod's respect for John greatly add to his criminality?** It did, as it showed that his conscience told him that John was right.

**3. What great miracle did Jesus do during this visit to Galilee?** He healed the nobleman's son by a word. John 4:46–54.

**4. What showed the faith of the father?** His believing Jesus' word, and starting for home in the assurance that his son had recovered.

**5. Where did Jesus then go?** To Nazareth, his childhood home. Luke 4:16.

**6. What was the passage he read in the synagogue there?** From Isaiah 61:1–3.

**7. Are these verses to be taken literally or as symbols?** They can with truth be taken in both ways.

**8. If symbols what is their meaning?** Those whose hearts are broken or crushed under godly sorrow for sin; those led captive by Satan; and those blind to the truth, because unable or unwilling to see it.

**9. What is "the acceptable year of the Lord"?** The time of grace (compared to the jubilee year), when God is ready to hear and forgive. Isa. 1:18, etc.

**10. Why did they wonder at Jesus?** Because they knew him only as the Nazarene carpenter's son. Luke 4:22.

**11. Why did our Lord's declaration in verses 24–27 so excite their wrath?** Because of their Jewish pride and contempt for all other races.

**12. Where did Jesus go from Nazareth?** To Capernaum, on the Sea of Galilee. Luke 4:31.

**13. Why did he enter a boat on the sea?** To be better able to talk to the multitudes which pressed around him.

**14. Whose boat was it?** It belonged to Andrew and Peter. Luke 5:3; Matt. 4:18.

**15. What miracle did Jesus now perform?** The wonderful draught of fishes. Luke 5:4–7.

**16. Did not Peter's exclamation show how much he realized the greatness of his Lord?** Yes, it made him deeply feel his own sinfulness in the presence of Christ's holiness and power.

**17. What disciples did Jesus now call to his service?** Peter, Andrew, James and John. Mark 1:16–20.

**18. Were not these the same as those mentioned in John 1:29–47?** (See 89. 7, 8). Yes, but now they were called to leave their business and devote all their time to Jesus.

**19. In what sense were they henceforth to catch men?** By drawing them out of the world to Christ in the gospel net.

**20. What two miracles did Jesus do on one sabbath day in Capernaum?** The healing of the demoniac in the synagogue, and of Peter's wife's mother. Mark 1:21–31.

**21. How do we see the completeness of the cure of Peter's wife's mother?** She was able to wait upon them immediately.

**22. Who came to Jesus there?** A great multitude of the sick. Mark 1:32–34.

**23. Why did they wait for sunset?** Because it was the sabbath which ended at sunset. Also perhaps because of the greater coolness, for the sick.

**24. Why did not Jesus allow the devils to speak?** Perhaps because they might make it appear that he was in league with them.

**25. Who was the great Example of fervent prayer?** Jesus, whose long and earnest prayers, by day and night, and especially before great duties or events, are often named. See Luke 4:42, 43.

**26. What wonderful cure is recorded in Mark 1:40–45?** That of a leper, whose disease was so rarely cured as to be considered practically incurable. Lev. 13:2.

**27. How could Jesus touch the leper**

**without being himself rendered unclean?** By his divine purity.

**28. What was palsy?** Paralysis, or some kindred disease. Mark 2:1–12.

**29. How did this man reach Jesus?** His friends dug a hole in the flat mud roof of the house, and let him down at Jesus' feet.

**30. Was this not a very bad thing to do?** No, the people of that country often dig a hole in the roof to let down what cannot be put in at the door; and it was very easily repaired.

**31. What is the argument of verse 9?** Saying the words of forgiveness and saying the words of healing are equally easy; but the power of the words of healing is most easily to be recognized.

**32. Why was our Lord's forgiveness of sins not blasphemy as the Jews thought?** Because he was God himself. Isa. 43:25.

**33. What other proof of his Godhead does this story contain?** His knowledge of people's thoughts.

**34. Who was the next disciple called by Jesus?** Levi, or Matthew, a publican or tax-collector. (See 87. 9, 10.) He became one of the twelve apostles, and wrote the Gospel of Matthew. Matt. 9:9; Luke 5:27, 28.

**35. What was the purpose of Matthew's feast?** To enable his friends and neighbors among the publicans to see and hear his Master.

**36. What miracle did Jesus do during passover week at Jerusalem?** The healing of the impotent man at the pool of Bethesda. John 5:2–47.

**37. What was Bethesda?** An intermittent spring in Jerusalem.

**38. For what was it famous?** It was considered to have a curative power while the waters were troubled.

**39. Explain verse 4.** It is not found in all the manuscripts of the gospel, and may be a comment written by a later copyist. If written by John it may easily have been the popular expression of the reason why the spring was intermittent. "Angel" means "messenger," and it may not here be intended to mean a heavenly being.

**40. Why did the Pharisees blame Jesus for this cure?** Because it was done on the sabbath, and was therefore against their law.

**41. What angered them still more in his reply?** He made himself equal with God.

**42. What indication of the connection of sin and suffering in the case of this man is there?** The warning of Jesus in verse 14 to sin no more, lest a worse thing happen unto him.

**43. Who is said to be the judge of all?** Christ is to be the judge that he may have equal honor with God.

**44. Were the disciples justified in taking the growing grain (Mark 2:23–28)?** They were.

*"When thou comest into the standing corn [grain] of thy neighbor, then thou mayest pluck the ears with thine hand; but thou shalt not move a sickle unto thy neighbor's standing corn [grain]."* Deut. 23:25.

**45. Why then did the Pharisees blame them?** Because they did it on the sabbath. It was forbidden as being a kind of reaping.

**46. How did the priests profane the sabbath and remain blameless?** They appeared to do so by killing the sacrifices on that day as on other days.

**47. What argument did Jesus give with regard to healing on the sabbath?** If a sheep fell into a pit on the sabbath it would be rescued; "how much then is a man better than a sheep?" Matt. 12:11, 23.

**48. What did Jesus teach at this time of the nature of the sabbath?** That "the sabbath was made for man, and not man for the sabbath"; the day being appointed, even in paradise, as a day of rest; a rest from earthly toil, and of special regard to the interests of our immortal souls.

## 92. THE SERMON ON THE MOUNT (Matt. 4:13–8:1; 10:2–4; Mark 3:7–21; Luke 6:12–49)

**1. What took place just before the Sermon on the Mount?** Jesus selected from his disciples twelve to remain with him constantly. Luke 6:12–20.

**2. Why was this selection made?** In order to have a small number prepared more fully for leaders of the church when Jesus should return to heaven.

**3. To whom was the Sermon on the Mount addressed?** To any disciples of Jesus who gathered there to hear him. Perhaps primarily to the twelve apostles just selected.

**4. What name is given to Matt. 5:3–12?** The Beatitudes, that is, The Blesseds.

**5. Who are the "poor in spirit"?** The humble-minded, not self-seeking nor over-confident.

**6. What is meekness?** Patience under provocation, after the example of Christ, "who, when he was reviled, reviled not again." 1 Pet. 2:23.

**7. What is it to hunger and thirst after righteousness?** To long earnestly for it, and to seek and to strive to obtain it.

**8. Who are the merciful?** Those who are kind to the poor, the hungry and the afflicted. See Isa. 58:10, 11.

**9. What is it to be "pure in heart"?** To have that "holiness, without which no man shall see the Lord." Heb. 12:14.

**10. Why are the peacemakers so distinguished?** Because of the difficulty in making and keeping peace, and as Christ is the Prince of Peace.

*"If it be possible, as much as lieth in you, live peaceably with all men." Rom. 12:18.*

**11. How does our Lord prepare his disciples for the future in Matt. 5:11?** By promising a blessing to all who endured persecution for his sake.

**12. What great precept does he teach in Matt. 5:16?** That his followers must so imitate Christ that men seeing them shall praise their Master.

**13. What great lesson of mutual forgiveness does Matt. 5:23–26 contain?** That we should come to the worship and service of God in peace and reconciliation with our fellow men.

**14. What rule against trifling with evil is found in Matt. 5:29, 30?** That we should make any sacrifice to be free from sin.

**15. What lesson of the largeness of the love of God have we in Matt. 5:45 and Luke 6:35?** "He is kind" to "the unthankful" and the "evil," and pours his daily blessings alike upon the wicked and the good.

**16. Compare the reward of Matt. 6:2 with that of verse 4.** The hypocrite's reward is the present and fleeting one of honor from man, while the true Christian's reward is the eternal one of acceptance with the Father, and glory in heaven.

**17. What encouragement for our imperfect petitions is there in Matt. 6:8?** That your heavenly Father knows what we have need of before we ask him.

**18. How do the first words of the Lord's Prayer adapt it to the whole human family?** They show that we have all one Father.

**19. What is it to "hallow" anything?** To treat it as holy.

**20. How is God's will to be done?** Men are to do God's will on earth as perfectly as do the angels in heaven.

**21. What does the petition as to daily bread teach us?** That we should not be over-anxious about the future.

**22. What condition is added to the petition for forgiveness?** That we should forgive those who have injured us.

**23. What does the word "debts" here imply?** That in each case the things are "owed."

**24. How can we judge how much we love God?** By thinking where our chief treasure is, whether on earth or in heaven. Matt. 6:21.

**25. Who takes care of our lives?** Our heavenly Father. Matt. 6:26, 30, 32, 33.

**26. What is meant here by "take no thought"?** The word so translated really means "anxious thought." It means we are not to worry over the future; it does not mean that we are not to plan ahead for our lives.

**27. What is the lesson of Matt. 7:1–5?** That we should not condemn those around us, since, knowing nothing of

their inmost hearts, we may prove more sinful ourselves.

**28. What wonderful promise is in Matt. 7:7–11?** That as a loving earthly father will do everything he can for the good of his children, so our heavenly Father is ready to give us all good things when we ask him.

**29. What is Matt. 7:12 often called?** "The Golden Rule," for if everyone obeyed it earth would be like heaven above.

**30. What is the meaning of the "strait gate"?** The narrow entrance into heaven, which "though wide enough for any sinner is too strait for any sin."

**31. What lesson do we learn about our conduct in Matt. 7:16, etc.?** That we shall be judged by our conduct rather than by our profession—by our fruits rather than our leaves.

**32. What parable did Jesus utter?** That of the destruction of the house built on the sand, and the safety of the house built on the rock. Matt. 7:24–27.

**33. What is the rock foundation on which we should build?** Jesus Christ.

*"For other foundation can no man lay than that is laid, which is Jesus Christ." 1 Cor. 3:9–15.*

**93.  THE SECOND PERIOD OF THE GALILEAN MINISTRY (Matt. 8:5–13, 23–9:1; 9:18–11:19; 12:22–15:20; Mark 3:19–7:23; Luke 7:1–9:17; John 6:1–71)**

**1. What is a centurion?** An officer in the Roman army, commanding 100 men.

**2. What did this man ask of Jesus?** That he should "say in a word" and heal his servant. Luke 7:7.

**3. What was this centurion's character?** He was praised very highly by the Jewish leaders, and was a man of humble and strong faith.

**4. What most wonderful miracle did Jesus do at Nain?** The raising from the dead of the only son of a widow of that place. Luke 7:11–17.

**5. What practical answer did Jesus give to John the Baptist's messengers?** That they were to conclude that he was the Messiah from the miracles that he did and the prophecies he fulfilled. Luke 7:21–23.

**6. How does our Lord sum up his reference to the greatness of John the Baptist?** By saying that the least of those in the kingdom of God was greater even than John. Luke 7:28.

**7. What great work of forgiveness is recorded here?** The forgiving of "the woman who was a sinner." Luke 7:36–50.

**8. What showed that she was ready for forgiveness?** She wept and washed Jesus' feet with her tears; and anointed them with costly ointment. But more sure than this was the knowledge Jesus had of her heart.

**9. In what manner did they sit at table?** They reclined on couches around it.

**10. How does Jesus compare this woman with Simon, his host?** Simon had invited Jesus from curiosity alone, and not only did not care to show him special respect, but had omitted several of the customary ceremonies.

**11. What terrible accusation did the Jews make against Jesus?** That his power came because he was in league with the prince of demons. Mark 3:22.

**12. What was his conclusive answer?** A house or a kingdom divided against itself cannot stand. If therefore Satan is divided against Satan, his kingdom must fall.

**13. Who will judge man's words?** Christ at the day of judgment, even every idle word.

**14. How do we see that discipleship is more than the closest family relationships?** By Christ's saying that those who did his Father's will were to him as brother and sister and mother. Mark 3:31–35.

**15. What new kind of preaching did Jesus now begin? and why?** He began to teach in parables, that he might make known the truth in a way which would not arouse the anger of his enemies.

**16. What is a parable?** A story of some natural event or condition which can be made to have a definite spiritual application.

**17. What name is given to the group of parables now spoken?** "The Parables by the Sea," because the greater part were probably spoken from a boat on the Sea of Galilee to a large multitude on the shore. Matt. 13:1.

**18. What was the first of these parables?** The seed sown in four kinds of ground. Matt. 13:3–9, 18–23.

**19. What is the seed?** The Word of God.

**20. Who are the wayside hearers?** The careless ones who forget immediately what they hear.

**21. Who are the stony ground hearers?** Those who hear and believe; but have no depth of character and do not remain faithful under trials.

**22. Who are the thorny ground hearers?** Those who hear and believe, but let this world's interests and cares destroy the seed.

**23. Who are they who truly receive the gospel?** Those who receive it into their hearts, as seed into good ground, and show its effects in their lives.

**24. What was the second parable?** The wheat and the tares. Matt. 13:24–30, 36–43.

**25. What are tares?** A poisonous grain much resembling wheat.

**26. What is the fate of the tares?** To be burned.

**27. What is meant by the harvest?** The end of the world (age).

**28. What is meant by the barn?** The heavenly treasure house and home.

**29. Who are the reapers?** The angels.

**30. How are the tares described?** As the children of the wicked ones.

**31. What other parables are given in this group?** The kingdom of heaven is likened to (1) the tiny mustard seed, which grows to be a large bush; (2) the leaven (yeast) which leavens all the meal; (3) the treasure hidden in a field, worth all else that a man has; (4) the one pearl, more valuable than all other jewels; (5) the net of fish, from which the good will be selected and the bad thrown away.

**32. What great deed was done after this teaching in parables?** Jesus stilled by a word the tempest on the lake. Mark 4:35–41.

**33. What ought we to learn from our Lord's words to his disciples?** That we ought to have strong faith at all times in his goodness and power.

**34. What did Jesus say to the sea?** "Peace, be still!" Mark 4:39.

**35. What man met them when they reached the opposite shore?** "A man with an unclean spirit," exceptionally fierce and dangerous. Mark 5:1–20.

**36. What did this man do?** He came and worshipped Jesus.

**37. What command did our Lord give to the demons?** He told them to go out of the man.

**38. Where did he allow them to go?** At their request they were allowed to go into a great herd of swine that was there feeding.

**39. What was the result?**
*"And the unclean spirits went out, and entered into the swine; and the herd ran violently down a steep place into the sea . . . and were choked in the sea."*

**40. How were those who saw it affected?** The keepers and owners of the swine were afraid and begged Jesus to depart; and the healed man wished to follow Jesus.

**41. What lesson is there for us in Jesus' command to the healed demoniac?** We should tell all our friends what Jesus has done for us.

**42. Who appealed to Jesus for help when he again reached Capernaum?** A leading man of the Jews, named Jairus. Mark 5:22–24, 35–43.

**43. What was his trouble?** His little daughter was at the point of death; but he believed that Jesus could even now cure her.

**44. What happened on the way to Jairus' house?** A sick woman in the crowd touched his garment in faith, and was cured. Mark 5:25–34.

**45. What messengers came to Jairus during this delay?** Those telling him that his daughter was dead.

**46. Had Jesus yet restored any from the dead?** Yes, one at Nain; but probably it was not widely known.

**47. What is death called in this story?** A "sleep" from which Jesus could "awake" her. See John 11:11.

**48. Was the life thus miraculously restored a natural life?** Yes, for Jesus told them to give her something to eat.

**49. Whom did Jesus next heal?** Two blind men and a dumb demoniac. Matt. 9:27–34.

**50. What was the proof of the faith of the blind men?** They acknowledged Jesus to be the Christ, the Son of David; and they prayed and persevered.

**51. What sad reception was given Jesus?** At Nazareth, his boyhood home, they refused to receive him. Mark 6:1–6.

**52. What common truth did Jesus state?** That a prophet, or any great man, is least honored in his own town, among his own people.

**53. Why did Jesus refrain from doing his mighty works?** Because of their obstinate unbelief.

**54. To what are sheep having no shepherd exposed?** To be "scattered" and destroyed. Matt. 9:36; Isa. 53:6.

**55. What commission did Jesus now give his twelve apostles?** He sent them by two and two out before him into the towns, to preach and heal in the same way as their Lord. Mark 6:7–13. Matt. 10:1–11:1.

**56. What command to the twelve also applies to us?**

*"Freely ye have received, freely give."*

**57. Why are Sodom and Gomorrah used in this comparison?** Because their privileges and opportunities were not so great as those of our Lord's time, and of our own.

**58. What is the end spoken of in Matt. 10:22?** The end of "the great tribulation." Matt. 24:21.

**59. What is meant by "taking the cross?"** Bearing without complaint every trial, large and small, that God appoints.

**60. What is the meaning of "finding life" (Matt. 10:39)?** Saving one's earthly life by giving up Christ.

**61. What encouragement have we for active love for the Lord's people?** Christ's assurance that the giver of even a cup of cold water to one of his disciples shall not lose his reward.

**62. What was the testimony of Herod's conscience when he heard of our Lord's miracles?** That they were done by John, whom he had beheaded, and who (he thought) had risen from the dead.

**63. Why was John in prison, and where?** At Machaerus, near the Dead Sea. See 91. 1, 2.

**64. Why was he beheaded?** To please Herodias' daughter; at Herodias' suggestion.

**65. Who was Herodias?** The wife of Herod's brother Philip, whom Herod had married.

**66. Why did Jesus go into retirement?** (1) Because the apostles had returned and needed a quiet talk with their Master; (2) because they were all in danger from Herod if they stayed in his province; (3) because the people might have been roused to revolt at the death of John, if Jesus had been among them, and this would have destroyed both Jesus and his disciples.

**67. What great miracle did Jesus do at this time?** The feeding of "about five thousand men, besides women and children" with five of their small loaves, and two tiny fishes. Matt. 14:21.

**68. Who had this food?** A little lad, who could have easily eaten that much himself. John 6:9.

**69. Did each have as much as he wanted to eat?** Yes, it says "they did all eat, and were filled," and a large number of fragments remained.

**70. Where did the disciples go after this miracle?** Jesus sent his disciples away in the boat.

**71. What happened after that?** There was a strong wind, and they could not reach their destination.

**72. What did Jesus do in the early morning?** He went to his disciples, walking on the water.

**73. What effect did it have upon them?** They were afraid, until Jesus said, "It is I; be not afraid."

**74. What did Peter try to do?** To walk on the water to meet Jesus. Matt. 14:28–31.

**75. Did he succeed in so doing?** Yes so long as he had faith to look to Jesus. When he failed in this he began to sink.

**76. Was Jesus ready to save him?** Yes, immediately.

**77. What sermon did Jesus preach the next morning, and where?** The "Sermon on the Bread of Life" at Capernaum. John 6:22–71.

**78. How did our Lord rebuke the insincerity of those who sought him?** By telling them that they came for the sake of the loaves with which he had fed them.

**79. What is meant by the "the meat which perisheth"?** Worldly comforts and riches.

**80. What is the meaning of the** word "sealed" in verse 27? Stamped, or approved as his own, by the miracles he wrought.

**81. Does not verse 29 show the true simplicity of the way of life?** Yes, it is only necessary to "repent and believe" (Mark 1:15), when all good works will follow.

**82. Did the Jews believe in Jesus?** No.

**83. What bread were the Jews willing to accept?** Bread from heaven, like the manna in the wilderness.

**84. Is there not in Jesus what will completely satisfy the soul?** Yes he is the Bread of Life, which satisfies all hunger and thirst.

**85. Does "eating with unwashen hands," Mark 7:2, mean that they were soiled?** Not at all; it means a ceremonial washing, as a symbol.

**86. Was it a part of the law of God?** No, it was a "tradition of the elders," or an addition to the law by the priests of earlier times.

**87. Did the tradition of the elders correspond with the law of God?** No, they made it of no effect. Mark 7:7–13. They dealt with the details of outward life, and lost the spirit and inward meaning of the law.

**88. What lesson of the necessity of sincerity toward God is here found?** The warning that God knows the heart, and that all hypocritical worship is "vain."

**94. THIRD PERIOD OF THE GALILEAN MINISTRY (Matt. 15:21–18:35; Mark 7:24–9:50; Luke 9:18–50; John 7:1–8:59)**

**1. Were Tyre and Sidon Jewish**

**cities?** No, they were in Phoenicia, on the seacoast to the northwest.

**2. Who asked Jesus' help there?** A woman of the country, Syrian by birth and Greek by race, who asked him to cure her daughter who was vexed by a demon.

**3. Who were meant by the children in Mark 7:27?** The Jews. Matt. 15:24, 26.

**4. Is there any limit to the power of faith?** No, it takes hold of the power of God. Mark 7:29.

**5. Where did Jesus go from this place?** Back to Palestine, to the neighborhood of the Sea of Galilee.

**6. What miracle did he do there?** He healed a deaf and dumb man. Mark 7:31–37.

**7. Did many come to hear Jesus there?** Yes, a great multitude. Mark 8:1.

**8. What did he do for them?** He fed them as he had the multitude before. Mark 8:1–9. See section 93. 67–79.

**9. What question did he ask his disciples at Caesarea Philippi?** First, who men said that he was; then, who the disciples thought he was. Mark 8:27, 29.

**10. What did Peter say?** *"Thou art the Christ, the Son of the living God." Matt. 16:16.*

**11. What is the meaning of Matt. 16:18, 19?** That Christ should build his church of his disciples, as foundation stones built together on the one great Rock foundation, Jesus Christ himself. 1 Cor. 3:9–15; Acts 4:11, 12; Eph. 2:20; Rev. 21:14. *"Neither is there salvation in any other: for there is none other name under heaven given among men, whereby we must be saved." "For other foundation*

*can no man lay than that is laid, which is Jesus Christ."*

**12. Is there any sign that Peter alone is meant?** All that is said here is said elsewhere of all the apostles. See Matt. 18:18; John 20:23; Matt. 19:28.

**13. What remarkable rebuke was addressed to Peter soon after his noble confession?** "Get thee behind me, Satan," because he voiced the temptation of the evil one.

**14. What great precept is given in Matt. 16:24–28?** *"For what is a man profited if he shall gain the whole world, and lose his own soul? Or what shall a man give in exchange for his soul?"*

**15. What is referred to in Mark 9:1?** Probably either the coming of the Spirit at Pentecost, which ushered in the beginning of the kingdom; or, as many think, the destruction of Jerusalem which closed this historical era.

**16. What wonderful sight were three disciples allowed to see?** The transfiguration of Jesus, and his conversation with Moses, representing the law, and Elijah, representing the prophets. Mark 9:2–8; Luke 9:28–36.

**17. Is there any other testimony than this to Jesus as the "beloved Son"?** Yes, at his baptism. Matt. 3:17.

**18. Whom did Jesus mean when he said Elias is indeed come?** John the Baptist.

**19. What service did they find to perform when they reached the foot of the mountain?** The demoniac boy, whose father had brought him for healing. Mark 9:14–29.

**20. Why could not the disciples cure**

**this boy?** For want of sufficient faith and prayer.

**21. Did not the father's faith almost fail?** Yes, he doubted Jesus' power.

**22. How did Jesus strengthen it?** By telling him that all things were possible to the one who believed.

**23. What is the "tribute money" referred to in Matt. 17:24–27?** Half a shekel, or about 30¢. "for the offering of the Lord," or the service of the temple. Ex. 30:13; 2 Chron. 24:9; Neh. 10:32.

**24. What is the meaning of "prevented? in verse 25?** It is the obsolete use of the word; the Revisions read "spake first" in this place.

**25. What lesson of considerateness does the Lord of all teach us?** Not to give needless offense, especially in little things.

**26. What dispute did the disciples have on the road?** As to who was the greatest in the kingdom of heaven. Mark 9:33–37.

**27. What lesson did our Lord teach them?** Humility.

**28. What great reward is promised to those who learn this lesson?** All the blessings that follow from receiving Christ and being his.

**29. Is not all intolerance discouraged in Mark 9:38–41?** Yes, we should not disown anyone as a disciple simply because he does not agree on all points with ourselves.

**30. Are great deeds done for Christ the only ones accepted by him?** No, even the giving of a cup of water for his sake shall have its reward.

**31. What further lesson have we against all persecution?** That any one who wilfully injures a weak or lowly believer in Jesus is liable to a greater punishment than even loss of life. Mark 9:42.

**32. How are we to deal with our sins?** To give them up, and every help and temptation to them, at any cost. Mark 9:43–49.

**33. What other great lesson did our Lord teach his disciples in Matt. 18?** The duty of forgiveness.

**34. How does Christ inculcate the duty of mutual forbearance and forgiveness?** By calling upon the injured to strive to gain over the offender by a quiet appeal to him when alone.

**35. Is there any limitation to the two blessed promises in Matt. 18:19, 20?** Only that what we ask of God must be "according to his will." 1 John 5:14.

**36. What was the utmost extent of forgiveness that seemed possible to Peter?** Forgiving seven times.

**37. Did the estimate of Jesus agree with him?** No, he commanded us to forgive "seventy times seven," which means, practically, times without count.

**38. In the parable in this chapter what was the amount of the debt owed to the master?** Probably about twelve million dollars; an amount worth much more then than now.

**39. Does this not show the greatness of our debt to God?** It indeed may give us some hint of it.

**40. Do we not also see the freeness of the divine forgiveness?** Yes, as compassion alone forgave the debt.

**41. How much did the fellow-servant owe?** About one hundred and sixty dollars.

**42. Does this represent the difference between the debts owed by man to**

man and those owed to God by man?
Yes, so far as we can imagine it.

**43. Are we not called upon to imitate the long suffering of God?** We are indeed; and if we know ourselves forgiven by him, we shall certainly do so.

**44. Where do we learn that the merciful God is also a God of judgment?** In the same parable, by his sentence of the ungrateful and unforgiving servant.

**45. When did Jesus utter the teachings recorded in John 7?** At the Feast of Tabernacles at Jerusalem.

**46. What was the Feast of Tabernacles?** One of the feasts of the Jews, when the people lived in booths to commemorate the forty years in the wilderness. See Lev. 23:39–43.

**47. Why were the people afraid of the Jews (verse 13)?** "Lest they should be put out of the synagogue," or excommunicated, if they confessed themselves followers of Christ. See Acts 5:13.

**48. What remarkable connection is there between obedience and the knowledge of right doctrine?** The man who really desires to do God's will shall have a fully sufficient understanding of the meaning of his word. John 7:17.

**49. Whom did the people mean by "the very Christ" in verse 26?** The true Messiah.

**50. Who are "the dispersed" of verse 35?** Those Israelites who had been scattered among all nations.

**51. Could the Jews bear to think that the gospel was to be preached to the Gentiles?** No, they considered themselves the only people of God.

**52. What is it to come to Jesus to drink (John 7:34–39)?** To receive him as our Saviour, and so to satisfy all the longings of the thirsty soul.

**53. Who was referred to as "the Prophet" (John 7:40)?** The one referred to by Moses in Deut. 18:15, 18.

**54. What is meant by "the law" in verse 49?** The law of Moses and the writings of the prophets.

**55. Who here took Jesus' part?** Nicodemus. Verses 50, 51; see John 3; 90. 5–11.

**56. What does Jesus say of himself in John 8:12?** He says that he is "the light of the world."

**57. Is this said of him in any other place?** Yes. John 1:4, 5, 9; 3:19; 9:5; 12:35, 36, 46.

**58. What does this mean?** That those who are his followers shall not now walk in the darkness of doubt and unbelief; nor be cast out later into the "outer darkness."

**59. What is it to judge after the flesh?** To judge by outward appearance and worldly notions. John 8:15.

**60. What does Jesus mean in verse 28 by being "lifted up"?** Being raised on the cross. See John 3:14; 12:32.

**61. What did Jesus mean by "the works of Abraham" in verse 39?** The "obedience of faith," which should have led the Jews to believe and obey Christ.

**62. Is death of the body referred to in John 8:51?** No, the death or ruin of the soul, "the second or everlasting death."

**63. How did Abraham see the day of Christ?** By the far-seeing eye of faith, looking at the promises of God. John 8:52–59.

**64. What does the Lord mean by "I am"?** That he was always in existence, from all eternity; as God called himself to Moses "I am." Ex. 3:14.

## 95. THE PEREAN MINISTRY: THROUGH THE FEAST OF DEDICATION (Matt. 11:20–30; Luke 9:51–10:42; John 9:1–10:12)

**1. What took place between the feast of tabernacles and the feast of dedication?** Jesus returned to Galilee, and spent some time in unrecorded work. Later he finally left Galilee.

**2. What incident is recorded in Luke 9:51–56?** The inhospitality of the Samaritans.

**3. Why is the term "steadfastly" used?** Because Jesus knew all the sufferings that would come upon him.

**4. Why would not the Samaritans receive him?** Because they knew that he was on his way to Jerusalem, and they hated the Jews.

**5. What made their conduct especially bad?** The universal duty of hospitality was violated; and still more they virtually denied his claim to be a religious teacher, and thus still more worthy of hospitality.

**6. What example of meekness did our Lord show?** He did not punish the Samaritans for their conduct though some of the disciples asked it.

**7. What proof have we of the poverty of Jesus?** He "had not where to lay his head." Luke 9:58.

**8. What proverb of faithfulness does Jesus give?**
"No man, having put his hand to the plough, and looking back, is fit for the kingdom of God." Luke 9:62.

**9. For what purpose were the seventy disciples selected?** To go two by two into every place where Jesus was to go, and prepare the way for him. Luke 10:1–24.

**10. Why were they to "salute no man by the way"?** Eastern "salutations" were very ceremonious and long.

**11. What is meant by "wiping off the dust of a city?"** It was an Oriental custom, meaning the entire casting off of responsibility and care for that city.

**12. Do not the directions for the seventy show the care of the Master?** Yes, for their bodily comfort as well as for their success in their ministry.

**13. How was Capernaum "exalted to heaven"?** As a prosperous city which had enjoyed the privilege of Christ's presence and teaching.

**14. What proof have we of the union of Christ and his people?** His saying that the hearing or despising of his ministers was the hearing or despising of himself.

**15. What is the truest cause of rejoicing?** That we have found Christ, and have our names written in heaven.

**16. May we not apply all these words to our own country and times?** Yes, to any place or time which has great advantages but does not serve God with the whole heart.

**17. Who is most likely to know the things of Christ?** Those who are humble and teachable, like a little child.

**18. What blessing come to those who take Christ's yoke upon them?** Rest for the soul.
"Come unto me, all ye that labour and are heavy laden, and I will give you rest. Take my yoke upon you, and learn of me; for I am meek and lowly in heart: and ye shall find rest unto your souls. For my yoke is easy, and my burden is light." Matt. 11:28–30.

**19. What is the teaching in the parable of the Good Samaritan, in Luke 10:25–37?** The true neighbor is the one who helps all in need, whatever their nationality or creed.

**20. How much was "two pence"?** About 33¢; but it was then two days' wages for an ordinary laborer.

**21. What great miracle of Jesus is recorded in John 9?** The healing of a man who was born blind.

**22. What belief of the Jews is indicated in the question of the disciples?** That all suffering is a penalty for sin.

**23. Did our Lord have this belief?** No, he said that there was no sin as the cause of this blindness; but the blindness gave an opportunity for showing the power of God.

**24. What does our Lord mean here by "day" and "night"?** Life, as the time of working for God; and death, as the rest from our labor.

**25. What is meant by expulsion from the synagogue?** Not allowing attendance upon the religious meetings, and so bringing disgrace and social privations.

**26. What was the great confession of this blind man?** *"One thing I know, that, whereas I was blind, now I see." John 9:25.*

**27. What beautiful parable is given in John 10?** The parable of the Good Shepherd.

**28. What sort of sheepfolds were in use in Palestine?** Very many of them were simply uncovered enclosures in the pasture grounds, for the protection of the sheep at night.

**29. Who is the door of the sheepfold?** Jesus Christ himself.

**30. What is promised to those who enter in by the door?** The supply of all their need; and protection from all harm.

**31. What was our Lord's object in coming into the world?** To lay down his life in order to give life.

**32. How is the atonement taught in this parable?** Jesus says that he lays down his life for the sheep, or in their stead, that they might live. John 10:11, 15–18.

**33. What shows the close care, and love for the sheep?** *"I am the good shepherd, and know my sheep, and am known of mine." John 10:14.*

**34. What was the feast of the dedication?** It was kept in memory of God's delivery of the temple from King Antiochus, in 165 B.C.

**35. What is the security of God's true people?** His assurance that they shall never perish. John 10:27, 28.

**36. Why cannot the scripture be broken?** Because it is the word of God.

**96. THE PEREAN MINISTRY: TO THE LAST JOURNEY TO JERUSALEM (Luke 11:1–17:10; John 11:1–54)**

**1. What is Luke 11:2–4 called?** The Lord's Prayer.

**2. Where else is it given? Is it the same?** In Matt. 6:9–13. It differs in minor points.

**3. What does this teach us?** That the words of a prayer are not of so much value as its sincerity.

**4. Why then is it of value to know the Lord's Prayer?** It is of great value to be able to unite with others in a simple, audible prayer. Also this prayer, given by our Lord himself, has within it all the essentials of any true prayer.

**5. What is importunity in prayer?** Feeling and speaking earnestly and perseveringly, as those who will not be denied whatever it may be God's will to grant.

**6. By what comparison does Christ help us to know God?** By comparing him with an earthly father.

**7. What is the "leaven of the Pharisees"?** Their bad principles and their hypocrisy. Luke 12:1.

**8. What proof of God's love and care have we in Luke 12:6, 7?** Even the sparrows are not forgotten by him.

**9. What blessing is promised to the confessors of Christ?** Those who are not afraid or ashamed to acknowledge Christ upon earth will be acknowledged by him before all the angels at the last day. Luke 12:8, 9.

**10. Against what are we warned in Luke 12:13–21?** Against the love of the riches and pleasures of the world.

**11. What does the soul's "being required" mean?** Being called away from earth to its great account.

**12. What is it to be "rich toward God"?** To be full of love to him and of good works for his sake.

**13. Against what are we warned in Luke 12:22–31?** Undue anxiety and worry about the future. Not ordinary forethought; but such worry as unfits us to do our Father's will today, in fear of what may come tomorrow.

**14. What is it to have a treasure in the heavens?** To have Christ there as our Saviour, and all his riches as our own through him.

**15. What great event is involved in the command to watch?** The sudden coming of our Lord. Luke 12:35–59.

**16. What responsibility is attached to the knowing of God's will?** The doing it.

**17. Is sin the cause of all the suffering in the world?** No, according to Luke 13:1–5 those who suffered were no more sinners than those to whom Jesus was speaking.

**18. Is it easy to enter the kingdom of heaven?** No, it means giving up our will to that of God, and striving against the temptations of the world around us. Luke 13:24–30.

**19. Must we do this in our own strength?** We cannot do it in our own strength; those who rely on that will fail. But our Saviour is ever ready to help us in every hard place.

**20. Who are they that shall be rejected?** Those who neglect or refuse to be received and saved. God does not will that any should perish. John 3:16.

**21. What is the meaning of Luke 14:30?** Originally, perhaps, that the Jews, who were the first to receive the light of the truth, should give place to the Gentiles, who were the last. It also means that many who seem in this world to hold and deserve the first place in the kingdom will in the judgment be obliged to give place to some who seemed here to be the least of all.

**22. What lessons are taught in Luke 14?** First, the true use of the sabbath; second, self-exaltation is not right or wise; and third, there is always room at the gospel feast for all who are willing to come.

**23. What may lawfully be done on the sabbath?** "Works of necessity or mercy"; and anything that may do real physical and spiritual good to those around us.

**24. What were the sabbath rules of the Jews?** They were very detailed and very arbitrary, so that it was impossible to be sure of keeping them fully.

**25. What gave rise to the parable in this chapter?** The fact that each guest chose the best seat at a feast.

**26. What rules for feasts did Jesus make?** The guests should be humble and take each the lowest seat; and feasts should be made for the poor and suffering rather than for the rich who will make a return for it.

**27. Who are meant by the invited guests in the parable?** The Jews, the original people of God.

**28. Why were their excuses so valueless?** Because according to Oriental custom, they had been previously invited and had accepted. But now the time had come to go "they all began with one accord to make excuse."

**29. How does this apply to the Jews?** The Scriptures and the prophets had foretold the coming and the manner of the Messiah. They should have been ready for him when he came, and have accepted his invitation.

**30. To whom was the offer of mercy then given?** To the Gentiles.

**31. What name is sometimes given to the parables of Luke 15?** "The Parables of the Lost and Found."

**32. How do we learn our preciousness in the sight of God?** By the joy in heaven that one repenting sinner creates.

**33. To what extremity was the prodigal son reduced in the service of sin?** He had spent all, and was perishing with hunger, and no man gave to him.

**34. What expression is used of the prodigal's change of mind?** "He came to himself"; as if before he had not been in his right mind.

**35. What did the prodigal intend to say to his father?** He intended in the deep penitence of his heart to ask to be one of his father's servants.

**36. Did the father's love give him time to say all he meant?** No, and equally ready is our heavenly Father to welcome his repenting and returning children.

**37. How is the sinner returning to God described?** As dead and lost, and then alive and found.

**38. Upon what principle did the unjust steward in the parable in Luke 16:1–15 act?** Upon the worldly one of making friends by any means, whether good or bad.

**39. What is meant by serving mammon?** Seeking riches or the favor of the world, as the main object of life.

**40. Does God's judgment of human affairs correspond with ours?** No, for he judges by the heart, which we cannot see.

**41. What is the lesson to be learned from the parable of the rich man and Lazarus in Luke 16:19–31?** To take care to make good use of our riches; and, to have a treasure in heaven.

**42. Does obedience to God warrant self-exaltation?** No, at the best "we have done that which was our duty to do." Luke 17:10.

**43. Who was the Lazarus of John 11?** Lazarus of Bethany, brother of Mary and

Martha, and a very dear friend of Jesus. See Luke 10:38–42; John 12:1–8.

**44. Is he the same Lazarus as is spoken of in question 41?** No. The name Lazarus is the Greek form of Eleazar, a very common Jewish name.

**45. What in this chapter is taught us about the right use of opportunity?** That time and opportunity will have an end, and we must use them before it comes.

**46. How is death spoken of?** As a sleep from which the people of God shall rise to a new life.

**47. What does Thomas mean in verse 16?** That he expected that Jesus would be killed by the Jews.

**48. How was Jesus himself the resurrection and the life?** Because his people by their union with him have a glorious resurrection to eternal life.

**49. Who are the dead spoken of in verse 25?** The "dead in Christ." 1 Thess. 4:16.

**50. Who are the living that shall never die?** Those who "are alive" at "the coming of the Lord." 1 Thess. 4:17. Or it means that those who live in Christ shall never really perish, but have eternal life.

**51. What proof of Jesus' love is there in verse 25?** His weeping at the grave of his friend.

**52. Why was Jesus compelled to go away again?** Because the Jews began to plan to put him to death.

**97. THE PEREAN MINISTRY: THE LAST JOURNEY TO JERUSALEM (Matt. 19:3–20:34; 26:6–13; Mark 10:2–52; 14:3–9; Luke 17:1–19:28; John 11:55–12:11)**

**1. Why did the lepers in Luke 17:12 stand afar off?** They were obliged by the law to keep separate from others.

**2. Why were they to show themselves to the priests?** To obey the Jewish law that the priests should examine all who thought either that they had the leprosy, or that, having had it, had been cured. Lev. 13:2.

**3. Was their cleansing previous to or after they had acted in faith?** After they had showed their faith by calling upon Jesus for mercy.

**4. What shows their ingratitude?** Of the ten only one returned to thank Jesus for the cure; and he was a Samaritan.

**5. What does the parable of the importunate widow teach?** That we should continue to pray, and never be discouraged. Luke 18:1–18.

**6. What should we learn from the parable of the Pharisee and the publican?** To be penitently humble, instead of self-righteously proud. Luke 18:9–14.

**7. What state of heart is acceptable in God's sight?**
*"The sacrifices of God are a broken spirit; a broken and a contrite heart, O God, thou wilt not despise." Ps. 51:17.*

**8. What is Jesus' teaching concerning divorce?** He spoke strongly against it. Matt. 19:3–12.

**9. What beautiful scene is recorded in Matt. 19:13–15?** The blessing of the little children who were brought to Jesus.
*"Suffer little children, and forbid them not, to come unto me: for of such is the kingdom of heaven."*

**10. What stood in the way of the young ruler who came to Jesus?** He thought more of his riches than of eternal life itself.

**11. Is the possession of wealth always**

**a blessing?** No, it is always a temptation and a snare. If the temptations are overcome, and the wealth rightly used, it may become a blessing.

**12. Does Jesus mean here that every one should give up all his property?** No, he told his young man to do what he most needed. Not all sick need the same medicine.

**13. How do we learn the deep-rooted nature of covetousness?** By our Lord's description of the extreme difficulty by which one who trusts in riches may enter the kingdom of God.

**14. What is to be understood by "the world (age) to come"?** Mark 10:30; Luke 18:30. The state or time after death.

**15. What blessed promise do you find in this story?** All who give up this world's riches for the sake of Christ have abundant reward.

**16. What fact shows the fairness of the householder in the parable of Matt. 20:1–16?** Those who came last came as soon as they were called; and were not made to lose because they had not been called earlier.

**17. What does it teach as to God's sovereignty?** That God is the Master of all, and will give to each man what he thinks fit. But his giving is not in mere justice, but in perfect justice tempered with perfect mercy.

**18. Who were the sons of Zebedee?** James and John, two of the apostles. Mark 10:35–40.

**19. What was the name of their mother?** Salome. Mark 15:40.

**20. What was their request?** That they should have the two highest places of honor at the coming of the kingdom. Mark 20:21.

**21. Was this entirely from wrong ambition?** It very likely included a desire to be very near to their Master, and to be of the greatest service to him.

**22. What was Jesus' answer?** His first answer was a question as to whether they could drink of his cup.

**23. What does this mean?** The sufferings and trials which Jesus was to endure for all men.

**24. What was their reply?** "We are able."

**25. Was this vain boasting?** No, they did suffer and endure for their Master. James suffered martyrdom.

**26. What was Jesus' second answer?** That these chief places were not given as gifts, but as rewards for those for whom they had been prepared.

**27. Does this mean that their request was refused?** No, there is no hint in the Bible as to that. They may be their true places. But they could not receive them in the way they asked.

**28. What is true humility?** Being ready to be last of all, and servant of all. Matt. 20:26.

**29. Whom did Jesus meet near Jericho on this journey?** Two blind men (Matt. 20:30), of whom one, Bartimaeus, was much the more prominent. Mark 10:46–52; Luke 18:35–42.

**30. Who was Zacchaeus?** A rich publican of Jericho. Luke 19:1–10.

**31. How did our Lord respond to the faith of Zacchaeus?** By noticing him, and making himself a guest at his house.

**32. What word of blame was said of Jesus?** That he had gone to be guest with a man that was a sinner.

**33. What was the answer?**
*"The Son of man is come to seek and to save that which was lost." Luke 19:10.*

**34. What is the meaning of the parables of Luke 19:11–27?** That when men are given equal opportunities they are rewarded according to the use they make of them.

**35. What great act of faith and love occurred at this time?** The anointing of Jesus' head and feet with costly ointment. John 12:1–8.

**36. By whom?** By Mary of Bethany, the sister of Lazarus. See XCVI. 43.

**37. Was this Mary Magdalene?** No, Mary Magdalene, or Mary of Magdala, was quite another person, as also was the "woman which was a sinner" of Luke 7:36–50. But they have often been confused.

**38. Of what value was the ointment used by Mary?** Three hundred pence; or the wages of a laboring man for one year.

**39. Who found fault?** Judas Iscariot.

**40. What did Jesus say?**
*"She hath done what she could: . . . Verily I say unto you, Wheresoever this gospel shall be preached throughout the whole world, this also that she hath done shall be spoken of for a memorial of her." Mark 14:8; Matt. 26:13.*

## 98. THE LAST WEEK

**A. Sunday (Matt. 21:1–11;**
     **Mark 11:1–11; Luke 19:29–44;**
     **John 12:12–19)**

**1. What was the special event of this day?** The triumphal entry of Jesus into Jerusalem as the Messiah.

**2. Where had this been prophesied?** In Zech. 9:9.

**3. What shows that he is the Prince of Peace?** His choosing an ass, used by civilians, instead of a horse, then used almost entirely by warriors.

**4. What indication is there that the owner of the ass was one of Jesus' disciples?** Jesus told his disciples to say, concerning the colt, that the Lord had need of him.

**5. What significant phrase is used by the Pharisees?** "Behold the world is gone after him." John 12:19.

**6. How was our Lord's prophecy about Jerusalem fulfilled?** In its destruction by the Romans about forty years later.

**B. Monday (Matt. 21:2–19;**
     **Mark 11:12–19; Luke 19:45–48)**

**7. Where did Jesus spend the nights of this week?** At Bethany. Mark 11:11.

**8. Why did Jesus expect to find figs on this tree when it was not yet the season?** Because the figs usually came before the leaves. Mark 11:12–14.

**9. Of what is this fig tree a type?** Of great pretensions with small results.

**10. What remarkable act of authority occurred on this day?** Jesus drove the buyers and sellers, and the money changers out of the temple.

**11. Had he ever done this before?** Yes, at the beginning of his ministry. John 2:13–25. See 90.

**C. Tuesday (Matt. 21:20–26:5, 14, 16;**
     **Mark 11:20–14:11;**
     **Luke 20:1–22:6; John 12:20–50)**

**12. What has this day been called?** Jesus' last great day of public teaching.

**13. What did he do during the day?**
He spent all the time in the temple, trying to persuade the Pharisees of the truth of his claim to be the Son of God and Son of man.

**14. What wonderful promise of faith did Jesus give?** *"And all things, whatsoever ye shall ask in prayer, believing, ye shall receive." Matt. 21:22.*

**15. Can this promise be taken literally?** Yes, on the just condition that we ask nothing that would be bad for ourselves or for others.

**16. What other indispensable condition is there?** That we forgive, if we have aught against any. Mark 11:25.

**17. How did Jesus answer the challenge of the Pharisees as to his authority?** By a counter-question as to the authority of John the Baptist. Matt. 21:23–27.

**18. How was this an answer?** If the Pharisees were willing to acknowledge John's authority they would be fair in judging Jesus; if not, there was no use in telling them.

**19. Why would they not answer?** They were unwilling to acknowledge that John came from God; and feared the people if they declared him an imposter.

**20. What lesson comes to us from Matt. 21:28–32?** That mere promises without their fulfillment are not obedience.

**21. Who is the householder who planted the vineyard?** God, the Father and Ruler of all. Matt. 21:33–46.

**22. Who are the husbandmen?** The chief priests and Pharisees.

**23. Who are the servants, and who the son?** The servants are the prophets and all others who sought to bring the people to a true service of God. The son is Christ himself.

**24. What does the parable of the marriage feast signify?** The rejection of the gospel. Matt. 22:1–14.

**25. Where else is found a parable of the rejection of the gospel feast?** In Luke 14:15–24. See XCVI. 22–30.

**26. What is meant here by the servants?** The prophets and teachers of the Jews, who were often persecuted, and even slain.

**27. Who were invited when the Jews proved unworthy?** The Gentiles, outcasts from the Jewish point of view.

**28. What was the wedding garment?** A garment given by the host, and worn over the other garments as the necessary preparation for the feast he gave. For us it is the garment of Christ's righteousness.

**29. Was it not unjust to send to punishment the man who had no wedding garment?** No, for it was the only condition made for entrance to the feast; it was a free gift offered to everyone; and refusal to wear it was a studied insult to the host.

**30. What was the snare laid for Jesus in Matt. 22:15–22?** The question was designed to bring an answer which would almost certainly offend either the Jewish or the Roman law.

**31. What was Jesus' wise answer?** *"Render therefore unto Caesar the things which are Caesar's; and unto God the things that are God's."*

**32. What does this mean?** Since you use the benefits from the government, pay your duties to the government, even though you do not approve of it. But also do your duty in obeying the laws of God.

**33. What was the scribe's tempting question?** "Which (literally, "what sort of a") commandment is the greatest?" Matt. 22:36.

**34. What did Jesus answer?** The greatest commandment is to love God wholly and entirely, without any reservation. Matt. 22:37, 38; Mark 12:29, 30.

**35. What is the second in importance?** To love one's fellowmen as one's self. Matt. 22:39.

**36. Why are these called "all the law"?** The first is the sum of the first four of the Ten Commandments; and if one obeys the second, he will obey the other six; and if one obeys perfectly the Ten Commandments he keeps all God's Law.

**37. How did Jesus at last silence his adversaries?** By asking them how the Messiah can be both David's son and David's Lord. It was unanswerable by any one with the Pharisees' beliefs concerning the Messiah.

**38. What followed the silencing of his adversaries?** A denunciation of the hypocrisy and evil doing of the scribes and Pharisees, the leaders of the people. Matt. 23.

**39. What was the character of his denunciation?** It was a very strong one, but uttered in love, and with a desire to show them their own hearts, so that they would repent and believe.

**40. What was the greatest sin of these leaders?** Their close attention to outward ritual while their hearts were at all times selfish and sinful. And still more that by their position and their actions they misled many of those they should have helped.

**41. What are phylacteries (Matt. 23:5)?** Slips of parchment with texts of Scripture upon them, which the Pharisees used in literal obedience to the command in Ex. 13:15, 16; Num. 15:38, 39.

**42. Was their wearing these as they did a sin?** No, but it should have been a symbol of the true wearing of the law of God in their hearts. To refuse to do the duty while wearing the symbol was to be a hypocrite.

**43. What is the difference between the long prayers of the Pharisees, which are condemned, and the "Pray without ceasing" commanded by the apostle?** The long prayers of the Pharisees were for a pretense of holiness to obtain praise from men, and were offered publicly where all could see them. The injunction of the apostle is for us to keep continually a spirit of prayer, so that we may raise our hearts to God in true secret prayer, even though in the midst of a crowd.

**44. Why did Jesus commend "the widow's mite"?** Because she gave with a true spirit of generosity and love, and the others with something of a spirit of ostentation. Mark 12:41–44.

**45. How is the truth that God looks on the heart illustrated by this?** Because he would not have commended the gift if he had not known the motive with which it was given.

**46. What are the only conditions under which a small gift is to be commended?** When it is large for the giver's circumstances; and is given out of love for God and his cause.

**47. Who were the "Greeks" in John 12:20–36?** Persons from Greece who had become Jewish proselytes.

**48. What connection is there between their wish to see Jesus and his declaration following?** Jesus meant that they must be prepared for his death and for any trials which that event must bring upon his followers.

**49. Why must a grain of wheat die before it can be fruitful?** It contains the germ of the new plant, and must die as a grain of wheat that the new plant may grow from it.

**50. For what cause did our Lord come to the hour of self-sacrifice?** Because he had willingly given himself up to die for the salvation of men and his own final glory.

**51. What is meant by "all men" in verse 32?** People of all kinds, of all nations, and of all times.

*"I beheld, and, lo, a great multitude, which no man could number, of all nations, and kindreds, and people, and tongues, stood before the throne, and before the Lamb, clothed with white robes, and palms in their hands." Rev. 7:9.*

**52. Does John 12:39 mean that God did not wish the Jews to believe?** Not at all; but because they continually hardened their hearts against his word they became unable to accept it.

**53. Who built the temple then standing?** Herod the Great. See 86. 11.

**54. When was it destroyed and by whom?** About forty years after Christ's death, by the Romans under Titus.

**55. What warning did Jesus give his disciples?** That many would seek to declare that they were the Christ, the Messiah; but they must preserve their faith in him to the end.

**56. Is the universal success of the gospel promised in Matt. 24:14?** No, only its universal preaching as a testimony of Christ. All men were to have the chance to repent and believe, but not all would accept of it.

**57. What was the "abomination of desolation" spoken of in Matt. 24:15?** This is probably a reference to Dan. 12:11 and perhaps refers to the banners of the desolating Roman armies, on whose banners were idolatrous symbols or images.

**58. Would not many who heard this prophecy be alive at its accomplishment?** Doubtless. Matt. 24:34.

**59. What is the lesson in the parable of the ten virgins in Matt. 25?** That we must be fully prepared for the coming of our Lord.

**60. Are the ten virgins blamed for sleeping?** No, those who had made full preparation could rest in peace until the cry came. The others were blamed, not for sleeping, but for insufficient preparation.

**61. Were the five wise virgins selfish?** No, for if they had shared their oil all the lamps would have gone out, and no honor done the bridegroom.

**62. Is it possible for us to share our "oil"?** No, for it means that grace and love of God which can only come into hearts prepared to receive it, and cannot be given away when once it is received.

**63. How does the parable of the talents in Matt. 25:14–30 differ from that of the pounds in Luke 19?** The pounds mean equal power and opportunity for all who received them. The talents mean the differing powers and opportunity we all possess.

**64. Did he who had but one talent have enough to be of value?** Yes for it was at least nearly $1,000, an amount it then would have taken a laboring man twenty years to earn.

**65. Is there any special lesson in this parable?** Yes, that inequality of power and opportunity does not excuse us from making the best use we can of what we have.

**66. Will any one be exempted from the final judgment?** No. It says, "All nations" shall be gathered before the Son of man for judgment. Matt. 25:31–46.

**67. What oneness of Christ and his disciples is shown in this parable?** *"Inasmuch as ye have done it [or 'as ye did it not'] unto one of the least of these my brethren, ye have done it [or 'did it not'] unto me." Matt. 25:40, 45.*

**68. How then may we judge whether we are truly serving Christ?** By our feeling and conduct toward his humble disciples.

**69. Does this reward and punishment depend on conscious service of Christ?** No, since the motive is the most valuable, those who do the least may be those who have served the best.

**70. What did Judas now plan?** To betray his Master for thirty pieces of silver (about $24, or six months' wages for a laborer). Matt. 26:1, 5, 14–16.

**D. Thursday (Matt. 26:17–35; Mark 14:12–31; Luke 22:7–38; John 13–17)**

**71. What was done on Wednesday?** There is no record, and it was probably spent in quiet retirement.

**72. Why was so indefinite a direction given to the disciples in Luke 22:10?** Probably so that Judas should not know long enough beforehand to arrange for the arrest there.

**73. What had the disciples to prepare for the passover?** The lamb, with unleavened bread, bitter herbs, wine, and a sauce made of dates, raisins, and other things. See 17.

**74. What strife took place on the way to the upper room?** The disciples again disputed as to who was the greatest. Luke 22:24–30.

**75. What service did they refuse to do when they reached the room?** To wash each other's feet from the dust of the street.

**76. Was this a formal service?** No, a necessary one, because they wore sandals, and had taken a long walk. But it was a most menial task.

**77. What lesson of true humility do we learn from Luke 22:26–28 and John 13?** To be as willing to serve as to rule, and to be ready to render any offices of kindness to our fellow Christians.

**78. What all-important declaration does Jesus make in John 13:8?** He said to Peter, "If I wash thee not thou hast no part with me."

**79. From what must we be washed before we can have part with Jesus?** From all our sins, in his own blood.

**80. Did Jesus mean his command in John 13:14, 15 literally?** Not necessarily. He meant that his disciples should be ready at all times to do even the most menial tasks, in order to help others.

**81. What did Jesus now tell his disciples?** That one of them should betray him. John 13:21–30.

**82. What is the meaning of "leaning on Jesus' bosom"?** Being the nearest to him in the order of reclining at the feast.

**83. How did the Lord indicate the traitor?** By the giving of a sop, that is a morsel of bread, dipped in the sauce. This was considered a great honor.

**84. Was the fact thus disclosed understood by the disciples?** Most probably not; else some plan would have been made to save Jesus. Perhaps, also, they had no idea of when the betrayal was to come; or what it truly meant.

**85. What wonderful rite did our Lord now institute?** The Lord's Supper. Matt. 26:26–29.

**86. Was Judas present at the institution of the Lord's Supper?** No, he "went immediately out," after receiving the sop. John 13:30.

**87. What is the object of the Lord's Supper?** That we may remember the Lord's death, till he come; and that our souls may be strengthened and refreshed by the fellowship with him, and with our fellow Christians of all ages. See 1 Cor. 11:23–26.

## CHRIST'S FAREWELL DISCOURSES (John 13:31–16:33)

**88. What is the true test of discipleship?** Love one to another. John 13:35.

**89. Was there not a wide difference between Peter's profession (John 13:37) and his practice?** Yes, a sad difference when he denied him in his hour of utmost need; but he repented under his Lord's forgiving look; was restored to his position as the Lord's apostle; and spent a long and arduous life in his service.

## John 14

**90. What is meant by "the Father's house"?** Our home in heaven.

**91. How must we come to the Father?** By Christ who is the only Way.

**92. How do we know that our Lord was a manifestation of the Father?** By Christ's assertion to Philip that whoever had seen him had seen the Father.

**93. Will our heavenly Father answer our petitions?** Yes if we ask in Jesus' name.

**94. Who was the promised Comforter?** The Holy Spirit.

**95. Was the Holy Spirit a temporary gift?** No, he was to abide with us forever.

**96. Why cannot the world receive him?** Because it knows him not, nor Christ, through whom he comes.

**97. How can we judge whether we love Christ?** By our constant obedience to his commands, and the witness of the Spirit within us.

**98. Did Christ mean that his disciples shall have peace and comfort on earth when he gave them his peace?** No, he told them that they should have tribulation in the world; but peace in their hearts. See John 16:33.

**99. Who only could say with truth that he had yielded no allegiance to the prince of this world?** Jesus Christ.

**100. Who is the "prince of this world"?** Satan, who rules over all the forces of evil.

## John 15

**101. Under what conditions only can we bring forth fruit?** By abiding in Christ by a living faith.

**102. What will be the consequence of our not bearing fruit?** As fruitless branches are cast aside and burned, so fruitless disciples shall be set aside as useless branches.

**103. What is the token of being Christ's friends?** The doing whatsoever he commands.

**104. Is love of the world compatible with love to our Lord?** There can be no true love for our Saviour in a heart that is full of worldly thoughts.

**105. What sin is referred to in verses 22 and 24?** The sin of seeing Christ's miracles, and hearing his words, and yet rejecting both God and him.

### John 16

**106. Compare verse 2 with Acts 26:9–11.** Saul thought he was doing God true service when he tried by persecution to crush out the followers of Jesus.

**107. What was the proof that satisfied the doubting disciples?** Jesus' knowing their wish or thought, and telling them plainly that he was going back to the Father.

**108. What is our consolation in trouble?** That Christ has overcome the world, and that in him we may have peace.

### JESUS' PRAYER FOR HIS DISCIPLES (John 17)

**109. What "hour" did Jesus refer to in verse 1?** The hour of his suffering for man.

**110. What is life eternal?** To truly know God as our reconciled Father in Christ. Union with Christ is eternal life already begun.

**111. Who was "the son of perdition"?** Judas, who was fast falling into complete ruin of both body and spirit.

**112. How do we know that believers of the present day are included in our Lord's petition?** *"Neither pray I for these alone, but for them also which shall believe on me through their word." V. 20.*

**113. What great petition is only now being answered?** "That they all may be one" (v. 21) is being answered in the growing unity and federation of the denominations in the Church of Christ, and in the great amount of truly Christian work that is being done "undenominationally."

### 99.  HIS LAST DAY: FRIDAY (Matt. 26:36–27:61; Mark 14:32–15:47; Luke 22:39–23:56; John 18:1–19:42)

### A.  The Agony in Gethsemane (Matt. 26:36–46; Mark 14:32–42; Luke 22:29–46; John 18:1)

**1. What and where was Gethsemane?** A garden on the slope of the Mount of Olives near Jerusalem, where Jesus and his disciples often retired for rest.

**2. What was Jesus' prayer in Gethsemane?** A prayer of the overburdened human frame for relief; but joined with a prayer of the devoted heart that God's will be done.

**3. What was the burden Jesus bore?** The burden of sorrow that pressed on him at the thought that he was laden with the sins of mankind.

**4. Did he have the sympathy of his disciples?** He found them sleeping; but Luke, the physician, says "for sorrow" (22:45).

**5. What command did he give to them, and what excuse for them?** *"Watch and pray, that ye enter not into temptation: the spirit indeed is willing, but the flesh is weak." Matt. 26:41.*

**B. The Betrayal and Arrest (Matt. 26:47–56; Mark 14:43–52; Luke 22:47–53; John 18:1–11)**

**6. Who came with Judas to the garden?** A band of soldiers and the authorities from the temple.

**7. How did Judas betray him?** He said, "Hail, Rabbi," and kissed him, as a sign.

**8. What unwise thing did Peter do?** He drew his sword to defend his Master. He could not do so singlehanded, and the action might have caused the death of all the disciples, who must be saved to carry on the work. John 18:10, 11; Matt. 26:51–54.

**9. What shows Jesus' majesty of appearance at this time?** Those who came to arrest him all "went backward and fell to the ground."

**C. The Jewish Trial (Matt. 26:57–27:10; Mark 14:53–72; Luke 22:54–71; John 18:12–27)**

**10. Where was Jesus' first trial held?** At a hastily called meeting of the Sanhedrin, or Great Council of the Jews at the house of Caiaphas, the high priest.

**11. What terrible thing happened here?** Peter denied his Master three times.

*"And the Lord turned, and looked upon Peter. And Peter remembered . . . and . . . went out and wept bitterly." Luke 22:55–62.*

**12. Was Peter forgiven and restored?** Yes, after the resurrection of the Lord. John 21.

**13. What was the charge and verdict of the Sanhedrin?** Blasphemy. "He is worthy of death."

**14. What became of Judas?** He returned the money to the priests, and went out and hanged himself.

**D. The Roman Trial (Matt. 27:11–31; Mark 15:1–20; Luke 23:1–25; John 18:28–19:16)**

**15. To whom did the Jews take Jesus for condemnation?** To Pilate, the governor of Palestine.

**16. What inconsistency is shown in John 18:28?** They were intent on crucifying their promised Messiah; but they refused to enter the house of a Gentile, because to do so during the passover feast would "defile" them.

**17. What charge did the Jews bring now?** Treason against Rome; because (1) he forbade giving tribute to Caesar; and (2) he claimed to be himself a king.

**18. Was there any truth in these charges?** No, the first was a falsehood, and the second was a misinterpretation.

**19. Why did they not bring now the same charge on which they had themselves condemned him?** The Romans would not consider that a cause for punishment.

**20. Why did not the Jews do as Pilate said (John 18:31) and punish him themselves?** The right to inflict capital punishment had been taken from them by the Romans; and nothing less would satisfy them.

**21. Did Pilate wish to condemn him?** No, he tried many times to persuade the Jews that Jesus was an innocent man, and should not be put to death.

**22. Could Pilate have refused to condemn Jesus?** He certainly had the authority; but he was afraid of the accusation of the Jews. John 19:12.

**23. Whom did the Jews choose instead of Jesus?** Barabbas, a popular leader, who had made an insurrection against Rome, and in it had committed murder.

**24. What happened when Pilate condemned Jesus?** The soldiers put on him a scarlet robe, the royal color, and on his head a crown of thorns, and mocked him.

**25. What final appeal did Pilate make?** He showed the Jews the suffering Jesus, crowned with thorns; but it was useless.

**E. The Crucifixion (Matt. 27:32–66; Mark 15:21–47; Luke 23:46–56; John 19:16–42)**

**26. What was done with Jesus?** He was crucified, the death of a slave.

**27. What petty revenge did Pilate take on the Jews?** The placard which bore the "crime" of the sufferer read "The King of the Jews."

**28. What were "the Seven Words from the Cross"?** The seven times which Christ is recorded to have spoken, while he hung upon the cross. They were: (1) Luke 23:34, (2) Luke 23:43, (3) John 19:26, 27, (4) Matt. 27:46, (5) John 19:28, (6) John 19:30, (7) Luke 23:46.

**29. What signs accompanied the crucifixion?** A great darkness from noon till three o'clock; the rending in twain of the veil of the temple, and of the rocks of the earth.

**30. Where and by whom was Jesus buried?** Joseph of Arimathea, until then a secret disciple, begged his body from Pilate, and laid it in his own new tomb.

**31. What happened on Saturday of this week?** The disciples rested, because it was the sabbath; and the Jews asked and obtained from the Roman governor a watch of soldiers to prevent the disciples from stealing the body.

**100. THE RESURRECTION DAYS (Matt. 28; Mark 16; Luke 24; John 20, 21)**

**1. On what day did Jesus rise?** On Sunday morning of passover week; our Easter Sunday.

**2. Who came early to the tomb, and why?** The women among the closest disciples; to prepare his body with spices for final burial.

**3. What does this prove as to the expectation of the disciples?** It proves conclusively that they did not expect that Jesus would rise again.

**4. What did the women find?** The stone of the tomb rolled away, the sepulchre empty, and an angel who told them that Jesus had risen from the dead.

**5. How many times and for how long did Jesus appear to his disciples after his resurrection?** Eleven times during forty days.

**6. Give them in their order.** (1) To Mary Magdalene on the morning of the resurrection, Sunday, April 9,

A.D. 30. John 20:11–18.

(2) To the women returning from the sepulchre, Sunday morning, April 9. Matt. 28:9, 10.

(3) To Peter alone, Sunday, April 9. Luke 24:34.

(4) To two disciples on the way to Emmaus, Sunday evening, April 9. Luke 24:13–31.

(5) To the ten apostles, Thomas being absent, Sunday evening, April 9. John 20:19–25.

(6) To the eleven apostles. Thomas being present, Sunday evening, April 16. John 20:26–29.

(7) To seven apostles fishing in the Sea of Galilee. The last of April or early in May. John 21:1–24. (It was at this time that Peter was restored to his apostleship.)

(8) To the eleven apostles on a mountain in Galilee. Early in May. Matt. 28:16–20.

(9) To more than five hundred brethren at once. Early in May. 1 Cor. 15:6.

(10) To James alone. May. 1 Cor. 15:7.

(11) To the eleven apostles at his ascension from the Mount of Olives, on Thursday, May 18, A.D. 30. Luke 24:50, 51; Acts 1:1–11.

**7. Did Jesus even appear again to men?** Yes to Paul at his conversion (Acts 9:1–7; 1 Cor. 15:8); and to John the apostle (Rev. 1:13–20).

**8. What is proved by these appearances?** That we worship a living, omnipresent Saviour, who is able and willing to conquer death.

## 101. THE ACTS OF THE APOSTLES. THE CHURCH AT JERUSALEM (Acts 1–7)

**1. Who wrote the Acts?** St. Luke 85. 7.

**2. What is the meaning of "passion" as used here?** Suffering, that is, the crucifixion.

**3. To what does the baptism of the Holy Ghost (Holy Spirit) refer in Acts 1:5?** To the coming of the Holy Spirit at Pentecost. Acts 2.

**4. How did the disciples understand the kingdom of God?** The restoring of the kingdom of David to Israel, with Jesus as king.

**5. What event took place at the close of this conversation?** Jesus ascended into heaven. Acts. 1:9.

**6. What promise did the disciples receive?**
*"This same Jesus, which is taken up from you into heaven, shall so come in like manner as ye have seen him go into heaven." Acts. 1:11.*

**7. To what does this refer?** To the second coming of Christ.

**8. What did the disciples do while they were waiting for the coming of the Holy Spirit?** (1) They had a continual prayer-meeting; (2) they chose by lot an apostle to take the place of Judas.

**9. When was the Day of Pentecost?** "Seven sabbaths," or "fifty days," from the Passover. Lev. 23:16–22; Acts 2:1.

**10. How long was this after the Ascension?** Ten days. See Acts 1:3.

**11. What were the signs of the coming of the Spirit?** (1) A sound as of a rushing, mighty wind; (2) a lame of fire which divided and hovered over each head; (3) a new power—to speak so as to be understood in all languages. Acts. 2:2–4.

**12. How was it that there were Jews "out of every nation"?** Because they were scattered "among all people" as

God had said, for their sins. Deut. 28:64.

**13. How did some explain the phenomenon?** They said the disciples were "full of new wine." Acts. 2:13.

**14. At what time was the "third hour of the day"?** At nine in the morning. Acts 2:15.

**15. Why was it not possible that Jesus should be holden of death?** Because of his divine power, and of the necessity of his body's rising again to prove his Godhead and complete his work.

**16. What is the meaning of "pricked in their heart"?** Having the conscience convinced of sin, and being brought to ask what they should do to be saved.

**17. What was Peter's command to them?** To repent and be baptized in the name of Jesus Christ. Acts 2:38.

**18. How many believed and confessed Christ on this day?** About three thousand. Acts 2:41.

**19. What does "had all things common" mean?** Held all their property at the disposal of the church, so that none need suffer. There is no indication that there was literally "one common stock."

**20. What is "singleness of heart"?** Sincerity.

**21. What time was the ninth hour?** Three in the afternoon.

**22. What attitude was always shown by the apostles to the regular Jewish services of religion?** All through the history we see them obeying exactly all the laws of their Jewish religion; and attending services in the temple and synagogues. They never broke with Judaism until they were driven out.

**23. Why was the miracle in Acts 3 especially notable?** Because the man was over forty years old, and had been lame from birth.

**24. To whom did Peter attribute the power which worked the miracle?** To Jesus Christ, and faith in his name.

**25. Who was the prophet predicted by Moses?** Jesus Christ, to despise whom would be to despise God who sent him. Luke 10:16.

**26. What was the effect of the miracle on the leaders of the Jews?** They were "grieved" at what the apostles taught the people and arrested them. Acts 4:1–3.

**27. Why were the Sadducees especially grieved?** They believed that there was no resurrection of the dead. Matt. 22:23; Acts 23:8.

**28. What in Peter and John most surprised the Jewish rulers?** That they, though of the "peasant class" were bold to proclaim their faith to their rulers. Acts 4:13.

**29. How does this fulfill the promise in Luke 12:11, 12?** Christ had promised that when brought before rulers "the Holy Ghost" would teach his disciples what to say.

**30. What general principle is laid down in Acts 4:19, 20?** That "we ought to obey God rather than men." See also Acts 5:29.

**31. What followed the release of the apostles?** Another downpouring of the Holy Spirit, and great power to the church.

**32. What spirit of generosity prevailed?** No one was needy, for those that had money or lands gave what was needed for the help of the poor.

**33. Why should there be need of this?** (1) Most of the converts were among the poorer class. (2) Converts from other countries would wish to stay and learn more, but could not support themselves there for long.

**34. What was the sin of Ananias?** He "sold a possession" ostensibly to give the money to the church. He then gave a part of the money, representing it to be the whole, that so he might have honor from the church, without entirely depriving himself. Acts. 5:1–6.

**35. What was the real sin of Ananias?** His lying not only unto man, but unto God.

**36. Could Sapphira have escaped punishment?** Yes, if she had answered Peter's question honestly. Acts 5:7–10.

**37. What was the result to the church?** Great fear, and great power, so that the leaders were again arrested. Act 5:11–18.

**38. Who delivered them from prison?** An angel, who commanded them to continue preaching. Acts. 5:19–21.

**39. Who was Gamaliel, and what was his advice?** A very learned man, a leader and teacher, or rabbi, of the Jews. He advised the council to let the apostles alone, for if the new teaching was not of God if would die of itself; if it was of God they could not overthrow it.

**40. What dispute now arose?** Some of the poor believers thought the food and other aid was not fairly distributed. Acts 6:1.

**41. How was the matter settled?** They chose "seven men of honest report," both Hebrews and Grecians, to have charge of this work and leave the apostles free for their especial work.

**42. Which of these men became prominent in other ways?** Stephen (Acts 6; 7) and Philip (Acts 8).

**43. What do we know about Stephen?** He "did wonders and miracles," and preached and argued for the gospel with wonderful power.

**44. What was the result?** The leaders of the Jews were so angry at his preaching that they stoned him; and he was the first martyr of the Christian church.

**45. What followed Stephen's death?** A great persecution which scattered the disciples, and really opened the way for the new era of the church. Acts 8:1.

**46. How long was this after Jesus' death?** About six years.

**102. THE ACTS OF THE APOSTLES. THE ERA OF HOME MISSIONS: ALL OVER PALESTINE (Acts 8–12)**

**1. Did the apostles leave Jerusalem at the time of this persecution?** No, they remained.

**2. How did the persecution defeat its own object?** The scattered ones everywhere preached the word. Acts 8:4.

**3. Who was one of the more prominent among the persecutors?** "A young man . . . whose name was Saul." Acts 7:58; 8:1, 3. See question 12, next page.

**4. What was Philip's first work?** He went to Samaria and preached with great success. Acts 6:5; 8:5–13.

**5. Who especially is named among the converts?** A sorcerer named Simon.

**6. Who went to Samaria to help in the work?** Peter and John. Acts 8:14–25.

**7. What happened after they arrived?** The new converts received the Holy Spirit.

**8. What was Simon's intention in offering Peter money?** That he might have the power of giving the Holy Spirit.

**9. What was Philip's next work?** To preach to the Ethiopian Eunuch. Acts 8:26–40.

**10. What more do we know of this man?** He was Court Treasurer for Queen Candace of Meroe; in Ethiopia; he was a Jewish proselyte; he was an earnest seeker after truth; he believed in Christ and was baptized.

**11. What commission did Saul receive?** To go to Damascus to arrest followers of Christ. Acts 9:1, 2.

**12. What vision did he see?** A bright light from heaven, and the voice of Jesus asking "Saul, Saul, why persecutest thou me?" Acts 9:3–30.

**13. What proof is there of Saul's immediate conversion?** His addressing Jesus as his Lord, and asking what he would have him do.

**14. What was the most striking change that had taken place in Saul?** His praying as a follower of Christ.

**15. Where did Saul obtain the ability to preach with the power recorded in verse 22?** "By the revelation of Jesus Christ" (Gal. 1:11, 12), added to his great natural ability as an orator.

**16. How did he escape the Jews of Damascus?** He was let down over the city wall in a basket.

**17. Why did Saul go to Tarsus?** The Jews tried to kill him, and Tarsus was his boyhood home.

**18. Why had the churches rest at this time?** The Jews were themselves much vexed by the Romans.

**19. What miracle of Peter's is next recorded?** The cure of a bedridden man at Lydda. Acts 9:32–35.

**20. Who was Dorcas?** A benevolent woman of Joppa who died and was restored to life by Peter. Acts 9:36–42.

**21. With whom did Peter live in Joppa?** Simon, a tanner. Acts 9:43.

**22. Why do we think he was a disciple?** Because the Jews greatly despised the trade of tanning and Peter was still a strict Jew.

**23. What is a centurion?** An officer of 100 men in the Roman army; about like our captain.

**24. What vision came to Cornelius?** An angel who told him to send for Peter. Acts 10:1–6.

**25. Where was Peter when the messenger arrived?** On the housetop where he had gone to pray. Acts 10:9–21.

**26. Why was the housetop convenient for prayer?** The houses there have flat roofs surrounded by a parapet.

**27. What vision did Peter have?**
*He saw "a great sheet knit at the four corners, and let down to the earth: wherein were all manner of four-footed beasts of the earth, and wild beasts, and creeping things, and fowls of the air. And there came voice to him, Rise, Peter; kill and eat."*

**28. What did Peter mean by "unclean"?** Forbidden by the Jewish law to be eaten.

**29. Why was the vision thrice repeated?** To make the lesson more emphatic.

**30. What was there strange in the visit of Peter to Cornelius?** Jews were forbidden by their law to visit Gentiles. It was for this that the vision had come to Peter. Acts 10:22–48.

**31. Were not the Jews very slow to**

**realize the calling in of the Gentiles?**
Yes, even believers in Jesus "were astonished" to find that "God also to the Gentiles" had "granted repentance unto life." Acts 10:45; 11:18.

**32. Where next was the gospel preached?** At Antioch in Syria. Acts 11:20.

**33. Who was sent there by the church at Jerusalem?** Barnabas. Acts 11:22.

**34. Whom did Barnabas get to help him?** Saul. Acts 11:25, 26.

**35. What name was given to the disciples at Antioch?** Christians. Acts 11:26.

**36. Under whom did the persecution again begin?** Under "Herod the King."

**37. What Herod was this?** Herod Agrippa I, grandson of Herod the Great, who was "king of Judea" when Jesus was born.

**38. What did he do?** He "killed James the brother of John with the sword" and put Peter in prison, expecting to kill him also. Acts 12:1–4.

**39. Which was the strongest, the prison or the prayers of the church?** Prayer. Acts 12:5–19.

**40. Did the Christians expect his release?** It seems not. Perhaps they were praying more for his steadfastness than for his release.

**41. What is the meaning of the word "examined" in verse 19?** Scourged to make them confess the truth. Acts 22:24.

**42. What example of pride follows?** Herod's being pleased with the gross flattery of his people, and being instantly and dreadfully punished by God. Acts 12:21–23.

**43. From what place and to what place did Barnabas and Saul "return"?** To Antioch from Jerusalem, whither they had gone to carry money from the church at Antioch for the poor Christians at Jerusalem. Acts 11:27–30; 12:25.

**103. THE ACTS OF THE APOSTLES. THE ERA OF FOREIGN MISSIONS: THE FIRST MISSIONARY JOURNEY (Acts 13:1–15:25)**

**1. Who were the first foreign missionaries?** Barnabas and Saul. Acts 13:1–3.

**2. Who sent them out?** The church at Antioch.

**3. What does "laid their hands on them" mean?** Consecrated them to this particular work.

**4. Whom did they take with them as helper?** John Mark. Acts 13:5; 12:25.

**5. Where did they go first?** Through Cyprus, Barnabas' early home. It is an island south of Asia Minor.

**6. What special event of interest occurred there?** Elymas the sorcerer tried to undo their work; and Saul rebuked him. Acts 13:8–12.

**7. Why was Saul's name changed to Paul?** Saul was Hebrew, and Paul, Latin. It was common to have a name in each language and to use the Latin name among Gentiles.

**8. Where did the missionaries go next?** To Perga on the southern shore of Asia Minor. Acts 13:13.

**9. What happened here?** Mark left them and returned to Jerusalem.

**10. What was their next stopping place?** Antioch in Pisidia. Acts 13:14–52.

**11. What shows that they kept the Jewish law?** They went to the Jewish synagogue on the Jewish sabbath.

**12. What illustration of the custom of the synagogue service have we here?** It was the custom for any one present to be asked to read or speak. See Luke 4:16.

**13. What did Paul call the gospel message?** "The word of salvation," "glad tidings," and "forgiveness of sins."

**14. Was the gospel preached at this time only to the Jews?** Hitherto only to the Jews. Here it was also preached to the Gentiles.

**15. What was the result of preaching to the Gentiles?** The bigoted Jews aroused the people, and expelled Paul and Barnabas.

**16. Where did they go?** First to Iconium (Acts 14:1–5); and then to Lystra. Acts 14:6, 7.

**17. What miracle did they do in the latter place?** They healed a lame man. Acts 14:8–18.

**18. What did the people of the city do?** They tried to sacrifice to them as gods.

**19. Why did the missionaries leave Lystra, and where did they go?** The Jews incited the people to stone Paul. They went to Derbe, and then retraced their journey. Acts 14:19–28.

**20. What question now arose in the church?** Whether Gentiles could become Christians without first becoming Jewish proselytes. Acts 15:1–31.

**21. What was the effect upon Paul and Barnabas?** They firmly withstood the idea of the necessity of becoming Jews.

**22. What was the witness of God to the disciples?** The giving them the Holy Spirit.

**23. How is the Jewish ceremonial law spoken of?** As a "yoke" that it was difficult to bear.

**24. Why did they so strenuously resist the rite of circumcision for the Gentiles?** It would be hard for the Christians to be obliged to keep all the Jewish law; and most probably only a few Gentiles would be won if that condition were made.

**25. Who was the Simeon here spoken of?** Simon Peter.

**26. To what conclusion did the apostles come?** To lay upon the disciples no greater burden of Jewish ceremonial law than the abstaining from some things that were chiefly connected with polluted idol-worship.

**104. THE ACTS OF THE APOSTLES. THE ERA OF FOREIGN MISSIONS: THE SECOND MISSIONARY JOURNEY (Acts 15:36–18:23)**

**1. Why did Barnabas and Paul separate now?** Because Paul felt it better not to take Mark with them again. Acts 15:36–39.

**2. Who went with Paul?** Silas. Acts 15:40.

**3. Where did they go first?** To the cities in Asia Minor where the first churches had been formed. Acts 15:41.

**4. Whom did Paul find in Lystra?** Timothy, who became Paul's help. Acts 16:1–3.

**5. Why did Paul circumcise Timothy when he had so earnestly opposed circumcision of new converts?** Timothy was half a Jew, and as such would have no influence in winning the Jews unless he was circumcised. Also, the missionaries did many things, for the sake of their work, which they did not require from the ordinary converts.

**6. What word of Paul in his epistles is illustrated in this incident?** *"I am made all things to all men, that I might by all means save some." 1 Cor. 9:22.*

**7. What vision did Paul have in Troas?** *"There stood a man of Macedonia, and prayed him saying, Come over into Macedonia, and help us." Acts 16:9.*

**8. What great difference was made by Paul's heeding this call?** The gospel was preached in Europe during the first generation of the Christian church.

**9. Who became a Christian in Philippi?** Lydia, a rich business woman. Acts 16:13–15.

**10. What girl did Paul often meet in the streets?** A slave girl who was "possessed with a spirit of divination." Acts 16:16–18.

**11. What is the meaning of "divination" and "sooth-saying"?** Pretended knowledge of future events and fortune telling.

**12. How does the account show that the deliverance from the evil spirit was a reality?** The "masters saw that the hope of their gains was gone." Acts 16:19.

**13. What was done with Paul and Silas?** They were accused before the magistrates, beaten, and put in prison with their feet in the stocks. Acts 16:19–24.

**14. What happened during the night?** A great earthquake opened the prison doors. Acts 16:25–34.

**15. Why was the jailer going to kill himself?** If his prisoners had escaped as he supposed, he would be put to death as a traitor. See Acts 12:19.

**16. What do his words in verse 30 mean?** He wished to become a follower of the leader who could do such wonders.

**17. Why did Paul not accept the release offered him?** Because they were both Roman citizens, and had been wrongly treated. Acts 16:35–40.

**18. What was the privilege of being a Roman?** Not to be bound or punished without a regular trial.

**19. Where did Paul go after leaving Philippi?** To Thessalonica, modern Salonica, in Macedonia. Acts 17:1.

**20. Why did he leave there?** The Jews raised a mob against him and other Christians. Acts 17:5–10.

**21. What is meant by the people of Beroea being more noble than others?** They were more ready to search the Scriptures and see if Paul spoke what was true. Acts 17:11.

**22. Did the Jews persecute Paul here also?** Yes, Jews from Thessalonica. Acts 17:13.

**23. Where did Paul then go?** To Athens, the capital of Greece. Acts 17:15–34.

**24. Before what important body did Paul speak at Athens?** Before the Areopagus, which had the power to determine whether a religion should be preached or not.

**25. What does "too superstitious" mean here?** It should read, as in the Revised Versions, "very religious."

**26. How were they "very religious"?** There were altars in Athens to almost or quite every known god and goddess. Then, lest they had inadvertently omitted one, they erected an altar "To an Unknown God."

**27. What does Paul preach in verse 26?** The natural brotherhood of all men.

**28. Who is to be the final judge of all men?** God by Jesus Christ.

**29. Who appoints the Day of Judgment?** God himself.

**30. Did the Athenians believe in a future life?** Very few of them did.

**31. What city did Paul visit next?** Corinth, also in Greece. Acts 18:1.

**32. What helpers did he find there?** Priscilla and Aquila, from Rome.

**33. Were the Jews now in favor with the Romans?** No, they had been expelled from Rome. Acts 18:2.

**34. How did Paul support himself here?** As a tentmaker. Acts 18:3; 20:34.

**35. How was he treated here?** The Jews opposed him and blasphemed. Acts 18:6.

**36. What then did he do?** He turned to the Gentiles.

**37. How long did Paul stay in Corinth?** At least a year and a half. Acts 18:11.

**38. Why did the Greeks beat Sosthenes rather than Paul?** Perhaps because Paul was a Roman citizen; perhaps in general hatred of the Jews because they had brought an accusation against Paul for preaching to the Gentiles. Acts 18:12–17.

**39. What is meant by "Gallio cared for none of these things"?** Considered disputes concerning the Jewish religion of too small account for him to be troubled with.

**40. What of Paul's Epistles were written at this time?** Those to the Thessalonians. See 107. 3–9.

**41. What act of Paul shows that he still kept the Jewish law?** His making a vow and shaving his head. Acts 18:18.

**105. THE ACTS OF THE APOSTLES. THE ERA OF FOREIGN MISSIONS: THE THIRD MISSIONARY JOURNEY (Acts 18:23–21:16)**

**1. What Epistle did Paul write while at Antioch before this journey?** Galatians. See 107. 10–15.

**2. What is the meaning of "mighty in the Scriptures" as distinguished from "eloquence"?** Well acquainted with them, and enabled to understand them, and to teach them by the Holy Spirit. Acts 18:24–28.

**3. What is meant by "knowing only the baptism of John"?** He had not heard of the baptism of the Holy Spirit at Pentecost.

**4. Where did Paul first stop on this journey?** At Ephesus in Asia Minor. Acts 19:1.

**5. How long a visit did he make there at this time?** About three years. Acts 19:1–20.

**6. What success did he have there?** Not many Jews believed, but the Gentiles came in large numbers.

**7. What example of practical repentance is shown?** The fortune-tellers and others burned their books that were the means of their profits, and of their sin.

**8. Was the worship of Diana a costly service?** Yes, her temple was filled with ornaments and gifts.

**9. What caused the great uproar in Ephesus?** A riot led by the silversmiths who feared that their business would be destroyed if Paul's preaching continued. Acts 19:23–41.

**10. Were the Jews held in honor at Ephesus?** No, for they despised all idolatry.

**11. What were the deputies?** Judges appointed by the Romans.

**12. What Epistle was written during this visit to Ephesus?** Paul's first Epistle to the Corinthians. See 107. 16–24.

**13. Where did Paul go from Ephesus?** To revisit the churches in Macedonia. Acts 19:21, 22; 20:1.

**14. What Epistle did he write while there?** The second Epistle to the Corinthians. 107. 25–28.

**15. Did he visit Corinth again?** Yes, and spent three months there. Acts 20:2, 3.

**16. What Epistle did Paul write during this visit to Corinth?** The Epistle to the Romans. See 107. 29, 30.

**17. Why did so many of the Christians accompany him to Jerusalem?** As delegates to the mother church, and to carry to her the gifts from the Gentile churches of Macedonia and Asia Minor. See Rom. 15:26; 1 Cor. 16:1–5; Acts 24:17.

**18. What incident is recorded of the stop at Troas?** A young man named Eutychus, overpowered by sleep, fell from a window of the third story, and was taken up dead. But he was restored to life by Paul. Acts 20:7–12.

**19. Who met Paul at Miletus?** The elders of the church at Ephesus whom he had summoned. Acts 20:17, 18.

**20. How far was Miletus from Ephesus?** Thirty-six miles.

**21. What did Paul mean by being "pure from the blood of all men"?** That as he had faithfully taught the whole truth

of God his hearers had only themselves to blame if they rejected it and were lost. Acts 20:26, 27.

*"When I say unto the wicked, Thou shalt surely die; and thou givest him not warning, nor speakest to warn the wicked from his wicked way, to save his life; the same wicked man shall die in his iniquity; but his blood will I require at thine hand." Ezek. 3:18.*

**22. With whom did Paul stay at Caesarea?** Philip. Acts 21:8. See 102. 4–10.

**23. What was strange about his daughters?** That, at that time, he should have four unmarried; and that they were engaged in active Christian work.

**24. What is meant here by "prophesying"?** Preaching, talking to others openly about the gospel.

**25. What prophecy was spoken to Paul at Caesarea?** That he should be bound at Jerusalem, and delivered into the hands of the Gentiles. Acts 21:11.

**26. What is meant by "took up our carriages"?** An old expression for took our baggage or things carried. Acts 21:15.

**106. THE ACTS OF THE APOSTLES. PAUL THE PRISONER (Acts 21:17–28:31)**

**1. What plan was proposed to Paul, and why?** That he should perform the Jewish rites regarding the Nazarite vow, in order to prove to the Jewish Christians that he was not false to the ancient faith. Acts 21:20–26.

**2. What charge was brought against Paul in the temple?** That he had brought Gentiles into the sacred parts of the temple. Acts 21:28.

**3. Was it true?** No, it was based on

the fact that he and a Gentile had walked together in the city. Acts 21:29.

**4. Who rescued Paul?** The "chief captain" or colonel of the Roman regiment at the Tower of Antonia adjoining the temple. Acts 21:31–36.

**5. What was it in Paul's speech that so provoked the Jews?** Paul's speaking of being sent to the Gentiles. Acts 22:21, 22.

**6. Why was Paul ordered to be scourged?** To make him confess what he had said to so anger the Jews. Acts 22:24.

**7. What saved Paul from this?** His Roman citizenship. Acts 22:25–29.

**8. What danger next confronted Paul?** Forty Jews took an oath to kill him. Acts 23:12–15.

**9. What did the chief captain do when he knew this?** He sent Paul off secretly to Caesarea to the Governor of Palestine. Acts 23:23, 24.

**10. Was the danger from the bigotry of the Jews unimportant?** No, it was thought prudent to give Paul nearly five hundred soldiers as a guard. Acts 23:23.

**11. How far was Caesarea from Jerusalem?** About sixty miles.

**12. Who accused Paul at his trial before Felix?** The high priest and the elders, with Tertullus, a lawyer, as spokesman. Acts 24:1.

**13. Which address to Felix was the more truthful?** The simpler words of Paul, as Felix's government was "a mean, cruel and profligate" one.

**14. How long did Felix keep Paul prisoner?** Two years; as long as he was governor. Acts 24:27.

**15. Did Felix hear Paul preach?** Yes, Paul often preached and talked with Felix. Acts 24:24–26.

**16. Did Paul spare the conscience of Felix?** No, he touched it till it trembled. Acts 24:25.

**17. How does the effect of Paul's reasoning upon Felix illustrate He. 4:12?** *It shows that "the word of God is quick, and powerful, and sharper than any two edged sword, piercing even to the dividing asunder of soul and spirit, and of the joints and marrow, and is a discerner of the thoughts and intents of the heart."*

**18. What mercenary motive influenced Felix?** The hope of a bribe from Paul to release him.

**19. Who succeeded Felix as governor?** Festus. Acts 24:27.

**20. What did the Jews ask of him?** That Paul should be brought to Jerusalem for trial. Acts 25:2, 3.

**21. Why was this request made?** Because they planned to lie in wait for him and kill him.

**22. Where was the trial held?** At Caesarea, the capital. Acts 25:6.

**23. What proposal did Festus make?** That he should take Paul to Jerusalem, and himself preside at his trial there. Acts 25:9.

**24. What was Paul's reply?** That he had done nothing whatever against Jewish law, and should not be judged by the Jews. Acts 25:10.

**25. What privilege of Roman citizenship did Paul claim?** Of having his cause judged at Rome by the Caesar, or his especially appointed representatives. Acts 25:11.

**26. Who was the Caesar referred to?** The Roman emperor or Nero.

**27. Who was this King Agrippa?** The second Herod Agrippa, and Jewish king or viceroy of the country to the north and east of Galilee.

**28. Why did Paul speak before Agrippa?** Festus wished him to hear Paul that he might advise him as to his report to Caesar.

**29. Why did Festus accuse Paul of insanity?** Because he had spoken of a resurrection from the dead.

**30. Who accompanied Paul on his journey to Rome?** Luke ("we" in Acts 27:1), and Aristarchus, a Macedonian. Acts 27:2.

**31. How was Paul treated by the centurion?** With much favor, as he was allowed at Sidon to go and see his friends. Acts 27:3.

**32. At what season was this voyage?** They reached Crete at some time in the latter part of September.

**33. Why was "sailing now dangerous"?** The ships of those days were usually small, and ill-fitted to cope with head winds, or any very strong wind.

**34. What did Paul advise?** That they pass the winter in the harbor where they were. See Acts 27:9–13.

**35. Why should Paul know anything about this matter?** He had done considerable voyaging, and had three times already been shipwrecked. See 2 Cor. 11:25, which was written nearly two years before this voyage to Rome.

**36. Whose advice was taken?** That of the master and the owner of the ship. Acts 27:11.

**37. What was the result?** After being tossed in a terrible tempest for over fourteen days the ship was wrecked on the island of Malta. Acts 27:14; 28:1.

**38. Why did the soldiers advise the killing of the prisoners?** Lest, if any escape, they should incur the penalty of death.

**39. What is the meaning of the term "barbarous," here?** Strange, foreign.

**40. To what did the people of Malta refer by the word vengeance?** Nike, the Greek goddess of vengeance.

**41. What was Paul's first work at Malta?** To heal the father of Publius, the chief man of the island. Acts 28:8, 9.

**42. What was the result?** They cared for Paul and his companions during the winter, and provided all necessities for them when they again set sail for Rome. Acts 28:10.

**43. What favor was granted to Paul on his arrival at Rome?** He was allowed to dwell as he pleased in a house by himself, only having with him always a soldier who was responsible for him. Acts 28:16.

**44. What was his first act after a brief rest?** He called the leaders of the Roman Jews and preached Christ to them. Acts 28:17–29.

**45. How long did he stay at Rome at this time?** Two years. Acts 28:30.

**46. What epistles did Paul write during these years?** Colossians, Philemon, Ephesians and Philippians.

**47. What was Paul's later history?** Nothing is known with certainty. It is thought, however, that he was released; spent three or four years in preaching in various places, during which time he wrote the first epistle to Timothy, and that to Titus. And then he was again arrested, and imprisoned in Rome, when he wrote the second epistle to Timothy; and then was martyred under Nero.

## 107. THE EPISTLES OF PAUL

**1. Name Paul's Epistles, in the order of the Bible.** Romans, 1 Corinthians, 2 Corinthians, Galatians, Ephesians, Philippians, Colossians, 1 Thessalonians, 2 Thessalonians, 1 Timothy, 2 Timothy, Titus, Philemon.

**2. Name them in the probable order of their writing.** 1 Thessalonians, 2 Thessalonians, Galatians, 1 Corinthians, 2 Corinthians, Romans, Colossians, Philemon, Ephesians, 1 Timothy, Titus, 2 Timothy.

**3. When were the epistles to the Thessalonians written?** During Paul's first visit to Corinth, shortly after his visit to Thessalonica. See 104. 31–40.

**4. What was their principal purpose?** As a comfort and encouragement in their persecution, and in their trouble at the death of some before the second coming of Christ. See 1 Thess. 4:12–18.

**5. What description of the second coming of Christ does Paul give them?** *"For the Lord himself shall descend from heaven with a shout, with the voice of the archangel, and with the trump of God: and the dead in Christ shall rise first: Then we which are alive and remain shall be caught up together with them in the clouds, to meet the Lord in the air: and so shall we ever be with the Lord." 1 Thess. 4:16, 17.*

**6. What is shown by the words "we which are alive"?** That Paul expected the second coming of Christ within his own lifetime, or the lifetime of some of those to whom he was talking.

**7. What confusion did he make?** Between the coming of the new era of the church, which he and others might live to see, and Christ's return to earth to reign.

**8. What did he say of the time in 2 Thess.?** He warns his readers against the idea that the day of the Lord was actually at hand.

**9. What great event must precede it?** *"For that day shall not come, except there come a falling away first, and that man of sin be revealed, the son of perdition"; etc. 2 Thess. 2:3–12.*

**10. When was the Epistle to the Galatians written?** At Antioch, just before Paul started on the third missionary journey. See section 105.1.

**11. Who were the Galatians?** The residents of that part of Asia Minor visited by Paul on his first missionary journey. See 103.

**12. What is the epistle's chief characteristic?** It has been called "the gospel's banner of freedom." It declares that salvation is by Christ alone.

**13. What does Paul describe in Gal. 5:19–21?** The "works of the flesh" against which we must strive if we wish to inherit the kingdom of God.

**14. What is the "fruit of the spirit" which we should show?** *"The fruit of the Spirit is love, joy, peace, long-suffering, gentleness, goodness, faith, meekness, temperance." Gal. 5:22, 23.*

**15. What universal law does Paul give in Gal. 6:7?** *"Be not deceived; God is not mocked: for whatsoever a man soweth, that shall he also reap."*

**16. When was the first epistle to the Corinthians written?** During Paul's long residence in Ephesus. See 105. 4–12.

**17. What was its purpose?** Largely to correct some errors into which the church had fallen.

**18. What in this epistle is most endeared to us?** Perhaps 11:23–26, Paul's account of the Lord's Supper; 13:1–13, the chapter on love; 15:1–58, the wonderful chapter on the resurrection; and many other shorter passages.

**19. What strong reason for purity does Paul give in this epistle?** *"Know ye not that ye are the temple of God, and that the Spirit of God dwelleth in you? If any man defile the temple of God, him shall God destroy; for the temple of God is holy, which temple ye are."* 1 Cor. 3:16, 17. See also 6:19, 20.

**20. Who is the Apollos mentioned here?** The Apollos who is mentioned in the Acts as in Ephesus and Corinth; a strong man and valued leader in the early church.

**21. What great renunciation does Paul make in the eighth chapter?** *Wherefore, if meat make my brother to offend, I will eat no flesh while the world standeth, lest I make my brother to offend."* 1 Cor. 8:13.

**22. Is this a model for us?** It surely is.

**23. What is the argument of 1 Cor. 15?** That if there is no resurrection Christ did not rise, and those who had given up all earthly good for faith in Christ had lost everything, and gained nothing but a vain dream.

**24. How does Paul picture Christ's second coming here?** That the trumpet shall sound and all believers, both living and dead, shall be changed into their immortal and spiritual forms.

**25. When was the second epistle to the Corinthians written?** From Macedonia, just before his second visit to Corinth. See 105. 13–15.

**26. What is "the ministering to the saints"?** The money which was being collected in Europe and Asia Minor for the poor of Jerusalem and Judea. 2 Cor. 9.

**27. What statement does Paul make which should influence our giving?** *"God loveth a cheerful giver."* 2 Cor. 9:7.

**28. What picture do we get in 2 Cor. 11?** A picture of Paul, who was not robust, living a life of such hardship as few of our missionaries have approached—persecutions, dangers of travel by sea and land. Yet with no desire for less, if only he may serve God and Christ the better.

**29. When was the epistle to the Romans written?** From Corinth, during this second visit. See 105. 15–16.

**30. What are some of the most wonderful passages in this epistle?**

*1. "Therefore being justified by faith, we have peace with God through our Lord Jesus Christ." Rom. 5:1.*

*2. "But God commendeth his love toward us, in that, while we were yet sinners, Christ died for us." Rom. 5:8.*

*3. "For the wages of sin is death; but the gift of God is eternal life through Jesus Christ our Lord." 6:23.*

*4. The entire eighth chapter, with its marvelous culmination: "For I am persuaded that neither death, nor life, nor angels, nor principalities, nor powers, nor things present, nor things to come, nor height, nor depth, nor any other creature, shall be able to separate us from the love of God, which is in Christ Jesus our Lord." Rom. 8:38, 29.*

*5. Two practical admonitions: "I beseech you therefore, brethren, by the mercies of God, that ye present your bodies a living sacrifice, holy, acceptable unto God, which is your reasonable service." Rom. 12:1.*

*"If thine enemy hunger, feed him; if he thirst, give him drink: for in so doing thou shalt heap coals of fire on his head." Rom. 12:20.*

**31. Where is the last admonition quoted also found?** In Proverbs 25:21, 22.

**32. When were the epistles to the Colossians, to Philemon, to the Ephesians, and to the Philippians written?** During Paul's first imprisonment in Rome, that recorded in the Acts. See Section 106. 43–46.

**33. What was the purpose of that to Philemon?** To urge him to receive with kindness his runaway slave Onesimus, who had been won to Christ by Paul.

**34. What is especially interesting about Philippians?** It was written to the first Christian church Paul founded on the continent of Europe.

**35. What special appeal does Paul make in this epistle?** To humbleness of mind by the example of Christ, who gave up all that he might serve men.

**36. What is the best-known chapter in Ephesians?** The sixth; especially the part, "Put on the whole armor of God."

**37. What are the three epistles to Timothy and Titus called, and why?** "The Pastoral Epistles"; because they contain Paul's admonitions and advice to these younger pastors.

**38. What epistle contains the last words of Paul, so far as it recorded?** Second Timothy.

*"For I am now ready to be offered, and the time of my departure is at hand. I have fought a good fight, I have finished my course, I have kept the faith; henceforth there is laid up for me a crown of righteousness, which the Lord, the righteous judge, shall give me at that day: and not to me only, but unto all them also that love his appearing . . . The Lord shall deliver me from every evil work and will preserve me unto his heavenly kingdom; to whom be glory for ever and ever. Amen." 2 Tim. 4:6–8, 18.*

## 108. THE EPISTLE TO THE HEBREWS

**1. Who wrote this epistle?** It used to be ascribed to Paul, but later evidence has questioned that. It is not certain to whom it should be ascribed.

**2. When was it written?** Probably just before the destruction of Jerusalem in 70 A.D.

**3. What was its purpose?** It was written to show that Christianity was the flower and culmination of the old Judaic ritual and symbolism; that Christ was the fulfillment of the symbols, a greater and everlasting High Priest, yet nearer and tenderer to his followers.

*"Seeing then that we have a great high priest, that is passed into the heavens. Jesus the Son of God, let us hold fast our profession. For we have not an high priest which cannot be touched with the feeling of our infirmities; but was in all points tempted like as we are, yet without sin. Let us therefore come boldly unto the throne of grace, that we may obtain mercy, and find grace to help in time of need." Heb. 4:14–16.*

**4. What does the first chapter prove?** That Christ, the Son of God, is greater than the angels, yea, even, he is God himself.

**5. What has the eleventh of Hebrews been called?** The roll-call of the faithful; the honor-roll of Israel.

**6. What conclusion does the writer draw from this honor-roll?**

*"Wherefore seeing we also are compassed about with so great a cloud of witnesses, let us lay aside every weight, and the sin which doth so easily beset us, and let us run with patience the race that is set before us, looking unto Jesus the author and finisher of our faith."* Heb. 12:1, 2.

**7. How is Jesus characterized in the thirteenth chapter?**

*"Jesus Christ the same yesterday, and today, and for ever." Heb. 13:8.*

## 109. THE EPISTLE OF JAMES

**1. Who was the author of this epistle?** The James called "the Lord's brother," who was for many years the head of the church at Jerusalem. He was not one of the Apostles.

**2. When was it written?** Probably shortly before his martyrdom, which was in A.D. 63.

**3. What are the leading ideas in the Epistle?** "Faith without works is dead"; and "Have not the faith of our Lord Jesus Christ with respect of persons."

## 110. THE EPISTLES OF PETER

**1. From what place was the first epistle written?** From "Babylon" (1 Pet. 5:13); but whether that means the famous Babylon in Asia, or, mystically, heathen Rome, is not known.

**2. Who was the author?** The apostle Peter.

**3. What is its date?** Between A.D.

63 and 67. Because 1 Peter makes use of Paul's Epistle to the Ephesians, written in A.D. 62 or 63, and Peter himself was martyred in A.D. 67.

**4. What was its purpose?** To comfort and strengthen the Christians during persecution; and to show the superiority of the gospel over the law on its true basis— that of spiritual development.

## 111. THE EPISTLES OF JOHN

**1. What John is this?** The Apostle John, the apostle of love.

**2. How many of the epistles are there?** Three.

**3. When were they written?** Near the close of the first century A.D.

**4. To whom were they written?** It is not known to whom the first Epistle was written. The second was addressed to an individual woman; and the third to Gaius, a layman of Ephesus.

**5. What was the purpose of their writing?** The first to declare the word of life in order that he and those he is addressing might be united in true communion with each other, and with God. The second was written to warn the lady against abetting a particular form of false doctrine. The third to serve as a letter of introduction for some Christian strangers.

**6. What is the especial characteristic of the first epistle of John?** Its frequent use of the word "love" both in description and exhortation: the love of Christ to us, and the love we should bear to him.

*"We love him because he first loved us." 1 John 4:19.*

## 112. THE EPISTLE OF JUDE

**1. Who was the author of this epistle?** Probably Judas, one of the brethren of Jesus. Matt. 13:55.

**2. When and to whom was it written?** Somewhere between A.D. 63 and 80, to the church at Antioch, in Syria; the first Christian church.

**3. Why was it written?** Because adversaries of the faith had crept into the church.

**4. To whom does he refer in verse 14?** To the patriarch Enoch. 4. 3–6.

**5. To what event does it refer?** To the second coming of Christ.

**6. Is this second coming spoken of in other parts of the Bible?** Yes, in 1 Thess. 4:16, 17, and fifty other places at least.

**7. What was the purpose of his coming?** To judge the world.

**8. Do we know when the Lord Jesus is coming?** No, Christ told us he would come "as a thief in the night."

**9. What effect would this uncertainty have on us?** We should "be diligent that we may be found of him . . . without spot and blameless."

## 113. THE REVELATION

**1. Who was the author of this book?** It is not certain, but probably the Apostle John.

**2. What is the meaning of the name?** "The unveiling of the mysteries of the unseen world."

**3. When and where was it written?** At Patmos, an island in the Aegean Sea, during a severe persecution. Probably during the time of Nero, A.D. 64–68 or the reign of Domitian, A.D. 90–96.

**4. Why was it written?** To give hope and guidance in hours of persecution and trial.

**5. From what sources did John take his imagery?** From Ezekiel, Daniel, Matthew 25, and several Jewish writings on similar subjects.

**6. Can it be explained?** Some of it is clear and easy to explain; but much of it is too symbolic. It is, in brief, the warfare of good and evil, with the ultimate triumph of good; the second coming of Christ, and the beginning of the heavenly kingdom. But no especial application to definite historical tacts can be made, and each of the many interpretations differs from all the rest.

**7. What promises are found in chapters 2 and 3?** Seven promises to "him that overcometh" the temptations and trials of earth. These promises are symbolical. Rev. 2:7, 11, 17, 26–28; 3:5, 12, 21.

**8. What is referred to in chapter 5?** The book of life, in which all the names of Christ's true followers are written, and which can be opened only by Christ himself, the "Lamb as it had been slain."

**9. What is the substance of the "New Song"?** Worthy is the Lamb to receive all power and honor, since he was slain to redeem mankind from the curse of sin.

**10. What shows that this redemption is for all mankind?** The multitude which had "washed their robes in the blood of the Lamb" was one "which no man could number, of all nations and kindreds and peoples and tongues." Rev. 7:9–14.

**11. What is promised to the followers of Christ?** They shall suffer neither hunger nor thirst, the most common of troubles; nor heat, which was often a cause of sickness in that semi-tropical land; nor tears—sorrow nor crying.

**12. What city is described in chapters 21 and 22?** The city of God, the capital of the Kingdom of God, in which God shall dwell among his people forever.

**13. Is the description literal or symbolical?** It is symbolical. We are not yet sufficiently spiritual to understand a literal description of such a city. It has characteristics of which we have here on earth no hint or parallel. The writer therefore takes the richest, and most beautiful, and most admired things of earth to symbolize the beauty, glory and grandeur of the city of God.

**14. Is there anything in its description which we can take literally?** Yes—much.

It is to come after the world has finally triumphed over evil. It is to be a place of joy and blessedness. God is to dwell in it himself. In it shall enter nothing evil. It has a place for everyone who wishes to enter.

*"Blessed are they that do his commandments, that they may have right to the tree of life, and may enter in through the gates into the city . . . And the Spirit and the bride say, Come . . . And let him that is athirst come. And whosoever will, let him take the water of life freely.*

*"He which testifieth these things saith, Surely I come quickly. Amen. Even so, come, Lord Jesus." Rev. 22:14, 17, 20.*

# GENERAL HINTS ON BIBLE STUDY

## Get Acquainted with the People in the Bible

Getting acquainted with the people in the Bible is a great thing. Ask your teacher to give you a list of persons to read about and then take up your Bible and hunt for them. Soon you will know something about Abraham, Isaac, Jacob, Esau, Moses, Aaron, Miriam, Joshua, Samuel, Eli, David, Saul, Jonathan, Solomon, Jonah, Daniel, and the three children of Israel who went into the fiery furnace. These persons are all in the Old Testament.

In the New Testament you will learn about Joseph, Mary, John the Baptist, Herod, Nicodemus, Peter, Judas, and, best of all, you will read the life of Jesus and how He came to earth to die on the Cross that all men might be saved. You will also learn about the great apostle Paul and the way in which he went about telling men how they might become children of God.

When you read about these men and women of the Bible try to make up in your mind a little story about them containing all the chief points that you have read.

## Find and Learn the Great Stories of the Bible

These stories are very wonderful indeed, because each of them points to a great moral. Each will help you later on when you take up a wider and larger study of the Bible. Take, for instance, the story of David and Jonathan. This will show you what a great thing is true friendship. Take also the story of Belshazzar's feast. This is one that will show the danger and punishment of sin.

In the New Testament look up the passages that tell of the boyhood of Jesus, how His earthly parents were forced to flee with Him from Palestine into Egypt to escape the men Herod had sent to murder Him, and how later on He was brought back. Seek out also the story of the first miracle and see for yourself for what a beautiful and kindly reason Jesus performed it.

Hunt also for the Sermon on the Mount and read the important things Jesus said in it. Next find the story about Jesus going up to Jerusalem for the last time and telling His disciples that He was to be crucified, and how Judas Iscariot sold His Master to death.

This will bring you to the story of how Jesus died, how His mother wept over Him and how the tomb wherein He was placed was watched, how it was found that He had risen from the dead and how He appeared to His wondering disciples.

Then you can turn to the life of the apostle Paul. Here you will see what a very great man this Paul was, how he persecuted the Christians and yet was called by God to go out into the world and spread the Gospel, how he realized what a great wrong

137

he had done and how he obeyed God's command, and how God made him one of the most remarkable persons in the Bible. These are only a few of the marvelous stories that you will read in God's Holy Book.

Always try to get everything exact. Don't read two stories at once. Finish one before you start another. Try to find in each story the particular lesson that it teaches, because there is no story in the Bible that does not teach a lesson. Learn to spell all the names that you find, even if you have to sit down and write a name out two or three times to get it fixed in your memory.

Another good way to get information about the Bible is to ask questions of your teacher. If something comes along in the lesson or what you have been reading that you don't quite understand, ask your teacher about it.

## Jesus, the Great Objective of the Bible Study

Another good thing to study is the list of miracles performed by Jesus. Each one has its particular story and moral. Read also Jesus' parables and study them. The parables were told by Jesus for the purpose of teaching a lesson and He told them quite as much for you as He did for the people that listened to Him tell them.

One great and important thing that you must never forget in reading and studying the Bible is to learn all about Jesus. If you don't learn this all your study of the Book of Books is not worth very much. You must understand that Jesus spoke as He spoke and acted as He acted for a very wonderful purpose. He promises that all who believe on Him will have everlasting life.

# THE BIBLE AS A BASIS OF RELIGIOUS BELIEF

## Foundation Teachings of the Bible

Every denomination that teaches Christianity, or the religion of Jesus Christ, bases itself on the Holy Bible. No system or creed calling itself Christian has been able to live without the Bible. This is because of two reasons. The first is that without it it would be impossible to tell of our Lord and Master, Jesus Christ, and the second reason is that no written book has ever been able to set forth the folly of being sinful and the wisdom of being good as has the Bible. From first to last it points out that sin always meets with punishment and that goodness meets with reward. This is the basis of every religion that is really a religion, and the Bible teaches it better than any other book.

In the Old Testament we are told that God chose the Jews as His own people, that is, the race of men He selected to do the things that He wanted them to do and to show others what a great and mighty God He was, so that they too might believe on Him. For doing this He promised to give them certain rewards. But they, in their pride and wickedness, failed. God then withdrew His promise and punished the Jews, sending them into captivity among their enemies and taking away from them their standing as a nation. Thus was sin chastised.

In the New Testament we are told of a new promise that God made. This time, instead of picking out one race of men, as He had with the Jews, He made the promise to all races. This promise was that all who would believe in His Son, who would be sent to earth to mingle with mankind and to live mankind's life, would have everlasting life.

Under God's promise in the Old Testament, man's sins were wiped out in the blood of animals that were offered up as sacrifices. In the New Testament and under the new promise the Son that He sent to Earth was to be the sacrifice, once and for all. Therefore, God ordained that His Son, Jesus, was to die upon the cross, thus shedding His blood, as the animals had shed theirs, for the sins of the world. All that was necessary for man, under this promise of God, was that man should believe that Jesus was the Son of God, and to follow His teachings. Thus was goodness rewarded.

This, in brief, is the whole of Bible teaching. Upon it the religious faith of all Christians is based. Following it no one can go astray, since it is God's own word laid down in His most Holy Book.

## General Bible Teachings

But there are many other things taught in the Bible as well as this. There are lessons of patience, forbearance, honesty, virtue, truthfulness, love, charity and a thousand other graces of character in the Book of Books.

Starting at the beginning we learn of the creation of the world and man. God had a great purpose in view when He made man "in His own image." He wanted man to live in a beautiful paradise, with every thing he could wish for at his command, but at the same time He wanted man to be good.

So God gave Adam, the first man, certain commands. Had man obeyed them, all would have gone well. But man disobeyed and was punished, by having "to earn his bread by the sweat of his brow," that is, by work, and by having to show God that he was worthy of the good things God had offered by being sorry for his sin and showing that sorrow by being righteous.

But man continued to be sinful and God punished him again by sending the flood. Still man was given a chance, because Noah and his family were saved to re-populate the earth. Then, after a while God chose one of Noah's descendants, Abraham, and made a promise to him and his children and their children. This was the choosing of the Jews.

Next we find God doing all that He could be expected to do in helping the Jews. He saved them from the bondage of the Egyptians and aided them in their wanderings through the wilderness toward the land of Canaan, which He told them would be their own. He gave them the Ten Commandments, the greatest and yet the simplest set of laws ever made, but still man persisted in disobeying.

Through hundreds of years we follow the Jews in the Old Testament as they disobeyed God. God was very patient, but finally he set His face against the Jews and punished them. He delivered them over to their enemies and sent them into captivity, because they had sinned. Then He had pity on them again and sent to them the great prophets, such as Isaiah, Jeremiah, Hosea, and the others whose words we read in the Bible. They exhorted the Jews to repentance, and told them what God would do if they were good and what He would do if were bad. But the Jews did not heed and were further punished by losing their standing as a nation and being placed under the rule of their enemies.

After several hundred years of this, God gave man still another chance. This time He was more generous than ever, because He sent His Son, Jesus, to live among men and to die for them.

We find the story of Jesus' life and teachings in the New Testament. Always sinless, always good, always thinking of His Father in heaven, always mindful of His human brethren, the Son of God lived His earthly life, and perished on the cross at Calvary, giving His life as an everlasting sacrifice for the redemption of the creatures God had made so many, many ages before "in His own image."

And then after the death and resurrection of Jesus we are told of the devoted band of apostles, chosen by Jesus Himself, to go out into the world and preach His religion. He set down only two or three rules, but they were great ones. "Believe in me and ye shall have everlasting life," "Do unto others as ye would have them do unto you," and "Love me and keep my commandments" were the things He ordered. Never did He turn a repentant sinner away, knowing that His Father would not do so. Thus is God constantly giving men chances to save themselves, as He has done from the time He first put Adam on earth. This, then, is the basic teaching of the Bible: that man always has a chance if he will repent of his sins and obey God's laws.

# A SHORT HISTORY OF THE HOLY BIBLE

## The Age of the Bible

The Holy Bible is not only the greatest and best of all books, but it is also the oldest. Its history has been very difficult to trace, yet the same Divine guidance that set its authors to work to write it has made Christians delve into the mists of the past to learn all about it. We find out more about it every day through the research of learned men, and things that are now hidden from us regarding it doubtless will be revealed in the course of time.

As to its authors and age, however, we know a very great deal. It was written by about forty different men and as it comes to us it took about sixteen hundred years to compose. We know pretty accurately that Moses began it about the year 1500 B.C. and that John, who wrote the last book, Revelation, finished it about the year 90 A.D., which estimate fills out the sixteen centuries.

The Bible gets its name from a Greek word which means "the little books." Gradually, in the course of many years, this word came to stand for something more than "little books," of which the Big Book was composed. It came to mean "the book," the "holy book," and finally it came to mean just what it means today—the Holy Book of Books.

This great work is composed of two parts—the Old Testament and the New Testament. The Old Testament has in it thirty-nine books or parts. It contains God's account of the creation of the world, a history of the Jewish people and God's dealings with them, a number of books written by the great Jewish prophets in which are foretold the things that happen in the New Testament, as well as a number of beautiful books of purely a religious character, such as the Psalms.

The men who wrote the Old Testament discontinued working on it about four hundred years before Jesus Christ was born. The New Testament begins with the birth of Jesus and covers a period of about seventy-five years down to the time when the faith of Christianity was being extended by the men Jesus Himself chose to go out into the world and tell about it. The New Testament contains twenty-seven books, four of which are known as Gospels, because they tell particularly of the life of Jesus. Some learned men think the word "gospel" means "God story" or "narrative of God," while some think it means "good story" or "good tidings," because of the tidings of salvation that it brings to those who read it.

## Formation of the Bible and Languages

The student of the Bible must not think that the Book as he reads it is its original form. The men who wrote it did so with much labor, just as letters are now written, and on the things which were used by them just as we use paper. Not until the great

141

art of printing was discovered was it possible to get a Bible such as we have. Instead, readers of the Bible used many thousands of written pages, kept carefully bound together. Of these there were many copies, but not nearly enough to go around among those who wished to possess a copy.

The men who wrote the Bible used two or three different languages. In the Old Testament the older books were written in Hebrew, while others were written in Aramaic, a language somewhat similar to Hebrew. The New Testament was written in a form of the Greek language. From these languages the Bible has been translated into almost every known tongue.

The growth of the Bible from two collections of smaller books into one grand whole was very slow, but God so directed the minds of men that they finally did the work and did it well. This was called forming the canon of Scripture. Canon is a word which means rod or rule. The term applied to the Bible means that it is the rule or form of God's word to mankind; in other words, the way God wants man to read what God has to say to him.

The canon of the Old Testament was formed first. This was done by the Jews themselves, probably about four hundred years before Christ's time. Their learned men gathered together all the nation's sacred writings and under Divine guidance made one work of them. After Jesus died began the preparation of the New Testament by the men God directed to do the work. Then these were also gathered together and councils of religious and wise men discussed them. It took several hundred years to get them arranged in their present form.

Of course, there have been many different translations of the Bible. The first ones were made into Greek and Latin. From the best of these—one called the Septuagint, made at Alexandria, Egypt, about 270 B.C. to 150 B.C.—is the present version of the Old Testament descended.

There are now two chief versions of the Bible printed in English. One is called the Authorized, or King James Version, because it was made by order of an English king, James, in the year 1611. The other version is called the Revised Standard Version. This was published in 1952 and differs from the Authorized Version in the use of some words and phrases which make the meaning a little clearer or which are closer to the meaning in the original languages of the men who wrote the Bible.

The chapter and verse subdivisions of the Bible, the descriptive headings of chapters and the presence of italics, or sloping letters, in the text, did not exist in the original. The division into chapters, which was for greater ease of reading and quotation, was made in the thirteenth century by either Cardinal Hug or Archbishop Langton.

At a later period, probably 1551, one Robert Stephens made the division into verses. They are very imperfect and sometimes greatly obscure the meaning. The presence of italics is due to the fact that in many instances it was necessary to introduce words to make clear a meaning which could not be translated easily, or to supply deficiencies due to differences in language.

## What the Books of the Bible Contain

The Holy Bible is divided into two great parts, called the Old Testament and the New Testament. Each is complete and distinct in itself as far as the subjects treated are concerned, but through both run God's revelation of Himself to man, His promise of salvation through righteousness and His laws and wishes for man to follow.

# NEW PRACTICAL COURSE IN BIBLE READING

## JOS. V. COLLINS, Ph.D.

## I. INTRODUCTION

The Bible is the greatest book in the world. It is interesting, highly instructive, and should be a handbook for all. As religion is the true basis for morals, no individual and no state is safe whose philosophy is not grounded in religious truth. All citizens should themselves know the foundation principles of right living in family, state, nation, and the world.

Perhaps the real reason why the Bible is not more widely read is that, side by side with the most important portions, are others which consist of lists of names or matter almost wholly devoid of interest to a modern reader. Obviously it should be easy to mark such passages for omission, and that is what this Course does.

For various reasons it is highly desirable to read the Bible through from Genesis to Revelation. Thus, the Old Testament prepares for the New, a cumulative knowledge of the Bible, so valuable in education, is secured, and a true perspective of religious history and truth is obtained. One who does this reading is prepared to understand and appreciate the myriads of allusions and references to sacred literature contained in secular history, literature, art, law, and life in general.

Every person's life is a success or a wreck, or something between the two, according as he does or does not govern it by the precepts of God's Holy Word. "The way of the ungodly shall perish, but the path of the just is as a shining light, that shineth more and more unto the perfect day." The foregoing should prove a powerful incentive to every seeker after truth to read the Bible through.

## II. SYSTEM OF MARKINGS

The course is divided into thirty-six lessons for a school year of forty weeks, and the markings give both the beginning and ending of lessons and the beginning and ending of passages or portions to be read. The following markings with the accompanying explanations will make the whole plain:

| —Genesis Markings | | Explanation |
|---|---|---|

—Genesis Markings

| | Ch. V. | | Ch. means chapter and V. means verse. Then 1:1 denotes |
| 1. | 1:1 | | the first chapter and first verse of Genesis. |
| | 9:29 | S | The 1. before the reference indicates that the first Lesson |
| | 11:1 | B | begins at this point. |
| | 11:9 | S | Next, opposite 9:29 is placed an S, which means that the |
| | 11:23 | B | Bible reading is to stop at the 9th chapter and 29th verse. |
| | 13:13 | S | Then the B opposite 11:1 means that the reading is to |
| | 14:13 | B | begin again at this point. Thus S and B follow one another |
| 2. | 19:1 | | alternately, B always marking a beginning point and S a |
| | 19:29 | S | stopping point. |

Attention to the following Rules will aid materially in the reading:

1. A letter B put in the margin marks a place to begin to read and a letter S a place to stop, always omitting all matter to the next B or figure.

2. A figure in the margin indicates the end of one lesson and the beginning of the next. If the reader is reading by lessons, it is advisable to insert a book-mark of some sort, so that the place to start the next time may easily be found.

3. When a new Book is started the readers should first examine the Introduction to it; next insert the markings for it if this has not yet been done; and then proceed to read it. When the reading of the Book is concluded the memory verses (if any) should be read and reread and, if possible, memorized.

## III. THE BOOKS OF THE OLD TESTAMENT
### Section I. The Pentateuch or Book of the Law

### BOOK I. GENESIS

The word "Genesis" means birth or beginning. The book of Genesis includes the following topics in order: The Creation, the Garden of Eden, the Antediluvians or peoples before the Flood, the Flood, the Tower of Babel, the dispersion or scattering of the races, and the lives of the patriarchs Abraham, Isaac, Jacob and Joseph. The book ends with the death of Joseph in Egypt. It has been called "the seed-plot of the Bible," for everything afterwards developed in the Word of God is first mentioned there. The Bible would have us understand that if God showed such great care for Abraham, Isaac, Jacob and Joseph He cares likewise for each of us, and this should be our point of view as we read, "The very hairs of your head are all numbered" (Matt. 10:30).

The importance of this book cannot be over-emphasized, and it is suggested that the reader make a list of all the beginnings he can find in it.

Before starting the reading of Genesis a map showing Mesopotamia, Canaan and Egypt should be carefully studied. Later it should be consulted also.

—Genesis Markings

| 1. | 1:1 | | 2. | 19:1 | | 31:1 | B | 3. | 39:1 | |
|---|---|---|---|---|---|---|---|---|---|---|
| | 9:29 | S | | 19:29 | S | 31:13 | S | | 46:7 | S |
| | 11:1 | B | | 21:1 | B | 32:1 | B | | 46:26 | B |
| | 11:9 | S | | 24:67 | S | 33:20 | S | | 50:26 | S |
| | 11:23 | B | | 25:19 | B | 35:1 | B | | | |
| | 13:13 | S | | 25:34 | S | 35:29 | S | | | |
| | 14:12 | B | | 27:1 | B | 37:1 | B | | | |
| | | | | 29:35 | S | 37:36 | S | | | |

—Memory Passages in Genesis: 1:1; 1:25; 4:9; 28:12-15; 31:49.

## BOOK 2. EXODUS

The word "Exodus" means going out and refers to the departure (the going out) of the children of Israel from Egypt. The book includes an account of the birth of Moses, the plagues by which God delivered the Israelites from Egypt, the journey to Sinai, the giving of the law there, and a description of the tabernacle.

The journey from Egypt to Canaan parallels in a wonderful way the life of every individual Christian, and it should be read with this thought in mind. Thus, the deliverance from Egypt pictures our redemption and the difficulties by the way it illustrates our experiences as we walk in the path of God's appointment. John Bunyon showed this most clearly when he wrote "Pilgrim's Progress." The reader will find it very interesting to compare the journey as described in the Bible with that of Christian in "Pilgrim's Progress."

For this book use a map of Egypt and the Sinai Peninsula.

—Exodus Markings

| 4. | 1:1 | | 6:28 | B | 5. | 23:1 | | 24:1 | B |
|---|---|---|---|---|---|---|---|---|---|
| | 6:13 | S | 22:9 | S | | 23:2 | S | 34:35 | S |

—Memory Passages: 12:13; 20:1-17.

## BOOK 3. LEVITICUS

The word "Leviticus" comes from Levite and Levite from Levi, one of the twelve sons of Jacob, and father of the priestly tribe of that name. This tribe had charge of the worship and of the teaching of the law. The Book of Leviticus gives the ritual of the tabernacle worship and the duties of the priesthood. Only short selections are made from it, merely to give an idea of its contents.

—Leviticus Markings

| 1:1 | B | 10:1 | B | 16:1 | B |
|---|---|---|---|---|---|
| 2:16 | S | 10:11 | S | 16:34 | S |

## BOOK 4. NUMBERS

Numbers (so called because it opens with the numbering of the people) beginning with the 10th chapter continues the narration of the journey from Egypt which was dropped in the 19th chapter of Exodus. A considerable portion of the book can be omitted because the matter is found elsewhere. Use a map of Canaan (Palestine) showing the Sinai Peninsula.

—Numbers Markings

| | | | | | | | | | | |
|---|---|---|---|---|---|---|---|---|---|---|
| 1:1 | B | 1:44 | B | 6. | 11:1 | | 26:2 | S | 32:1 | B |
| 1:4 | S | 1:47 | S | | 14:45 | S | 27:12 | B | 32:33 | S |
| 1:17 | B | 6:1 | B | | 15:32 | B | 27:25 | S | 33:50 | B |
| 1:23 | S | 6:27 | S | | 17:13 | S | 31:1 | B | 33:56 | S |
| | | 10:1 | B | | 20:1 | B | 31:12 | S | 35:1 | B |
| | | | | | | | | | 35:34 | S |

## BOOK 5. DEUTERONOMY

"Deuteronomy" means second law, that is, the second giving of the Law. The first five books of the Bible, called the Pentateuch, or the Books of Moses, give the history of the world from the Creation to the death of Moses. Deuteronomy is in the form of four addresses by Moses, repeating matters which have been already given in the previous books, and for this reason much of it is omitted from the Readings.

—Deuteronomy Markings

| | | | | | | | | | |
|---|---|---|---|---|---|---|---|---|---|
| 1:1 | B | 5:1 | B | 31:1 | B | 32:48 | B | 34:1 | B |
| 2:8 | S | 5:33 | S | 31:30 | S | 32:52 | S | 34:12 | S |

## Section II. The History of Israel in Canaan

## BOOK 6. JOSHUA

The book of Joshua is named after the successor of Moses, and tells, among other things, how the children of Israel entered the land of Canaan from the east, passing through the river Jordan, whose waters miraculously opened for them by the power of God. It also relates how the inhabitants of the land were conquered, and how their land was divided among the tribes of Israel. A considerable part of the book is taken up with Joshua's advice to the people as to how they should live and honor God. Use a map of Canaan showing the location of the Twelve Tribes.

—Joshua Markings

| | | | | | | | | | |
|---|---|---|---|---|---|---|---|---|---|
| 7. | 1:1 | 14:1 | B | 18:1 | B | 20:1 | B | 21:41 | B |
| | 11:23 | S | 14:15 | S | 18:10 | S | 21:4 | S | 24:33 | S |

## BOOK 7. JUDGES

The book of Judges gives the history of Israel from the death of Joshua to the days of Samuel. During this time the people disobeyed and forgot God again and again, resulting in their being overcome by their enemies. But when they repented and turned again to Him God raised up leaders, judges, who delivered them. The names of Gideon, Jephthah and Samson stand out prominently in this book.

—Judges Markings

| 8. | 4:1 | | 10:17 | B |
|----|------|---|-------|---|
|    | 9:22 | S | 16:31 | S |

## BOOK 8. RUTH

The book of Ruth describes an episode in the time of the Judges. It gives a lively picture of ancient life, with its manners and customs. Ruth was a great-grandmother of King David, and so is in the earthly ancestry of Jesus Christ. The passage of 1:16, 17 is one of the most pathetic in literature. This book is full of interest to modern readers.

The whole book is to be read.

## BOOKS 9 AND 10. I AND II SAMUEL

These two books are one in the Hebrew Bible, and they relate in detail the closing days of the theocracy (in which God ruled directly, through the Judges) and the early days of the kingdom. Israel rejected Jehovah their God and desired a king like other nations. Their first king was Saul, a man of goodly appearance and a skillful warrior, but not a man after God's own heart. At his death after a long reign, David, God's own choice as king, was proclaimed ruler. The life and activities of David are given fully, together with an account of Samuel, the last of the Judges.

—I Samuel Markings

| 9. | 1:1 | | 10. | 24:1 | | The whole of the book is to be read. |
|----|-----|---|-----|------|---|---|

—II Samuel Markings

| | 1:1 | B | 11. | 16:1 | | 24:1 | B |
|---|-------|---|-----|-------|---|-------|---|
| | 12:31 | S | | 23:23 | S | 24:25 | S |
| | 15:1 | B | | | | | |

## BOOKS 11 AND 12. I AND II KINGS

These two books, one in the Hebrew Bible, continue the history of the people of Israel from the accession of Solomon, David's son, to the carrying away of the people into captivity. They record the death of David, the accession of Solomon, the revolt of Jeroboam and his ten tribes during the reign of Rehoboam, Solomon's son, and from this time on the narrative intermingles the histories of the two kingdoms up to the captivity of each. The lives of the prophets Elijah and Elisha are found in these books.

Use a map of Canaan for the times of the kings, showing the northern and southern kingdoms.

—I Kings Markings

| 1:1 | B | 12. | 8:1 | |
|------|---|-----|-------|---|
| 3:28 | S | | 22:53 | S |
| 4:20 | B | | | |

—II Kings Markings

| 1:1 | B | 4:1 | B | 17:1 | B | 13. | 18:1 | S |
|------|---|------|---|------|---|-----|-------|---|
| 2:25 | S | 9:37 | S | | | | 25:30 | S |

## BOOKS 13 AND 14. I AND II CHRONICLES

The two books of Chronicles are, to a large extent, a repetition of matter found in other parts of the Scriptures, especially in I Samuel and II Kings. The first nine chapters give a genealogy, or list of names, beginning with Adam. The author lays most stress on the history of the kingdom of Judah, with special reference to the temple worship. Because of the similarity of the matter to that of the other books no references for reading are given.

## BOOK 15. EZRA

The book of Ezra gives an account of the return of some of the Jews from their captivity in Babylon and the rebuilding of their ruined temple. This work was carried out with difficulty because of the enmity of some of their neighbors and the lack of a spiritual religion among many of the Jews.

—Ezra Markings

| 1:1 | B | 2:64 | B | 8:15 | B |
|------|---|-------|---|-------|---|
| 2:1 | S | 7:28 | S | 10:14 | S |

## BOOK 16. NEHEMIAH

The book of Nehemiah outlines the events connected with the rebuilding of the wall of Jerusalem, and describes certain social and religious reforms. Nehemiah (God Comforts) was governor of Jerusalem under Artaxerxes of Persia, 455—424 B.C.

—Nehemiah Markings

| 1:1 | B | 14. | 7:66 | | 12:27 | B |
|------|---|-----|--------|---|--------|---|
| 3:3 | S | | 9:38 | S | 12:30 | S |
| 4:1 | B | | 10:28 | B | 13:1 | B |
| 7:6 | S | | 11:2 | S | 13:31 | S |

## Section III. The Literary Books of the Old Testament

Of the books of the Bible which may be classified under this section the book of Esther alone is written entirely in prose, while the book of Job contains only a small amount of prose. The others—Psalms, Proverbs, Ecclesiastes, Song of Solomon, and Lamentations—are written entirely in poetry, though only the revised versions show the fact.

## HEBREW POETRY AND ITS PECULIARITIES

The greater part of the poetry of the Bible is either lyric (song-like) or didactic (teaching). The Psalms illustrate lyric poetry and the Proverbs illustrate didactic poetry.

Hebrew poetry differs from that of western nations in its form. The western nations divide the matter in their poetry into lines of a fixed number of syllables, and usually require these lines to rhyme, that is, their final syllables must have the same sound. Hebrew poetry is altogether different. The lines are of varying length, and instead of two successive lines ending in the same sound, the second of a pair of lines is a repetition of the idea of the first, or a contrasting idea. The poetry of western nations makes much of accent; the Hebrew poetry does not.

The characteristic of Hebrew poetry mentioned above has been called parallelism. Three kinds of parallelism have been noted:

(1) When the second line, or clause, repeats the idea of the first in other words. See Psalm 6:1. The first clause has "rebuke" and the second "chasten."

(2) When two contrasted ideas come together. See Psalm 1:6.

(3) When the second clause extends or expands the meaning of the first, or deduces something from it. See Psalm 119:2, 9.

## BOOK 17. ESTHER

The book of Esther is a gem, read alike by young and old with interest and pleasure. It shows the hidden providences of God defending and delivering His people from their enemies.

The whole book is to be read.

## BOOK 18. JOB

The book of Job is thought by many to be the oldest book in the world, and deals with its most difficult question: "Why do the righteous suffer?" The early chapters, in prose, tell of great misfortunes that came upon Job. Some of his friends come to condole, or express their sympathy with him, and argue that as the laws of nature are unchangeable Job himself was to blame for the troubles that have come upon him. Job undertakes to prove that he is not to blame, or, at most, is only partly to blame. The book shows that Job was right. Here and there the style reaches the sublime.

—Job Markings

| 1:1 | B | 6:12 | S | 38:1 | B | 42:17 | S |

—Memory Passages: 12:1; 13:2, 15; 14:7, 10, 12, 14; 19:20, 23-26; 28:12-28; 31:35, last clause; 33:14, 15, 23, 24; 38:1-11.

## BOOK 19. THE PSALMS

The book of Psalms is the principal devotional book of the Bible. In some churches it is used in ritual worship, public and private. Many of the Psalms appeal to the deepest emotions of the human heart. Not a few of them are among the very finest gems in literature; for example: Psalms 1, 19, 23, 46, 90, 100, 103.

A great many verses or short passages are striking in their thought and expression, and are widely quoted. Many of the Psalms and passages from them have been made familiar to us in modern hymns and anthems.

—Psalms Markings

| 15. | 1:1 | | 16. | 40:1 | | 17. | 100:1 | | 18. | 121:1 | |
|-----|------|---|-----|-------|---|-----|--------|---|-----|--------|---|
| | 6:10 | S | | 42:11 | S | | 100:5 | S | | 128:6 | S |
| | 8:1 | B | | 45:1 | B | | 103:1 | B | | 132:1 | B |
| | 9:20 | S | | 51:19 | S | | 107:13 | S | | 139:24 | S |
| | 13:1 | B | | 53:1 | B | | 110:1 | B | | 144:1 | B |
| | 16:11 | S | | 53:6 | S | | 150:6 | S | | | |
| | 17:15 | B | | 61:1 | B | | | | | | |
| | 18:36 | S | | 61:8 | S | | | | | | |
| | 19:1 | B | | 65:1 | B | | | | | | |
| | 20:9 | S | | 67:7 | S | | | | | | |
| | 22:1 | B | | 79:1 | B | | | | | | |
| | 29:11 | S | | 79:13 | S | | | | | | |
| | 32:1 | B | | 84:1 | B | | | | | | |
| | 34:22 | S | | 87:7 | S | | | | | | |
| | 37:1 | B | | 90:1 | B | | | | | | |
| | 37:40 | S | | 92:15 | S | | | | | | |
| | | | | 95:1 | B | | | | | | |

—Psalms to be memorized, or reread many times: 1, 8, 19, 22, 23, 46, 51, 67, 84, 90, 91, 100, 103, 121, 122, 133, 137, 139, 146, 148, 150

## BOOK 20. PROVERBS

A proverb is a saying condensing into a few words the wisdom of experience. Wise men of old studied things around them and watched the lives of their neighbors. What they learned from years of observation, study and experience they condensed into single sentences. Their advice is of special value to the young. Were this advice to be studied and followed generally the world would be saved a great amount of trouble, suffering, shame and punishment, for much of the truth set forth by them is as applicable to-day as it was three thousand years ago.

—Proverbs Markings

    1:1   B         19.   7:1               31:31

—Memory Passages: 6:6-11; 12:24; 13:7, 12, 15, 24; 14:34; 15:1; 16:32-33; 20:1; 22:1-6, 15, 29; 23:5, 29-35; 25:11; 21, 22; 26:17, 20; 27:1, 6; 31:10-31.

## BOOK 21. ECCLESIASTES

The word "Ecclesiastes" means preacher or speaker. The book seems to have been written as a soliloquy, or a talking to one's self. The word "vanity," which appears many times in his book, does not have its usual meaning, but rather means transitoriness, that is, when the author says that such and such things are vanity he means that they will pass away, they are not lasting. Solomon is usually credited with being the author of this book.

—Ecclesiastes Markings

    1:1   B               12:14   S

—Memory Passage: 12:1-14. In this remarkable passage the references are to parts of the body; thus the pitcher at the fountain is the heart, etc.

## BOOK 22. SONG OF SOLOMON

This book is also called the "Songs of Songs" and "Canticles." The Jews interpreted it as picturing the love of God for His people.

—Song of Solomon Markings

    1:1   B          2:17   S         4:1   B         8:14   S

## THE HEBREW PROPHETS, MAJOR AND MINOR

A prophecy, as commonly understood, is a foretelling of the future. This is one element in the writing of all the prophets, but it is usually a minor one. The more correct view of the prophets is to regard them as men called by God when people were forgetting Him, to speak His word to the people and to turn them to Him in repentance and obedience to His will.

### Section IV. The Major Prophets: Isaiah, Jeremiah, Ezekiel, Daniel

## BOOK 23. THE PROPHECY OF ISAIAH

The Prophecy of Isaiah is one of the world's greatest masterpieces. It is elevated in style, vivid in description, vehement in its development of thought, emotional in sentiment and full of striking figures of speech. Its moral and religious teachings are keen and pure, and the prophecies of Christ's coming in the eleventh and fifty-third chapters are startling in their accuracy.

—Isaiah Markings

| 20. | 1:1 | | 9:7 | S | 40:1 | B | 55:15 | S |
|---|---|---|---|---|---|---|---|---|
| | 6:15 | S | 11:1 | B | 43:12 | S | 60:1 | S |
| | 9:1 | B | 11:10 | S | 51:1 | B | 64:12 | S |

—Memory Passages: 1:18-20; 9:1-8; 11:1-10; 40:1-8; 42:1-9; 53:1-12; 55:1-13.

## BOOK 24. THE PROPHECY OF JEREMIAH

Jeremiah prophesied "in the days of Josiah the son of Amon" and continued to prophesy up to the carrying away of Jerusalem captive. He faithfully proclaimed the word of the Lord, calling on Jerusalem to repent and turn from their sins. When the remnant left in Judah by Nebuchadnezzar fled to Egypt they took Jeremiah with them, and he probably died there.

—Jeremiah Markings

| | 1:1 | B | 16:11 | B | 23:1 | B | 21. | 35:1 | |
|---|---|---|---|---|---|---|---|---|---|
| | 3:25 | S | 16:21 | S | 23:8 | S | | 40:6 | S |
| | 7:1 | B | 18:1 | B | 24:1 | B | | 42:1 | B |
| | 7:15 | S | 18:8 | S | 24:10 | S | | 42:17 | S |
| | 13:1 | B | 20:1 | B | 27:1 | B | | 50:1 | B |
| | 13:14 | S | 20:6 | S | 28:17 | S | | 50:20 | S |

## BOOK 25. LAMENTATIONS OF JEREMIAH

Lamentations in the Hebrew Bible is in poetic form, and each of the first four chapters is an acrostic, the first verse beginning with the first letter of the alphabet, the second with the second letter, and so on. In the third chapter there are three verses to each Hebrew letter.

—Lamentations Markings

| 1:1 | B | 1:22 | S | 3:1 | B | 3:22 | S | 5:1 | B | 5:22 | S |
|---|---|---|---|---|---|---|---|---|---|---|---|

## BOOK 26. THE PROPHECY OF EZEKIEL

Ezekiel was carried away captive to a point near Babylon when Nebuchadnezzar conquered Judah in 597 B.C., and he prophesied "among the captives by the river of Chebar."

The book has been divided into three parts: 1. God's dissatisfaction with the kingdom of Judah, chapters 1-24. II. Woes pronounced on neighboring nations, chapters 25-32. III. Prophecies of a return of the exiles and a glorious future, chapters 33-48. For the historical connection see II Kings 23-25.

—Ezekiel Markings

| 1:1 | B | 18:1 | B | 30:1 | B | 34:20 | B | 47:1 | B |
|------|---|-------|---|-------|---|--------|---|-------|---|
| 4:17 | S | 18:20 | S | 30:13 | S | 34:31 | S | 47:23 | S |
| 7:1 | B | 26:1 | B | 33:1 | B | 37:1 | B | | |
| 8:18 | S | 26:21 | S | 33:6 | S | 37:28 | S | | |

—Memory Passage: 37:1-14

## BOOK 27. DANIEL

Daniel is one of the most readable books in the Bible. Its stories are vivid and exciting, and the visions in the later chapters are most significant. In the Hebrew Bible Daniel is found with the poetical and devotional books of Section III. The four beasts of Daniel 7:3 are commonly thought to be the four great world powers,—the Babylonian, the Medo-Persian, the Greco-Macedonian, and the Roman. The second vision, Daniel 8:1, is thought to refer to the Greek power under Alexander the Great. Greece is the he-goat that overcame the Persian ram, and Alexander is "the notable horn" between its eyes. The kingdom in chapter 9 is understood to be the Messianic, or Christ's kingdom. The visions in chapters 10-12 refer to "the latter days."

—The whole book is to be read. (Lesson 22.)

—Memory Passages: 5:1-6, 25, 31

### Section V.  The Twelve Minor Prophets

### BOOK 28.  HOSEA

The first three chapters of the book of Hosea give an account of the prophet's family troubles, which were intended to picture Israel's sins and Jehovah's love. The remaining chapters contain denunciations of the people for their idolatry and sins. For contemporary history see II Kings 14—20.

—Hosea Markings

| 1:1 | B | 6:11 | S | 14:1 | B | 14:9 | S |
|------|---|-------|---|-------|---|-------|---|

## BOOK 29.  JOEL

The book of Joel is divided into two parts. In the first a great calamity caused by an army of locusts is predicted in striking language. In the second part is given God's answer to the people's prayers.

The book of Joel contains a prophecy frequently found in the writings of the prophets, that the Jews shall establish a great nation in Palestine in later times.

—The whole book is to be read.

—Memory Passage: 2:28-32.

## BOOK 30. AMOS

Amos was one of the earliest of the writing prophets. He prophesied that God loves mercy and not mere formal sacrifices, such teaching being like that of Christ. He was born 12 miles south of Jerusalem, but prophesied in the Northern Kingdom. He taught that Israel's future greatness was not to be secured through power and wealth, but through justice and judgment. For historical connection see II Kings 14.

—Amos Markings

| 23. | 1:1 | | 3:1 | B | 5:18 | B | 9:1 | B |
|-----|-----|---|-----|---|------|---|------|---|
|     | 1:5 | S | 4:1 | S | 7:17 | S | 9:15 | S |

## BOOK 31. OBADIAH

Obadiah lived in Jerusalem after Judah's deportation to Babylon. He was God's messenger announcing the doom of the Edomites, the descendants of Esau, who had gloried over Judah's downfall. He also prophesied a future when the Jews should again rule over all the lands formerly under David's control.

—Read all of the 21 verses of Obadiah's prophecy.

## BOOK 32. JONAH

The book of Jonah is quite the most readable of all the Minor Prophets. Two views of it have been held. One regards it as a historical narrative, while the other looks upon it as a symbolic story, teaching that as Jonah failed to do his duty by the people of Nineveh, so Israel failed in its moral and religious obligations to other nations. However, the testimony of our Lord Jesus Christ is conclusive that Jonah is a historical narrative (Matt. 12:38-41).

—All of the book is to be read.

## BOOK 33. MICAH

Micah lived in the time of Isaiah. Like Isaiah he preached against the sins of his time, especially against the oppression of the poor by the rich. He prophesied the destruction of both Israel and Judah just before the punishment fell on Israel. For historical connection see II Kings 15-20.

—Micah Markings

| 1:1 | B | 1:15 | S | 4:1 | B | 5:15 | S |
|-----|---|------|---|-----|---|------|---|

## BOOK 34. NAHUM

Very little is known about Nahum. He lived about 505 B.C., when Nineveh was destroyed by the Medes, thus ending the Assyrian Empire.

—Nahum Markings

| 1:1 | B | 1:15 | S |
|-----|---|------|---|

## BOOK 35. HABAKKUK

It is not known when or where Habakkuk lived. It was probably about the time Jerusalem was taken by Nebuchadnezzar. The last reference given contains Habakkuk's prayer.

—Habakkuk Markings

| 1:1 | B | 1:17 | S | 3:1 | B | 3:19 | S |

## BOOK 36. ZEPHANIAH

Zephaniah lived in the time of Jeremiah, Habakkuk and Nahum, and prophesied, as did they, against the sins of the people of his time. Among his other prophecies he includes a great doom that shall come on the whole world. After that Jehovah shall reign and His people shall prosper. For the contemporary history see II Kings 22, 23.

—Zephaniah Markings

| 1:1 | B | 1:18 | S | 3:1 | B | 3:20 | S |

## BOOK 37. HAGGAI

The book of Haggai contains four prophecies, all dealing with the rebuilding of the temple under Zerubbabel. God raised up Haggai and Zechariah to stir up the people to build His house. For a picture of the conditions during this period see the early chapters of Ezra.

Read the entire book.

## BOOK 38. ZECHARIAH

Zechariah has been divided by scholars into two parts, chapters 1-8 and chapters 9-14. The first part deals with the same topic as Haggai's prophecy; the last part with the Messianic or Christ's Kingdom.

—Zechariah Markings

| 1:1 | B | 3:10 | S | 14:1 | B | 14:21 | S |

## BOOK 39. MALACHI

Malachi is best known as the last book of the Old Testament. It contains promises of the coming of the Messiah, or Messenger of the Covenant. Malachi lived after the temple had been rebuilt and the worship restored, but he found the people sinning in various ways, and his ministry was addressed to their consciences to turn them to God.

—Read the entire book.

Note: A period of several hundred years elapses between Malachi and the books of the New Testament.

## IV. THE BOOKS OF THE NEW TESTAMENT

### INTRODUCTION

A period of about four hundred years has elapsed since Malachi, whose book is the last of the Old Testament Canon, wrote. During this time the Old Testament books were collected, and were in use in the synagogues, or churches, in New Testament times.

It does not seem necessary in the New Testament Notes to give Introductions to the several books, since they are nearly all self-explanatory. It is desirable, however, that the reader should early get a good understanding of the different kinds of books in the New Testament and a brief connected history of the events described in it.

The New Testament includes: (1) The Four Gospels, covering about the first third of the First Century. (2) The Acts of the Apostles, or history of the early church, from about 30 A.D. to about 63 A. D. (3) The Epistles or letters to churches and individuals, from about 40 A.D. to perhaps 80 A.D. (4) The Revelation, written close to the end of the First Century.

Because the Four Gospels are all alike in giving the life of Christ, and the twenty-one Epistles are alike in dealing largely with doctrines and the conduct of Christians, it is possible to frame a Short Course which will give in three lessons a good idea of the whole of the New Testament.

Before beginning the reading the learner should study a map of "Palestine in the time of Christ," finding on it: Judea the southern portion, Samaria the middle part, and Galilee the northern country, also the country east of Jordan River. He should locate: the Lake of Gennesaret or Sea of Galilee, the Jordan River with its valley, the Dead Sea, and the seacoast country along the Mediterranean Sea. Next he should fix in mind the position of the following cities; Jerusalem, Nazareth, Bethlehem, Capernaum, Sychar in Samaria, Jericho, and Tyre and Sidon. He should find Mt. Moriah in Jerusalem itself, the Mount of Olives just east of Jerusalem, and Mt. Hermon in Galilee.

Before beginning the reading of the Book of Acts a map of the "Travels of St. Paul" should be studied, locating on it Jerusalem, Joppa, Cæsarea, Antioch in Syria, the island of Crete, the peninsula of Asia Minor (now Turkey), with its cities, Macedonia, Greece and Rome.

Also before beginning the reading of the New Testament it should be helpful to study the following little biography of Christ, using the map of Palestine while doing so.

### THE LIFE OF CHRIST IN THE GOSPELS

The life of Christ, as told by the four Evangelists who wrote from thirty to sixty years after His death, is in one sense easy to follow, the narrative being always interesting and highly instructive. It is not easy to follow in the sense of knowing when and where many events happened. A little outline should have some value as the reader begins with the Gospel story.

Jesus was probably born in December, B.C. 5, which is practically four years before the beginning of our era. He was born in Bethlehem, a few miles south of Jerusalem, but soon thereafter was carried by Joseph and Mary to Egypt to escape death, Herod the king having commanded the killing of all the male children of Bethlehem under two years of age. After staying a short time in Egypt Joseph and Mary returned with the child, going to their home in Nazareth, which lies some distance west of the Sea of Galilee. Here Jesus grew up, aiding Joseph, who was a carpenter, until He was about thirty years old. The only event recorded of Him in all this time was a trip to Jerusalem when He was twelve years old.

When about thirty years of age He went to the river Jordan where He was baptized by John the Baptist. After that He went into the wilderness where He was tempted by the devil. Returning from the temptation He walked by the Sea of Galilee, where He called six of His apostles-James and John, Andrew and Simon Peter, Philip and Nathanael. After some time spent in teaching and healing in Galilee, Jesus went to Jerusalem to be present at the first Passover Feast of His ministry. After this feast He went about Judea teaching and then returned to Galilee. From about this time till about six months before His crucifixion it is very difficult to fix on dates and periods. What are called Harmonies of the Gospels have been constructed which attempt to arrange the events which occurred in chronological, or time, order. Owing to the lack of proper information this is difficult to do.

In the late winter or spring of probably A.D. 30, the master left Galilee in the north and came to Jerusalem to be present at the Passover Feast. On the Sabbath before the Passover Christ made a triumphal entry into Jerusalem, riding on an ass. From that day events followed each other in quick succession. On Thursday evening He ate the Passover with His disciples, and later in the Garden of Gethsemane was taken by officers to be tried, first by the Jewish Sanhedrin and then, the next day, by the Roman Governor, Pilate. At nine a. m. on Friday He was crucified on Calvary, and on the following Sunday morning He rose from the dead. After that He was seen by many of His disciples and conversed with some of them. Forty days from the resurrection He led His disciples from Jerusalem, at which time He ascended into heaven. He gave the promise when He left that the Holy Ghost, the third person of the Godhead, should remain and comfort the disciples, and be in His Church.

## LESSON MARKINGS FOR THE WHOLE NEW TESTAMENT

Because the whole text is to be read the letters B and S will not appear. The first lesson extends from 24 to 25, the second from 25 to 26, and so on. However, on account of the two courses certain directions are necessary for skipping what will be read later, or what has been read. The reader is advised to insert at first the markings for the First Course only, and those for the Second Course when it is reached, after erasing those for the First Course.

### First Course

Matthew 1:1. Omit
Matthew and Mark in
First Course, passing
directly to Luke 1:1.
24. Luke 1:1.
25. Luke 22:1.

Luke 24:32. Omit John's
Gospel in First Course,
passing to Acts 1:1.
26. Acts 22:1.
    Acts 28:31.
    Pass from here to
    Ephesians.

1:1 in First Course,
Ephesians 6:24. Pass
from here to Revelation
1:1 in First Course.
Revelation 4:1. Pass to
Revelation 20:1.
Revelation 22:21.

Return now to Matthew 1:1, where the Second Course is begun.

### Second Course

27. Matthew 1:1
28. Matthew 25:1
    Mark 16:20. Omit
    Luke's Gospel in
    Second Course.
29. John 1:1.
30. Acts 1:1.

31. Acts 22:1
32. I Corinthians 1:1.
33. Galatians 1:1.
    Galatians 6:8. Omit
    Ephesians in Second
    Course.

34. 1 Timothy 1:1.
35. James 1:1.
36. Revelation 1:1.

Important Note: As soon as a book is finished the memory passages (references for which follow) should be looked up and studied.

—Memory Passages in the New Testament

Matthew: The Beatitudes, 5:3-12; The Lord's Prayer, 6:9-13; The Gracious Invitation, 11:28-30; The Great Commandment, 22:36-40; The Parable of the Talents, 25:13-30; The Great Commission, 28:18-20.

The Gospels are full of passages that are frequently quoted.

Mark: The Gospel of Power, 1:1-28.

Luke: The Birth of Jesus, 2:7-18; The Twelve Apostles, 6:13-16; The Sinful Woman, 7:37-50; The Seventy sent out, 19:1-11.

John: 1:1-18; 6:48-58; 15:1-14; 19:1-19

Acts: Peter's Address, 2:13-41; Paul's Speech, 17:22-34; Paul's Speech before Agrippa, 26:1-32.

Romans: The Natural State of Man, 1:28-32; 8:28; 8:36-39; The Christian Life, 12:1-21.

I Corinthians: 2:1-4; Love, or Charity (Charity = Love), 13:1-13; Resurrection, 15:40-58.

II Corinthians: 3:2-4; 4:8-10; 5:1; Paul's Glorying, 11:21-12:11.

Galatians: 1:11-24; 6:1-10.

Ephesians: 6:18-19.

Philippians: 1:21-24; 2:1-11; 3:4-6.

Colossians: 3:1-25.
I Thessalonians: 4:13-5:3; 5:15-28.
II Thessalonians: 3:8-18.
I Timothy: 6:6-12.
II Timothy: 1:1-7.3:16-17; 4:6-8.
Hebrews: 1:1-14; 4:12-16; 9:9-15; 11:1-16, 32-40.
James: 1:22-25; 2:14-26; The Tongue, 3:2-14.
I Peter: 1:1-9; 2:1-9, 3:14-18.
II Peter: 1:3-10; 3:8-18.
I John: 2:12-17; 4:16-21.
Revelation: 1:9-16; 22:1-21.